CAPTIVE PASSAGE

CAPTIVE PASSAGE

The Transatlantic Slave Trade and the Making of the Americas

Published by

SMITHSONIAN INSTITUTION PRESS

Washington and London

in association with

THE MARINERS' MUSEUM

Newport News, Virginia

Library of Congress Cataloging-in-Publication Data
Captive passage : the transatlantic slave trade and the making of the Americas.
        p.   cm.
    "The Mariners' Museum."
    Includes bibliographical references and index.
    ISBN 1-58834-037-6 (alk. paper)—ISBN 1-58834-017-1 (pbk. : alk. paper)
        1. Slave trade—Africa. 2. Slave trade—America. 3. Slave trade—Europe. I.
    Mariners' Museum (Newport News, Va.)
    HT 1322.C35   2002
    382'.44—dc21   2001049647

British Library Cataloguing-in-Publication Data available

Printed in Singapore, not at government expense

07 06 05 04 03 02   5 4 3 2 1

⊛ The paper used in this publication meets the minimum requirements of the American
National Standard for Information Sciences—Permanence of Paper for Printed Library
Materials ANSI Z39.48-1984.

Beverly C. McMillan developed and edited this volume for The Mariners' Museum and
wrote the accompanying boxed features, except where otherwise noted. Special appreciation
goes to the following individuals at The Mariners' Museum: Publications: Betty Zattiero,
Department of Photographic Services and Licensing: Claudia Jew, Jason Copes, Greg Vicik,
Lisa Flick, John Pemberton, Collections and Collections Management: William B. Cogar,
Lyles Forbes, Randy Wyatt, Jeanne Willoz-Egnor, Michelle Clawson, Library and Archives:
Cathy Williamson, Josh Graml, Jennifer Kirch, Lester Weber.

Except where otherwise noted, the illustrations, paintings, and artifacts shown in this book
are from the Collections of The Mariners' Museum.

Smithsonian Institution Press
Caroline Newman, Executive Editor, Museum Publications
Martha Sewall, Production Manager

Design: ThinkDesign, Buellton, CA

Front Cover: (top) Engraving showing slaves being taken by canoe to Dutch ships anchored
near Elmina on the west coast of Africa. From Awnsham and Churchill, *Collections of Voyages
and Travels*, vol. 5, London, 1746. (center) Detail of a map included in *The English Pilot*,
1799. (bottom) View of Cape Santo Domingo, Hispaniola (Dominican Republic), in 1801.
(inset) Wood carving of a bound African man, from Ghana. (Sample Pittman Collection,
New York City.)

Back Cover: Detail of a map included in *The English Pilot*, 1799.

Half Title Page: Detail of Charleston, South Carolina, c. 1767. From *Scenographic Americana
or A Collection of Views of North America and the West Indies, 1768* by T. Mellish with engrav-
ings by Charles Canot.

Title Page: Detail, *Ten Views of Antigua* by William Clark. (Hamilton College.)

This book is a companion volume to the travelling exhibition *Captive Passage: The Transatlantic Slave Trade and the Making of the Americas* organized by The Mariners' Museum in Newport News, Virginia, in association with South Street Seaport Museum in New York City and the National Museums and Galleries on Merseyside in Liverpool. While not an exhibition catalog, *Captive Passage* provides a foundation for understanding what became one of the most odious economic enterprises in human history. As audiences throughout the United States experience *Captive Passage* in the coming years, the organizers hope that the perspectives it offers will inspire a fuller appreciation of the complex origins and enormously varied impacts of the transatlantic slave trade. That history remains incomplete, and perhaps this telling also will inspire the discovery of new material that can further illuminate both the enigma of how such activity could have been so widely accepted for so long, and the paradox of how, in the end, the extraordinary contributions of millions of enslaved Africans bequeathed a legacy of triumph.

John B. Hightower
President and Chief Executive Officer
The Mariners' Museum

The exhibition *Captive Passage: The Transatlantic Slave Trade and the Making of the Americas* was underwritten in part by a generous grant from The National Endowment for the Humanities. We also express our appreciation to The Rockefeller Foundation for support provided to South Street Seaport Museum.

C O N T

To the Reader

The transport of slaves from the west coast of Africa to the Americas was the largest forced migration in human history. And because the millions of African captives were carried across the Atlantic Ocean in ships, the transatlantic slave trade also stands as history's greatest maritime tragedy.

When the trade was launched in the fifteenth century, the taking of slaves, often as spoils of war, had long been a staple of human interactions. To a great degree, the elements that set the new regime of slavery apart from such historical practices were its vast scale, systematic operation, and global impact. Beginning in the mid-1440s, the trade was launched for the specific purpose of providing labor to European colonies in Central and South America and the Caribbean. The precious minerals, such as gold and silver, and exotic agricultural products, such as sugar and tobacco, that flowed from those colonial outposts were sold or traded in many other parts of the world, generating wealth on a scale never before imagined. Ultimately the trade encompassed a massive enterprise that engaged every major maritime nation in Europe—Portugal, Spain, Holland, Britain, France, Denmark, Sweden—and eventually involved a suite of fledgling American nations including the United States, Brazil, and Cuba.

The Atlantic slave commerce also was fluid, with captains or ship-owning syndicates adjusting their procedures to increase the survivorship of their human cargoes (and hence profits) and always making careful calculations—not always accurate—of the types and value of trade goods their vessels should carry. Its economic and technological

Opposite:
Detail of "Sugar Mill."
(Deroy after Lugendas, from *Illustrated London News*, March 1845.)

parameters evolved over time, with different trade items falling into and out of favor in different eras and places, and vessels becoming faster and more seaworthy. Like other ships engaged in other trades, those carrying enslaved Africans benefited from technological advances in navigation and ship construction; in the latter decades of the trade, slaves were even transported across the Atlantic in steamships. On each of the continents that participated in the trade, it garnered fabulous riches for a relative few, in stark contrast to the unspeakable personal and cultural losses inflicted on millions of captive Africans.

Scholars have spent decades attempting to determine with some precision how many Africans were forcibly shipped to European colonies in the New World. At this writing, based on available records in Europe, Africa, and the Americas, some consensus has formed around the range of 11 to 13 million transported Africans who eventually set foot on colonial shores. Yet respected scholars differ, and ongoing research may well refine current views on the numbers of Africans who were sold into slavery at different stages of the trade, how many of those individuals died awaiting shipment, and how many perished during the Middle Passage.

An enduring myth about the trade is that most enslaved Africans were transported to North America. In fact, only about 6 percent of those confined in the holds of slave ships were destined for that continent. Regardless of their destination, however, the experience of slavery was always violent and degrading. Made captive initially by other Africans, the men, women, and children loaded onto slave ships waiting in West African harbors all passed through the crucible of the Atlantic crossing. Of those who survived that appalling journey, most would never live another day in freedom.

Yet the story of the transatlantic trade is also the story of how people stripped of all human rights managed to resist the psychic and cultural ravages of enslavement. Instead they endured, and then moved beyond simple endurance to forge new cultures, establish religions, and evolve rich art forms. In ways dramatic or more subtle, the larger societies in which slaves lived and worked became infused with African heritage.

Some of the essays presented in this book help us understand the economic and social forces that gave rise to and sustained nearly four centuries of commercial trafficking in human beings. Others examine the experiences of enslaved Africans from the time of their initial captivity, through the Middle Passage, and on the foreign shores where survivors were consigned to lives of forced labor. Another probes the birth of anti-slavery sentiments and efforts to outlaw the trade. A final case study of how black Africans fashioned identities as seafarers underscores what perhaps are the ultimate lessons of the transatlantic slave trade. Not only were the spirits of the captives indomitable, but their unpaid toil and that of their descendants created fortunes that were key to the building of New World economies—the making of the Americas.

The Mariners' Museum

1

Human Commerce

Edward Reynolds

In the beginning, gold was the magnet that attracted Europeans to Africa. It was soon followed by ivory, pepper, beeswax, gum, and the skins of tropical animals. Yet for well over three centuries, it was a trade in human beings that cemented the continents of Europe, Africa, and the Americas together in a commercial relationship.[1] Fueled by the demand for human labor in European enterprises in the New World, the transatlantic slave trade would bring millions of Africans to bondage in the Americas[2] from eight major slave-trading regions—Senegambia, Upper Guinea, the Windward Coast, the Gold Coast, the Bight of Benin, the Bight of Biafra, the Congo, and Angola. At markets situated along a great arc of the west coast of Africa, from Senegal in the north to Angola in the south, ships flying the flags of Spain, Portugal, Holland, England, France, and Denmark all took on cargoes of African captives. Thus began a journey to colonies in the Americas where slave labor would be used to build and sustain mining operations and plantations producing lucrative agricultural commodities—tobacco, cotton, coffee, rice, and, most of all, sugar.

Scene depicting African slaves digging for ore, possibly gold, in a Spanish colony in the New World. ("Nigritae in Scrutandis Venis Metallicis ab Hispanis." Theodor de Brys, Collection of Voyages to the East and West Indies, 1594.)

Opposite:
An ivory hip mask from the Kingdom of Benin in Africa, c. 1550. At the top are figures of Portuguese visitors, while the brow shows ritual scarification—a pattern of shallow incisions in the skin. Like other masks of this type, this one was intended to be worn on the belt of the oba, or king. (Metropolitan Museum of Art, Michael C. Rockefeller Memorial Collection, Gift of Nelson A. Rockefeller, 1965.)

BEGINNINGS

Portuguese traders had introduced African slaves to Europe starting with Portugal's exploration of the west coast of Africa in the fifteenth century. The transport of millions of Africans across the Atlantic Ocean to the Americas did not begin until Spanish explorers and settlers arrived in the New World during the last decades of the fifteenth century and the first decades of the sixteenth.[3] Lured by the prospect of finding gold, Spanish entrepreneurs and others created permanent settlements in various parts of the Americas, and Spain established a provisional form of government centered on a system of labor and tribute grants (called *encomiendas.*) In theory the grantee was given the responsibility for protecting workers—initially, local Amerindians—and in turn received labor and money tribute from them. In reality, the punishing work in the mines, a form of toil previously unknown to Amerindians, took an often deadly physical toll. In addition, the native peoples' lack of immunity to European diseases such as smallpox, typhus, measles, and influenza cruelly increased Indian deaths.

When the Spanish conquistadores had sailed to the Americas, they had brought with them a few black slaves, and early Spanish settlers soon were reporting that in mining operations the work of one African was equal to that of four to eight Indians. In general, they began promoting the idea that black slaves would be essential to produce goods needed for European colonization. Fueling their demands was the introduction into Spanish America of valuable tropical crops, notably sugarcane. By 1509 the first sugar mills had been established in Spanish colonies, with more soon to follow. Such operations required a substantial initial outlay of capital, and to produce enough sugar to be profitable they demanded a workforce that was both large and controllable. Hence, as Amerindians began to perish in large numbers (and Spanish clerics began interceding on their behalf), the Spanish crown turned to Africa—and African slaves—as a source of labor.

With the labor needs of its New World settlements growing, Spain began regulating the slave trade, granting special licenses known as *asientos* for the importation of slaves into the colonies. The first organized transport of slaves directly from Africa took place in 1518, when Spain's King Charles I granted an asiento to a member of his household. It allowed the importation of 4,000 African slaves into the Caribbean islands known as the Greater Antilles: Hispaniola (now Haiti and the Dominican Republic), Cuba, Jamaica, and Puerto Rico. It was a portentous beginning, for during the next two centuries slave merchants representing various European countries would vie for asientos and the opportunity to participate in a profitable trade in human beings. Indeed, during this period asientos became a great international prize, with wars sometimes fought to secure them. The licenses were filling a substantial demand: large numbers of black slaves were being employed in Spanish

Map of seventeenth-century Africa, showing the region Europeans called Negroland, Guinea, and the area that came to be called the Slave Coast.

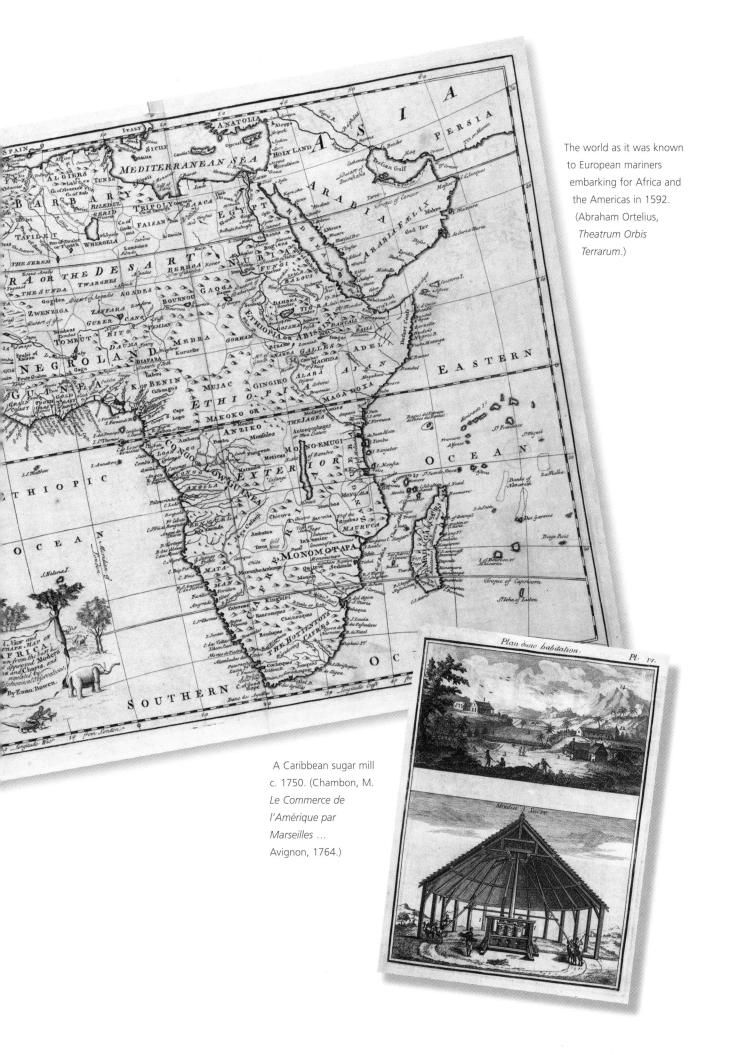

The world as it was known to European mariners embarking for Africa and the Americas in 1592. (Abraham Ortelius, *Theatrum Orbis Terrarum*.)

A Caribbean sugar mill c. 1750. (Chambon, M. *Le Commerce de l'Amérique par Marseilles …* Avignon, 1764.)

In Brazil, Pernambuco was the locale for a thriving commerce in enslaved Africans, many from the western African region known as Angola. In 1648 the Brazilian cleric Frei Antonio Viera recognized the central role of both the slave trade and its source when he wrote, "Without blacks there is no Pernambuco, and without Angola, there are no blacks." ("Gate and slave market at Pernambuco" c. 1822. Library of Congress.)

gold mines in Peru, Venezuela, and Chile, in sugarcane fields of Mexico, Colombia, Peru, and the Antilles, and in the production of cocoa in Venezuela, grapes and olives in Peru, and wheat in Chile. And although the Spanish crown would stop issuing asientos in the mid-1700s, by then the transatlantic slave trade was an entrenched reality of New World commerce, with slavers from a variety of nations freely supplying slaves not only to the Spanish colonies, but to those of other European nations as well.

SUGAR AND SLAVERY SPREAD

Like Spain, Portugal had visions of New World empire, the Portuguese explorer Pedro Álvares Cabral having "discovered" Brazil in 1500. For several decades before Portugal established a foothold there, however, Portuguese planters had been using African slaves to grow sugarcane on Atlantic islands off the coast of Africa, including Madeira, the Azores, the Cape Verde islands, and São Tomé. Starting around 1516, this experience with the technical requirements of sugarcane cultivation began to prove useful in the development of Portuguese plantations in Brazil, confirming the utility of using slaves for the arduous toil the field work and processing exacted.[4] Meanwhile, problems including high production costs, heavy local consumption, and marketing difficulties suppressed sugar exports from Spanish colonies, and after about 1550 Brazil became the main exporter of sugar from the Americas— and a major importer of black slaves. The success of the Brazilian sugar industry was linked to several factors: excellent soil, adequate rainfall, and the proximity of Brazilian ports to the cane fields, which made it easy to ship sugar to market. In addition, from the end of the fifteenth century marketing channels available in Europe offered

SOME
OBSERVATIONS
ON THE
Affiento Trade,
As it has been Exercised by the
South-Sea Company;
PROVING THE
DAMAGE,
Which will accrue thereby to the
British Commerce and Plantations
in AMERICA,
And particularly to
JAMAICA.
To which is annexed,
A Sketch of the Advantages of that Ifland to Great Britain, by its annual Produce, and by its Situation for Trade or War.
ADDRESSED TO
His Grace the Duke of NEWCASTLE, One of his Majefty's Principal Secretaries of State.
By a Perfon who refided feveral Years at Jamaica.
LONDON:
Printed for H. WHITRIDGE, at the Corner of Caftle-Alley in Cornbill. MDCCXXVIII.

Pamphlet referring to the asiento trade to Jamaica, 1728. (Sample Pittman Collection, New York City.)

Brazilian growers optimal distribution of their commodity.

The surge in slave trading to Brazil in the middle 1500s coincided with growing dominance of the Brazilian sugar export business by Dutch traders. The Dutch ascendance in turn reflected the fact that at the time, Holland was the only European nation with the commercial organization and capital to adequately finance sugar distribution; importing African slaves for the plantations became a natural extension of their business operations.[5] Business boomed, and in 1632 the Dutch effectively seized Brazil from the Portuguese, while looking to solidify their trade domination in other ways. Around the same time they took the Caribbean islands of Curaçao, St. Eustatius, and Tobago, and established settlements in Surinam, Demerara, Berbice, and Essequibo in northeastern South America. These outposts, too, developed into productive sugar colonies.

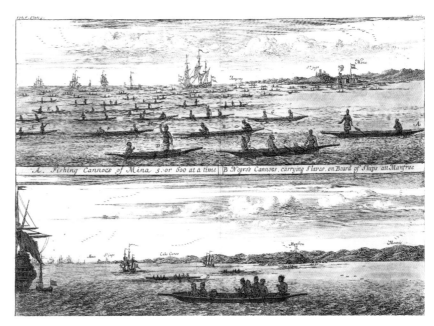

This colored engraving depicts slaves being taken by canoe to Dutch ships anchored near Elmina. (J. Kip, artist. Engraving: Awnsham and John Churchill, *Collections of Voyages and Travels*, vol. 5, London, 1732.)

Across the Atlantic other conquests also beckoned, for the Dutch had no trading posts on the West African coast, the source of black slaves. To remedy this deficiency and secure a supply of slave workers, Dutch forces captured the town of Elmina (or El Mina, "the mine") on the Gold Coast in 1637 and took Angola four years later.

All the while, Brazil's sugar industry was thriving. Indeed, the period from 1629 to 1660 saw the heyday of Brazilian sugar production as Dutch merchants strove to maximize sugar exports. Their dominance, and sugar's, was not to last, however. Finally expelled by Portuguese forces in the late 1600s, the Dutch left behind a Brazilian sugar industry that would begin slipping into decline. Yet as it did, other labor-intensive forms of economic activity were developing. For example, as the eighteenth century opened, Brazilian gold mine operators sought both unskilled and skilled slave laborers, including carpenters, masons, and smiths. So, in the 1700s, although Brazil was losing its position as the world's leading sugar producer, the result was another surge in slave imports to its shores.

In all, the Atlantic slave trade brought an estimated 3.5 million Africans to Brazil, including slaves shipped during the 1800s as commercial cultivation of coffee took hold. Like sugarcane planters and mine operators, coffee growers required reliable, efficient labor, and the nineteenth-century slave trade from Africa—as well as internal slave trading from northern to southern Brazil—made the rapid expansion of that nation's coffee agriculture possible.

Having lost Brazil, the Dutch simply took their sugar expertise to the Caribbean and set up operations there. Already in place were fledgling sugar enterprises mounted by other European nations, to which Dutch traders provided technological aid and credit to finance the purchase of equipment, land,

and African slaves. In fact, despite their extensive efforts at colonizing the New World, Dutch traders delivered most of the captives they transported from Africa to colonial outposts of other European nations. Among these were British colonies on the islands of Barbados and Jamaica, and the French colony of St. Domingue.

Until the early 1600s, only Spain had possessed colonies in the West Indies. However, those islands were less significant to the Spanish crown than were mainland colonies such as Peru and Mexico. So, while Spaniards had settled on large islands such as Cuba and Hispaniola, the smaller islands of the Lesser Antilles had essentially been left to the native Carib Indians. It was on these islands that the British and other Europeans settled, and during the seventeenth and eighteenth centuries Britain's colonies would become by far the most successful.[6]

The British founded colonies in Barbados in 1627, in Nevis in 1628, in Montserrat and Antigua in 1632, and in Jamaica in 1655. The first farms on the islands tended to be small, grew mainly tobacco, and employed few slaves. Instead, agricultural labor in the British colonies was performed by workers drawn from Britain's white, lower middle classes, either as voluntary immigrants or as kidnap victims. Working as indentured servants, such people were bound to a plantation owner for four or five years, after which they would receive a plot of land in the colonies.

Around 1640, however, this system started to change as planters began shifting from tobacco and cotton to sugarcane. In Barbados, for instance, with their sugar finding ready markets, Barbadian plantations began to grow larger, eventually averaging 200 acres. Like similar efforts in Brazil, they needed a sure, plentiful supply of workers to maintain the grueling pace of operations. Barbadian planters who had visited Pernambuco to learn how to refine sugar had not failed to notice that Brazilian sugar plantations were operated by African slaves and that slave labor offered clear advantages over employing white workers. They knew also that the substantial revenues to be earned from sugar could justify the purchase of slaves. Even so, for a time British ethnocentrism and a strong aversion to living among black people deterred Barbadian planters from using Africans.

When those attitudes changed, it was in part because white labor was proving increasingly unreliable. Whereas Barbados originally attracted a large number of indentured servants, as time went on the island developed a reputation for cruel conditions and free workers were less and less willing to go there. White labor also was becoming expensive, because wage advances in England had boosted the cost of indentured servants. Slave prices, by contrast, were falling. By the mid-1600s, for example, the cost of purchasing a captive African—which had been the equivalent of about $25 in the 1640s—had dropped to $15, making black slaves simply a better value than white servants. With Dutch traders waiting in the wings, willing and able to provide a steady supply of slaves, once the planters of Barbados started using slaves on their sugar plantations they never looked back.

With the marriage of sugar and slavery, the Barbadian plantation economy could flourish. Moreover, the Dutch merchants who had educated British would-be sugar producers not only supplied their clients with slaves on easy terms, but also sold British sugar on the continent at profitable prices. So successful was the British plantation effort that by 1700 British planters in Barbados, Jamaica, and the Leeward Islands were supplying almost half of the

A slave market on the Rue du Valongo, the "shopping district" for African slaves in Rio de Janeiro in the 1830s. ("Boutique de la rue du Val-Longo," J. B. Debret, *Voyage Pittoresque et Historique au Brésil*, vol. 2, Paris, 1835. Library of Congress.)

Vüe du Cap S.ᵗ DOMINGUE , prife en rade , du fond de la petite An...

View of the port of St. Domingue in the West Indies around 1801. ("Vue du Cap St. Domingue, prise en rade, du fond de la petite Anse, le 15 pluviale X-ième Expedition de Le Clerc.")

An illustration of the "landing of Negroes at Jamestown" from a Dutch man-of-war in 1619. (Howard Pyle, in *Harper's Monthly*, January 1901.)

Terms of Trade

Black Africans were sold to Europeans in exchange for a vast assortment of goods—seashells, rum, brandy, wine, guns and gunpowder, tobacco, knives, and a whole host of metal goods ranging from copper, silver, and pewter to gold and ingots of Swedish iron. Most slavers also carried various kinds of cloth, for while West African weavers produced their own fine-quality textiles, their output could not meet the demand. Africa had ready buyers for cottons, linens, and other fabrics woven in Britain, France, Holland, and India. Representatives of the Dutch East India Company even traded for slaves with exotic Chinese silks. Africans also prized Swedish amber and glass beads manufactured in Italy and England, using them along with precious metals or shells to create exquisite items of personal adornment.

Certain trade items came to be broadly used as currency. Iron bars and copper or brass manillas were in this category at times, as were cowrie shells. Collected mainly from the Maldive Islands in the Indian Ocean, the glossy, brightly marked shells were small and therefore readily portable, and could not easily be counterfeited. It has been estimated that in the 1700s Europeans traded more than 25 million pounds of cowries for slaves and other merchandise, paying over 150,000 shells for a single slave. During that same period, a slave might also be purchased for firearms at the rate of three to six guns per captive. The number of guns required to buy a slave increased along with the European demand for slave labor. As a result, guns manufactured in England and other slave-trading nations allowed some African rulers to outfit large armies for fighting their internal wars—conflicts that produced prisoners of war who were then sold as slaves to purchase more guns.

Surgeon John Atkins, recounting his observations aboard British slave ships in the 1720s, notes that different sorts of items were wanted in different places: "Crystals, orangos, corals, and brass-mounted cutlasses are almost peculiar to the Windward Coast. … Cowries [are wanted] at Whydah, copper and iron bars at Callabar; but arms, gun powder, tallow, old sheets, cottons of all the various denominations, and English spirits are everywhere called for. Sealing wax, and pipes are necessary in small quantities [because] they serve for dashees [tips] and a ready purchase for fish, a goat, kid, or a fowl."

During one voyage Atkins also kept track of equivalent values of slaves and trade goods. During a port call in Sierra Leone, he recorded that a woman slave for his vessel's cargo was purchased for three pieces of chintz, one piece of "handkerchief stuff," another piece of "planes" cloth (a material typically woven in Wales), and seven large brass kettles. A boy cost seven smaller kettles, five pieces of cotton cloth, a length of fabric called "brawls," and one iron bar. At another trading town farther down the West African coast, an adult male slave cost his British buyers "8 trading guns, 1 wicker bottle, 2 cases of spirits and 28 sheets." Additional trade items in Atkins's record include brandy, rum, gunpowder,

Copper Katanga crosses of a type used in trade in the 1730s in the region of modern Nigeria. Their value at the time is said to have been sufficient to purchase several slaves. (Sample Pittman Collection, New York City.)

"pacato beads," beef tallow, pewter tankards and washbasins, small and large brass pans, musket shot, cutlasses, and beer.

A different trader in a different time and place would have encountered other trade terms, and in general the prices Europeans paid for African slaves varied over time. In order to measure profits, traders ultimately converted slave prices into their own currencies. While it is difficult to figure modern equivalents (for example, the United States dollar did not even exist until rather late in the trade), the relative prices paid for slaves during different periods are revealing. In 1550, when the trade was still in its infancy, the average cost of a slave in Africa was the equivalent of £10, increasing 40 percent (to £14) by 1600. Prices remained steady until the 1630s and then declined, falling to less than £5 in the 1670s (a sum nonetheless equal to a year's wages for some English workers of the day). Sixty years later, in the 1730s, New World sugar plantations were thriving, demand was high, and the cost of a slave in Africa had jumped to £25. While wars preoccupied Europe during the 1790s, the slave price dropped sharply (to about £15), and by the 1860s, when the transatlantic trade in slaves had been outlawed in much of the Americas, slaves could once again be purchased for about £10—the same price as 300 years earlier. On the other side of the Atlantic, however, in those places where slavery continued to exist, prices skyrocketed as illegal traders' risks grew. In the waning decades of the nineteenth century, a slave purchased in Africa for the rough equivalent of $15 might sell in Cuba for $1,500. —B.C.M.

An artisan of the Kuba peoples (Congo) used cowrie shells, glass beads, and raffia to create this hat. (Hampton University Museum of Art.)

sugar consumed in Europe. By 1724, all available land on Barbados was under cultivation or had been granted. As the plantation system in the British West Indies peaked in the eighteenth century, the interdependence of sugar and slavery was an accepted fact.

Despite the great need for slaves, the supply to British colonies was not always consistent. Jamaica was a case in point. Because of that island's vast area of land suitable for agriculture, the demand for slaves there was especially keen, and during the 1600s British and Dutch slave ships called regularly with cargo holds laden with captive Africans. In 1713, however, British slavers received Spanish asientos obligating them to supply Spain's colonies with 4,800 slaves a year. As a result, instead of receiving slaves for its own plantations, Jamaica became merely the depot for through-shipping slaves to Spanish holdings. Sweetening the pot for the British slavers was the ready payment offered by the Spaniards, whereas resident British planters expected long periods of credit. To secure enough labor for their plantations, in 1732 Jamaican planters even attempted (unsuccessfully) to impose duties on slaves exported from the island.

SLAVERY IN FRENCH AND DANISH COLONIES

French pirates and privateers were operating in the Americas as early as 1504. It was not until the seventeenth century, however, that France acquired colonies there.[7] The French occupied three islands in the West Indies, settling St. Christopher, Guadeloupe, and Martinique by 1635. They secured the western part of Hispaniola, or Santo Domingo, from the Spanish in 1697, renaming the new French colony St. Domingue. After initially growing tobacco, indigo, cotton, and ginger, colonial French planters, like their British neighbors, shifted to sugar production and proceeded to organize supply monopolies to provide their operations with slave labor. Beginning in 1664, sugar was the primary export of the French West Indies, an activity that transformed the islands' economies. Land values soared and, as in British colonies, smallholders were eventually replaced by large plantations.

The heart of French sugar production lay in Guadeloupe, Martinique, and St. Domingue, and for the first few decades plantations there relied on indentured labor. As a result, the scale of sugar production in the French Caribbean was slow to increase and there were few slaves on the French islands until after 1700. Around that time in St. Domingue, for example, most planters owned at

"A Liverpool slave ship," painted by William Jackson around 1780. (Courtesy Board of Trustees, National Museums and Galleries on Merseyside.)

most twelve slaves—a paltry number compared to the slave populations of other European colonies of the time.

In 1710 St. Domingue exported just 2,920 tons of sugar. By the 1740s, however, the island had become the most productive of the French colonies; by 1791, at the pinnacle of its success as a sugar exporter, annual sugar production had grown to 78,696 tons. Given this sizeable enterprise, during the eighteenth century much of the French transatlantic slave trade was directed to that colony. In the end, France became the third most active European slave-trading nation, accounting for just over 20 percent of African slaves imported to the Americas, most coming from Angola and the Bight of Benin.

In 1671 Danish entrepreneurs also had established Caribbean sugar plantations, on the islands of St. Thomas and St. John.[8] By comparison with the French and British, however, their success was limited, and by 1725 there were only about 6,000 slaves on those two Danish islands. On nearby St. Croix, which the Danes purchased from France in 1733, sugar also was produced on a relatively small scale and in 1754 that island claimed a population of only 7,600 slaves.

SLAVES COME TO NORTH AMERICA

The first black people to arrive in the mainland colonies of North America came before the systematic importation of slaves began. As early as 1526, Spain had attempted to establish a North American colony, landing 200 colonists and 100 African slaves near Cape Fear, North Carolina. The venture failed as harsh conditions and disease took their familiar toll, and when a remnant of the Spanish expedition returned to Hispaniola it left behind Africans who subsequently became assimilated into local Indian groups.

The organized delivery of slaves into British North America dates to 1619, when a Dutch slaver sold twenty black Africans to the settlement at Jamestown in Virginia. The year 1625 saw the first Dutch shipment of Africans to New Amsterdam, the settlement that would grow into New York. Indeed, until 1654 enterprising Dutch slavers dominated the supply of captive labor to North America. Later, after the enactment of the Navigation Acts in 1651 (which regulated shipping to Britain's colonies) and the establishment of British monopoly trading companies, providing slaves to American colonial planters would become the business of British and American merchants.

In North America the demand for slaves was relatively limited until the 1700s. By and large, the British colonies there shared a similar climate with the mother country, which hampered efforts to find a new and profitable agricultural export crop that could justify the required investment. In the long term, however,

This leather handbag decorated with cowrie shells would have belonged to an important African personage. (Danny Drain Collection, Walterboro, South Carolina.)

Don Álvare, who became the king of Congo in 1567, is shown here giving an audience to Dutch ambassadors. In addition to selling captive Africans to European slave traders, Álvare used slaves to work his land and as servants in his household, as concubines and soldiers, and to serve in other capacities as well. (Thomas Astley, ed., *A New General Collection of Voyages and Travels*, London, 1745–47.)

cultivation of tobacco, rice, and later, cotton, in the southern colonies of British North America would bring both economic rewards and large numbers of African slaves to the country.[9]

The need for agricultural labor first became clear as commercial tobacco production increased. In 1627 Virginia exported £500,000 worth of tobacco, grown mostly by white workers. By the eighteenth century, however, Virginia and neighboring Maryland had responded to the increasing difficulty of obtaining indentured servants by turning in earnest to slave labor, a change that was reflected in growth of their exports. The colonists shipped £20 million worth of tobacco to England in 1700, £80 million by the mid-1730s, and £220 million in 1775.

Colonial South Carolina's economic base also grew slowly until rice became a viable export crop in 1695. And as with tobacco agriculture in Virginia and Maryland, the cultivation of rice in South Carolina came to rely almost entirely on the efforts of black slaves. Beginning in the early 1690s, African slave imports boosted the black population so that it equaled, then surpassed, the white population. By 1708 blacks comprised the majority of South Carolina's population, most of them toiling in the rice fields.

A slave mother and her children being sold at auction, probably in the Caribbean. (John Carter Brown Library at Brown University.)

It is interesting to note that initially South Carolina's white settlers had been unable to grow rice because they understood little about how to cultivate it. Their African slaves, however, knew well how to plant and care for the crop because an indigenous variety of rice (*Oryza blaberrima*) was grown in African rain forests. In fact, African rice was routinely part of the provisions loaded aboard slave ships headed for the Americas. Thus enslaved Africans, who before 1700 faced food shortages and had been encouraged to grow their own food, apparently succeeded with rice crops where their white masters had failed.

While the use of slave labor allowed various crops to be produced profitably over a wide swath of the American South, the region's land area dedicated to plantations—and the concomitant use of slaves—remained small until the end of the eighteenth century, when Eli Whitney's cotton gin suddenly transformed green-seed upland cotton into a commercial crop. The economic rewards of growing cotton also expanded the plantation region from the narrow confines of the southern Atlantic coast to the rest of the South. Even so, cotton plantations were not a major factor in bringing slaves from Africa to North America, because the spectacular expansion of cotton farming in southern states came mere years before the trade was abolished. The same phenomenon

Slaves harvesting rice. (*Harper's New Monthly Magazine*, November 1859.)

applied to North American sugar; sugar production in Louisiana began to boom in 1795, just a little over a decade before international slaving became illegal. As a result, much of the labor needed for North American cotton and sugar production in the nineteenth century came from the existing slave population, rather than from fresh imports from Africa or elsewhere.

Despite the comparatively slow development of African slavery in North America, American maritime merchants showed interest in participating in the Atlantic slave trade as early as 1643. Their involvement was modest at first, with most slaves being transported north from Barbados and other West Indian islands. Around 1680, however, when the American colonies' need for agricultural workers began to burgeon, slave buyers began showing a preference for slaves from Africa and entrepreneurs eager to fill the demand soon entered the arena. Between 1698 and the outbreak of the American War of Independence in 1775, Boston, New York, and Newport (Rhode Island) became the major ports from which ships were launched into the Atlantic slave trade, with vessels coming also from New London (Connecticut), Providence (Rhode Island), and Philadelphia. After the United States of America came into being, the new nation's major slave-trading ports were Newport, Boston, and Charleston (South Carolina).

DEMAND AND SUPPLY

Whatever the destination of slaves in the New World, the purpose of their enslavement and transport across the Atlantic was purely economic, and their lives in slavery were often brutal. The demands of sugar plantations in particular, which called for sixteen to twenty hours of daily labor in the harvesting seasons, led almost inevitably to high mortality among slaves. Many survived only eight to ten years, and some sugar planters periodically had to replace entire populations of enslaved workers. Gold mining, especially in Brazil, claimed thousands of lives. There, a punishing regimen of prospecting in icy mountain streams brought rapid physical deterioration, and the combination of overwork and disease killed most slaves within ten or twelve years. It is therefore not surprising that overall, the largest number of African slaves went in a steady stream to the mining and sugar-growing areas of Brazil and the Caribbean. During the course of the transatlantic slave trade, Brazil imported about 38 percent of the slaves who came from Africa; another 51 percent were divided roughly equally among the British Caribbean, the French Caribbean, and Spanish America; some 6 percent went to North America, and another 6 percent to the Caribbean colonies of Holland, Denmark, and Sweden.

Initially, the African seacoast furnished a large number of the captives Europeans purchased. With increasing demand, however, African suppliers of those human cargoes were obliged to resort to the backcountry. Regardless of where slaves came from, they were acquired mainly through warfare or subsequent tribute arrangements, through kidnapping, and through judicially sanctioned enslavement. In some places, for example, legal infractions that could lead to enslavement included adultery and the unauthorized removal of sacred and religious objects. Among groups like the Tio and the people of Iboke in what is now the Democratic Republic of Congo (formerly Zaire), slavery was often the punishment for convicted adulterers who were unable to pay a fine, which was equal to the value of a slave. The Akwamu kings and chiefs of the Gold Coast could exploit anti-adultery laws for personal gain, taking as wives women who were married to them in name only. At the end of the year, the

Working the Mines

When Christopher Columbus made his second voyage to the New World and disembarked onto the Caribbean island of Hispaniola in 1495, he promptly enslaved local Amerindians for a largely fruitless effort to extract gold from the island's mountainous terrain. In the ensuing decades, however, Europeans would indeed discover New World gold, and would learn that the indigenous people generally did not make good slaves: not only were they combative, but they succumbed quickly to overwork and disease. Many black Africans, on the other hand, came from cultures in which precious metals such as gold were mined, and they were accustomed to working with horses and other domestic livestock. Africans also gained a reputation for their ability to endure punishing working conditions.

By the early 1500s a few Africans had been shipped across the Atlantic to work in Spanish mines, with seventeen of the "best and strongest" consigned to gold mining operations in Hispaniola. As Spanish adventurers located new sources of precious metals and stones, the trickle of African slaves to New World mines became a sizeable stream. In 1524 some 300 enslaved Africans arrived in Cuba to work mines there, and within twenty years forced African labor was sustaining gold, silver, and diamond mining operations in Brazil, Mexico, Peru, Honduras, Venezuela, Puerto Rico, and elsewhere. Diamond mining, which is depicted in the accompanying drawing, was a profitable but short-lived enterprise, for by the middle of the sixteenth century European colonies in the Americas had begun to focus largely on an even more lucrative venture: the cultivation of sugarcane. —B.C.M.

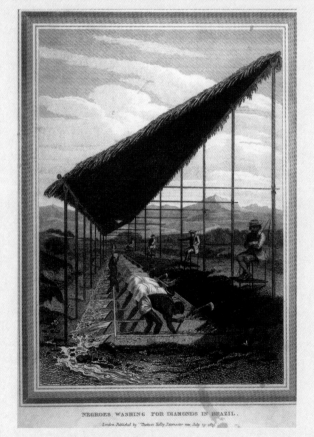

NEGROES WASHING FOR DIAMONDS IN BRAZIL.

London Published by Thomas Kelly Paternoster row July 9 1815

Slaves in a diamond mine in Brazil.
(Mary Evans Picture Library.)

women were asked to identify men who had slept with them during that time, and these transgressors were then sold into slavery unless relatives ransomed them. Also on the Gold Coast, religious objects were often laid in pathways, and those displacing them could be seized and sold or be required to forfeit the price of a slave.

On the Upper Guinea coast, by the late 1500s a slew of infractions were legal grounds for enslavement. Examples included administering poison to or placing a fetish on others, committing adultery with a wife of the king, soliciting war against the king, or asking the gods to bring about his death. Indebtedness and offenses against taboos were other accepted routes to forced labor. These practices allowed ample opportunity for fraud and abuse, especially in cases involving adultery and witchcraft. In some instances, whole families had to follow the convicted individual into slavery as though they also had committed sins for which their descendants must suffer. In some areas of Africa, misfortune brought on by drought or famine caused children or even entire families to be sold into slavery. As the commerce in slaves stimulated a desire for exotic trade goods that Europeans could provide, it was not uncommon for people to sell their children to gratify new desires or relieve financial difficulties. Among the Tio, for instance, a maternal uncle could approach the father of his niece or nephew for money and if the father could not provide it, he was asked to sell one of his children. These youngsters and other individuals who had been sold by their own people were unlikely to attempt escape, since they had no place to go.

The slave delivery system within Africa was generally characterized by monopolistic restrictions. In the savanna that extends from the Senegambia basin to Lake Chad in central Africa, as in other areas beyond the forest, the trade was controlled by Muslims who, with their agents, formed trading caravans that at times included up to 1,000 people, with slaves bought and sold en route. From the Bight of Benin to the Gold Coast, strong states like Akwamu and Oyo in the seventeenth century, and Oyo, Dahomey, and the Asante nation during the eighteenth century, controlled the procurement and sale of slaves.[10] The king of Oyo and his court prevented merchants in the area north of them from passing through their territory, a restriction that allowed the king's traders uncontested access to the trade. In Dahomey the commerce in slaves was not as complete a monopoly, but the state had a strong commitment to controlling it and severely restricted the internal movements of European traders on the Dahomey coast. The Asante also maintained a state monopoly over the slave trade; after conquering coastal lands they collected ground rent from Europeans who maintained forts there. The same monopolistic practices extended from the area of the Benue River to the Bight of Biafra.

One trading organization, that of the Aro, has particularly intrigued historians of the slave trade. The Aro originally came from the Nigerian town of Arochuku, but from about the seventeenth century they established extensive commercial networks in the interior of southeastern Nigeria. Their trade dominance has been attributed to their exploitation of the respected oracle Arochuku, who demanded from supplicants human "sacrifices" who eventually were sold into the slave trade. While the Aro were heavily involved in the integration, supply, and wholesale aspects of the slave delivery

Included in an anonymous book of charts prepared in 1720 for ships plying "the Western Ocean," this map includes many major ports of call for vessels engaged in the triangular trade from Europe to West Africa and thence to South America and the Caribbean. A legend (lower left) provides distance equivalents in English, Dutch, and Spanish—the languages of three of the most prominent slave-trading nations at the time. (In *The English Pilot*, vol. 5.)

system, agreements and cooperation with various groups and neighboring communities facilitated their slave transport operation. And although the Aro were one of the most successful slave-trading groups, there were others in southeastern Nigeria that blocked Aro expansion and maintained their own trading networks.

A different delivery system operated around Angola during the early 1600s. Agents were sent to the interior to buy slaves on the region's borders with Congo. Among the most important markets were fairs of the Mpumbu near Stanley Pool. Agents—mulatto sons or trustworthy slaves of the Portuguese—were called *pombeiros* (or *pumbeiros*) from an indigenous word meaning hawker. In some instances, the pombeiros remained in the interior trading for years, periodically receiving merchandise from the coast. Portuguese governors themselves obtained slaves through raids and from tribal chiefs. Slaves were also transported from the Angolan interior by merchants who accompanied Portuguese soldiers during Portuguese wars of conquest and purchased war captives from them.

Whatever the mechanism by which slaves were procured, they were always brought to the coast of Africa for sale. Chained to prevent their escape, many first passed through various markets and masters, some being used along the way as domestics or as field hands during the planting or harvesting season.

European ship captains and slavers who arrived at the African coast were required to obtain a trade license, typically by paying fees or purchasing a number of slaves at a specified price from the local chief. In addition, some form of permission was often necessary for "breaking trade," as this procedure was sometimes called. The fees and numerous presents European slave traders were obliged to give Africans to pave the way for business were governed by a complex protocol and were subject to change at the behest of the local people. In general, customs and dues were payable on all imports and exports, and Europeans strove to comply with such demands to avoid jeopardizing their ability to trade.

Because of the role Europeans played in the transatlantic slave trade, and the fact that it was the need for labor in the Americas that fostered the commerce in human beings, the trade has sometimes been called the European slave trade. It also has been termed the "triangular trade," reflecting the fact that the trade route often involved a voyage of three legs: from Europe to Africa where trade goods were exchanged for slaves; on to the Americas where slaves were sold for cash, promissory notes, or agricultural products; then back to Europe, where the New World commodities would be sold. Not all slave voyages conformed to this pattern, however; for example, some slave ships originating in Brazil and North America participated in what amounted to a bilateral trade, from the Americas to Africa and back.

On arrival at their American destination, slavers could sell their cargo in three ways: by private treaty, by "scramble," and by public auction. In private treaties, slaves were sold either directly to planters or to specialized wholesalers at an established price. During the early years of the trade, island merchants served as go-betweens, arranging slave sales to planters on commission. Later, the merchants traded for themselves, buying captives from arriving ships and reselling them. When slaves were sold by scramble, prospective buyers rushed on board to select slaves they liked at a fixed price. For the captives a scramble sale could be a frenzied, terrifying event as buyers frantically grabbed and roped their quarry. At public auction, Africans were examined, poked, and prodded, and sold to the highest bidder. Having disposed of its slave cargo, a ship would return to Europe with colonial products such as coffee, sugar, and cotton. Sometimes, though, ships returned to Europe simply in ballast, their economic mission apparently satisfied.

The number of Africans sold into slavery across the Atlantic is great enough to have had significant implications for political development in Africa, for retarded economic growth there, and for what has been called Africa's underdevelopment.[13] Because it was difficult to procure both slaves and ordinary trade goods from the same area, during the decades of the slave trade normal economic activities could not be pursued. At the same time, the threat of enslavement increased fear and insecurity and stifled creativity that might otherwise have led to improvements in Africa. Furthermore, African rulers and the few other key individuals who established the demand for imports to Africa favored consumable goods and luxuries that did little to foster economic diversification or create new wealth in their homelands.

It is sometimes asserted that the goods Africans accepted in return for their slaves were of poor quality or, in some cases, essentially worthless. However, whereas African slave sellers may have been greedy or shortsighted in selling the best asset of their societies, they cannot be accused of stupidity. In fact, Africans met European traders on the coast on equal terms and could accept or reject the commercial items they had to offer. Ample evidence exists that European traders selected their trade goods carefully to suit African tastes and interests. That said, the availability of some products offered in exchange for slaves, especially textiles, iron, guns, and liquor, has been blamed for forestalling their manufacture in Africa.

In the end, African slave traders organized a far-flung commercial network that delivered many millions of their countrymen into the hands of European slavers who would disperse the human cargoes throughout the Americas. Both Europeans and Africans reaped economic profit from this trade in people. And although scholars may debate the level of profit it yielded and the distribution of those profits among the participants, none can deny the profound contribution of African labor to the development of the Americas.

Europeans used the bronze or copper bracelets called manillas to barter for slaves, especially in the Bight of Benin from the Gold Coast to Nigeria. In the early days of the trade a slave might cost between twelve and twenty-five manillas, depending on the captive's age, sex, and health, as well as current market values. By about 1520, when colonial sugar operations were expanding rapidly and the demand for slaves was burgeoning, slave prices had risen sharply to more than fifty manillas for one captive African. Eventually, foundries in Birmingham, England turned out the bracelets in large quantities. The manillas shown here were recovered from the schooner *Douro*, which sank in 1843.

2

Africa:
The Source

John Thornton

The people who were transported to the Americas during the Atlantic slave trade were drawn from a vast region of western and central Africa, with a few even coming from the southeastern part of the continent. From the lower fringe of the Sahara Desert, the area of modern Senegal, in the north, to the upper reaches of the Kalahari Desert in Angola, in the south, a great river of people embarked on what was by far the greatest forced migration in history.

At its height the slave trade was a huge business enterprise, directly and indirectly employing thousands of people. They ranged from the businessmen and bankers in Liverpool, Lisbon, Nantes, and Boston who financed the trade, to humble peasants in Africa who sold their farming surpluses to feed the captives awaiting export on the coast. It was also a moral disaster, for even as it flourished a good many observers felt a tinge of guilt at the violence, greed, and cruelty that such a forced passage required. The transatlantic slave trade also remains a puzzle for historians, for the more it is studied the harder it is to fully explain.

Wood carvings of bound African men and women, from Ghana. (Sample Pittman Collection, New York City.)

AFRICAN CONTROL

The slave trade was not simply a matter of Europeans staging attacks on the African coast and enslaving their captives. The first Portuguese to visit West Africa in the middle of the fifteenth century tried this tactic, but were quickly undone. An ocean-going sailing ship cannot easily approach the African coast, and African coastal navies, whose shallow draft canoes were well adapted to the waters and small creeks of the coastal zone, quickly and decisively defeated such forays. Although other mariners in later times would try the tactic of raiding, none were successful beyond the short-term gains obtained by surprise, and most regretted their attempt.[1]

In fact, only in Angola did military forces led by Europeans—the Portuguese—play a significant role in the capture and enslavement of people. Even there, Portuguese involvement was a slow process that began in 1491. Initially it involved mercenaries in the service of African rulers; only after a long preliminary period did European forces begin seizing territory and launching wars, in 1579. And even then, the period when European-led armies were the primary means of enslavement was relatively short, lasting only about a century.[2]

Where circumstances did allow Europeans to participate directly, they could not force Africans to furnish them with slaves. For example, Africans in the region between modern northern Liberia and the eastern end of Côte d'Ivoire (Ivory Coast) never participated in the trade in any significant way, even though the area was fairly densely populated and Europeans did trade there for ivory, pepper, wood, and cloth. Similarly, most of what is today Cameroon and Gabon did not export slaves, though they exported other commodities. The Kingdom of Benin in the southeastern part of today's Nigeria dropped out of the slave trade from about 1550 until perhaps 1710, and the Kingdom of Congo in modern northern Angola barely exported any slaves of its own taking between 1580 and 1650. Both kingdoms contributed significantly to the slave trade at other times, however, and others participated actively in some periods, and much less so in others.

Where European merchants were allowed to build fortifications, as they did in the area of Senegambia and on the coast of modern Ghana, the forts were to protect the merchants and their cargoes from seaborne attack by pirates and not to serve as raiding bases against the Africans. Initially, many forts were constructed to protect gold awaiting shipment rather than as slave-trading entrepôts. Occasionally, Africans might engage fort garrisons as mercenaries, as often happened on the Gold Coast. But the garrisons were too weak to enforce their will against even petty African states. On more than one occasion, Europeans found out to their cost that Africans could take these forts by storm if they were determined to do so.[3]

African rulers, therefore, controlled the wars and raids that led to the sale and transport of captives abroad. Everywhere except Angola, African slaves were acquired by European slave dealers through peaceful trade that was regulated by African governments. Hundreds of thousands of pages of commercial records left by European slave-trading companies such as the English Royal African Company or the Dutch West India Company document the process of purchase in great detail.[4] European traders paid taxes, tribute, and tolls to conduct their business, often dealt directly with the coastal political authorities or their representatives, and conducted their trade strictly in accordance with

English slave trader Thomas Golightly served as mayor of Liverpool and was active in the trade until it became illegal in 1807. (Courtesy Board of Trustees, National Museums and Galleries on Merseyside.)

Map of the west
coast of Africa in the 1600s. The cartographer noted growing
European intrusions on the coastline, including the Portuguese fortress known to the British
as El Mina ("the mine") or Elmina Castle. This outpost was the first such trading center that
Europeans established in Africa.

African law. They recorded purchases of agricultural goods to feed themselves and to supply the thousands of slaves destined for export. Likewise, in the few African locales for which there exist written African records, rulers themselves describe their activities in acquiring and selling slaves. For instance, in a letter written in 1514, King Afonso of Congo described gifts of slaves to various Portuguese, as well as the capture and sale of slaves by his armies.[5] Three centuries later in 1810, King Adandozan of Dahomey described for his "brother," the king of Portugal, a number of his campaigns and the many captives and slaves he took.[6]

Clearly, it was the African political and economic elite, leaders who were capable of defending their countries from seaborne European marauders, who did the primary work of enslaving, transporting, and selling the Africans who would be traded on the coast. Yet this fact creates the central paradox of the Atlantic slave trade. Given the slave trade's strong negative effect on Africa, why did African leaders who controlled the trade permit it to continue?

CONSEQUENCES

The negative impact of the slave trade can be seen clearly in its demographics. Because slave buyers in the Americas were anxious to use African captives as laborers, in general they wished to buy adult males. On average, enslaved men outnumbered women two to one, and children or older people rarely made up even a tenth of exports. Thus the slave trade's drain on the population of Africa was all the worse because it targeted the most productive adults. While modern historians have gradually learned roughly how many people were boarded on ships in West Africa during the period of the slave trade, it is far from established how many people lived at the time in the areas most deeply affected. Thus we do not know what percentage of Africa's population was lost to the trade. Still, some hints suggest that in addition to a fairly small decrease in the overall population of the hardest hit areas such as Angola and the Bight of Benin, there was a significant impact on the demographic structure of the population. For example, late eighteenth-century census material from Angola, one of the areas most deeply involved in trading slaves, shows that among the adult population women had come to outnumber men by more than two to one. Few areas suffered as much as Angola did, but at least some population distortion of this sort took place in most regions that were trading slaves extensively.[7]

To some extent African laws and customs helped offset population losses. African marriage law did not limit the number of wives a man could have, and by the 1700s polygamy was widespread in many African countries, for humble and rich alike. The practice of men taking multiple wives allowed fertility to remain close to normal, so birth rates did not decline. In the same populations, the ratio of boys to girls among the children was fairly normal, although the ratio of adults to children was relatively low. This population distortion, in turn, probably had a number of results: there were fewer women, and many fewer adults in general, to take care of the large child population, and work

Captain John Newton made three slave voyages between 1745, when he was only twenty, and 1755. In middle age he married, became a clergyman, and wrote of his regret at having participated in and profited from the trade. Newton left as a legacy the words to the hymn "Amazing Grace," which he wrote around 1770. (Mary Evans Picture Library.)

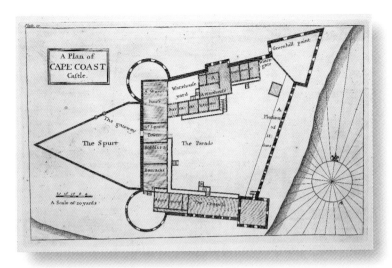

Cape Coast Castle as drawn by William Smith around 1727. The Royal African Company appointed Smith to survey its West African trading posts, called "factories." (In *Thirty Different Drafts of Guinea*.)

that adult males should have performed would have had to be done by women or not done at all. Under these circumstances productivity had to fall, and some scholars suggest that Africa's relative backwardness in the nineteenth and twentieth centuries was due to this diminished economic capacity, an economic disaster from which Africa has yet to recover.[8]

Other negative impacts were less tangible. People did not accept enslavement voluntarily —virtually all those who crossed the Atlantic had been forcibly seized, either in war or illegally by bandits. To reap such a harvest of human beings, there must inevitably have been a great sowing of violence, with its related destruction and disruption. Additional evidence suggests that those who were not forcibly seized were enslaved through court action, and in many areas the courts were corrupted to increase the numbers of people enslaved.[9]

AFRICAN SOURCES OF SLAVES

Because of the role of violence and judicial corruption in the process of enslavement, it is tempting to add condemnation of the African elites who ran the courts, conducted the wars, and sold the enslaved victims, to the censure of European merchants and their backers. Such a solution is not very satisfying, however. The slave trade lasted some 400 years; it involved at least 200 sovereign states in Africa, and thus many thousands of leaders. In many African societies, decisions such as the one to engage in the slave trade were made not just by rulers acting alone, but also by a large class of powerful, wealthy, and influential people. The decision to go to war and to sell slaves was made hundreds of times each year, and it is impossible to believe that so many African rulers were so irresponsible that they took such portentous steps simply to sell slaves. This is especially true because, in African traditions, some of these leaders are remembered as being wise and just and appear so even in contemporary records. For example, Queen Njinga, ruler of Ndongo and Matamba from 1624 to1663, is remembered today as a heroine and a staunch patriot against Portuguese intruders in her realm, yet she unhesitatingly engaged in the slave trade.[10] It strains the imagination to suppose that all those leaders over all that time made decisions that were consistently wrong or guided solely by sordid principles of gain and power.

One explanation might be that African rulers waged wars simply to acquire slaves, much as a hunter attacks game. But war is not hunting, and the military situation in Africa was rarely so unbalanced that one country could raid its neighbors with impunity. In fact, many African leaders began wars that they could not be sure of winning at all, which is hardly rational if their objective was only to obtain slaves. The Kingdom of Dahomey, whose eighteenth-century rulers sold thousands of slaves acquired mostly in wars, engaged in a war or some other military operation virtually every year. Yet before one dismisses these operations as slave raids designed to garner income to satisfy the rulers' greed, one must consider that Dahomey actually *lost*

Peoples of Art

In the 1430s, when Portuguese explorers in the service of Prince Henry the Navigator first touched on West African shores in search of gold, they found a continent of diverse cultures and highly developed artistic traditions. The city-state of Benin was an example. Benin astonished the Portuguese explorer João Afonso Aveiro in 1486, and later the Dutch writer Olfert Dapper, with its size, complex architecture, sophisticated trading networks and monetary systems, and vibrant customs. Counted among its Bini people were artists highly skilled in casting bronze, carving ivory, and weaving cloth. Elsewhere in West Africa, as in Sierra Leone, the extraordinary delicacy with which African carvers were crafting objects from ivory amazed the Europeans, who returned home bearing saltcellars, spoons, and other objects fashioned from "elephants' teeth," sometimes commissioned from European designs.

Just south of Benin, in what today is part of Nigeria, Igbos apparently had a long tradition of bronze working; several objects uncovered in the course of excavations are the oldest West African bronzes found to date. Gold working was another African specialty, notably among the Asante in the region comprising modern Ghana. Royal personages might adorn themselves lavishly, studding their fingers and toes with intricately carved gold rings. A king's young male attendants, who would precede him in ceremonial processions, wore finely worked pectoral disks—gold pendants etched with images of animals or other designs that were thought to ward off evil spirits.

Due in part to the damp West African climate, it was inevitable that many art works created from perishable materials such as cloth, wood, and grasses would not survive. Also, in some African cultures, objects we might think of today as "art" were created specifically for transitory use in rituals and ceremonies. Many preserved West African wood carvings from the colonial and precolonial periods were originally acquired by Europeans, gradually finding their way into museums and private collections.

Just as inevitably, the decades and then centuries of contact with Europeans influenced African artistic expression. As European missionaries energetically began converting Africans to Christianity, Christian motifs such as Madonna figures and crosses began appearing in artistic works. As foreign traders introduced materials such as beads and coral to West African peoples, the artists among them readily incorporated those novel materials into their repertoires. By the 1500s, the creators of Benin bronzes were fashioning images of Portuguese soldiers, and it would not be long before ivory carvers were documenting scenes of slavery in creations that were at once astonishingly beautiful and chilling reflections of human misery. Today such works bear powerful witness to the sensitivity of African artists to the new social and economic realities that emerged from the international trade in their countrymen and women. —B.C.M.

Mounted king with attendants, brass, c. 1600–1700. Bas-relief plaques were a common art form created in and around Benin. (Metropolitan Museum of Art, Michael C. Rockefeller Memorial Collection, Gift of Nelson A. Rockefeller, 1965.)

Carved tusk from the Loango coast (Angola), fashioned around 1860. Its creator depicted numerous scenes of the slave trade, including captives shackled together in a coffle and European ships at anchor. (National Museum of African Art, Smithsonian Institution, photograph by Franko Khoury.)

A procession of the *oba* (king) through the City of Benin. (Olfert Dapper, "De Stadt Benin," from *Nauwkeurige Beschrijvinge de Afrikaansche ewesten*, Amsterdam, 1668.)

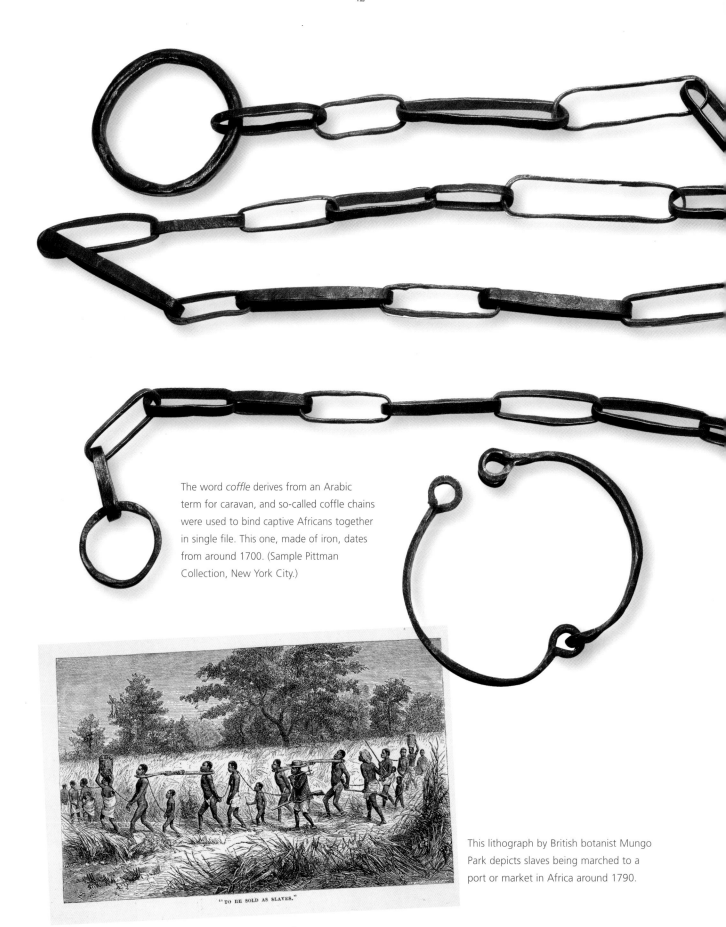

The word *coffle* derives from an Arabic term for caravan, and so-called coffle chains were used to bind captive Africans together in single file. This one, made of iron, dates from around 1700. (Sample Pittman Collection, New York City.)

"TO BE SOLD AS SLAVES."

This lithograph by British botanist Mungo Park depicts slaves being marched to a port or market in Africa around 1790.

one-third of its wars, sometimes with heavy casualties. In another third the results were indecisive and Dahomey's armies returned with few or no captives.[11] It also is not difficult to see that at least some of Dahomey's wars were waged to secure territory, extend royal power, or even obtain peace.[12]

Rather than dismiss all African rulers as selfish tyrants, one must attempt to consider the slave trade from an African perspective. It helps to start by recognizing that in Africa, the condition of slavery was not regarded as aberrant or immoral. Most African legal systems recognized slavery as a social condition: slaves constituted a class of people, captives or their descendants, over whom private citizens exercised the rights of the state to make law, punish, and control. These rights were alienable, that is, they could be transferred by sale. The exercise of such rights by private citizens (or by the ruler and state officials in their private capacities) was crucial, for African law did not recognize the right of a person to draw income from the rent or sale of land, as many other societies did. Thus, in many parts of Africa slaves were the prime source of private income.

In general, African slaves were probably treated better than slaves in the Americas. African slavery was mild, more like serfdom in medieval Europe. As the principal form of private income-bearing property, slaves were used in many more activities than were similar classes of people in Europe or the Americas. In addition to their roles as agricultural laborers and personal servants, African slaves sometimes performed administrative tasks or served in the military, occasionally in positions of command.

Although there was a slave class in Africa, this does not mean that Africans simply sold off an existing slave community in their dealings with Europeans. In fact, most available information suggests that people of the slave class who had been settled in one location for sufficient time (often less than one lifetime) came to possess a number of rights, including immunity from resale or arbitrary transfer to another owner or location. Moreover, most of the Africans sold as slaves for export were not from the established slave class, but were newly enslaved captives taken in war or purchased from bandits. The existence of the class in African societies simply meant that there was a legal basis for selling slaves to Europeans, and an apparatus for acquiring, controlling, and moving enslaved people.[13]

Africans who made decisions about the slave trade did not necessarily imagine that they were transferring people to America to serve in the same ways that they did in Africa. African leaders probably knew that the type of slavery exported captives would know in America was harsh compared to the slavery of Africa. African leaders often sent ambassadors to Europe, and many African elites had their children educated abroad. Because

Hand-colored etching showing Lisbon's harbor around 1580. (Georg Braun and Franz Hogenburg, *Civitas Orbis Terrarum*.)

of the routes vessels took to reach Europe, such travelers crossed the Atlantic on the very ships that made the Middle Passage. In fact, it was impossible to travel from Africa to Europe and not pass through Brazil or the West Indies, where the harshest forms of American slavery—work in sugar production— were practiced. In 1643, it was just such an itinerary that Miguel de Castro, ambassador from the Congolese province of Soyo, followed during his diplomatic mission to Holland.[14] During layovers that might last months, travelers such as de Castro had ample opportunity to observe first- hand the horrors of American slavery, horrors they could and doubtless did report back to their families and sponsors upon their return to Africa. But although Africans were aware of the problems of American slavery, they were not selling their own subjects or usually even their own slaves abroad. They were selling foreigners and even enemies, people captured in wars waged for a wide variety of reasons.

SPOILS OF WAR

Seventeenth- and eighteenth- century observers who interviewed numerous African slaves in the Americas all testified to the important role warfare played. In fact, war was at the heart of the paradox of African enslavement, the means by which most of those who were enslaved were captured.

Wars in Africa were waged for much the same reasons as conflicts in other parts of the world. From the available evidence, African rulers waged war to increase their territory, to avenge wrongs done them by neighbors, to gain influence in a region, or to control key resources or travel routes. African wars often were civil wars between rival members of a ruling elite to secure power. Beyond the reports of elite Africans to Europeans or those preserved in chronicles, we know relatively little about the causes of many African wars during the era of the slave trade. African oral tradition, the source of much of our understanding of precolonial African history, indicates that African wars had origins that appear quite conventional in the seventeenth- and eighteenth-century world.

While African wars apparently were like those elsewhere, however, the slave trade was not merely an outgrowth of warfare that would have been waged anyway. It may well have been influenced by the European demand for

This "Meeting with the King of Sestro" was drawn from a description in the journal of French Huguenot slave captain Jean Barbot, who plied the Atlantic slave trade in the service of English interests in the late 1600s. Barbot, like many others, justified his choice of livelihood in part by citing how slaves would benefit from being con- verted to Christianity. (Awnsham and John Churchill, *Collection of Voyages and Travels*, vol. 5, London.)

"Prospect of St. George's Castle at Elmina," on the Gold Coast, c. 1732. (Awnsham and John Churchill, *Collections of Voyages and Travels*, vol. 6, London, 1746.)

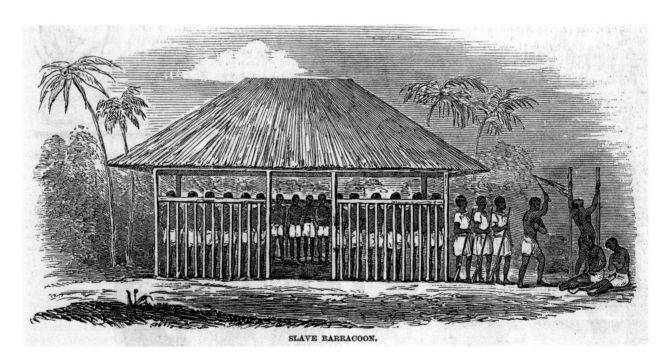

SLAVE BARRACOON.

A slave barracoon in Sierra Leone in the 1840s. Chained by the neck and legs, recently captured Africans could be held under guard in a barracoon and flogged, sometimes fatally, if they resisted or tried to escape. (*Illustrated London News.*)

slave labor. One clue that this was so comes from the fact that Europeans sold munitions as an important item of commerce, suggesting that the African decision to wage war was often made with an eye to the trade in weapons. In disposing their troops, planning battles, and making their attacks, African generals might consider the military and financial implications of capturing and deporting people. The slave trade may not have caused wars, but it played a big role in the way that wars were waged.

An example of this planning logic comes from the war in 1730 between Akwamu and Akyem, two small states on the Gold Coast (modern Ghana). As the threat of war built in the late 1720s, Dutch, English, and Danish traders predicted that it would be a big showdown and would yield a great haul of slaves. Yet when the war ended with total victory for Akyem, few slaves were forthcoming. This was because, a Danish factor complained, the Akyem authorities had decided not to "eat the country"—a local expression for the policy of complete devastation of a defeated country, especially the capture and export of its population. The practice had two effects. First, eating the country helped defray the costs of war and repay loans the victors had taken to finance it, including loans from European traders for munitions. Second, the devastation of the population so weakened the defeated country that it would be unable to recover its political initiative—an important point given that Akyem had no chance of absorbing and garrisoning Akwamu.

The rulers of Akyem decided not to "eat" Akwamu because they felt they needed its military resources for a new war that was brewing with their more powerful neighbor, Asante. They were confident that Akonno, the late ruler of Akwamu, had sufficiently alienated his own people that they would be loyal to Akyem if they were spared. In the end, Akwamu did support Akyem in the war with Asante when it finally came in 1742, although Asante won anyway.[15]

As this example shows, a combination of ordinary motives, such as the desire to capture territory and defeat rivals, might feed into the slave trade. The economic demands of waging war, as well as the politics of demography, made selling captives into the slave trade a principal goal even when the war's fundamental purpose was something else. So whereas in many instances the decision to make war, with the accompanying risk of defeat, was not driven by the slave trade per se, the conduct of that war was shaped by the slave trade. Europeans did not operate a "gun-slave cycle" whereby they fostered African wars by selling guns to one power in order to persuade it to fall upon its neighbors, using the guns to ensure victory. But they did benefit from the fact that both the purchase of guns and the sale of slaves made sense in the course of seeking other, more conventional outcomes.

The idea of "eating the country" worked as a strategic principle in international wars; so could the decision not to do it, as with Akyem and Akwamu. Similar strategies might also be employed in civil wars, or in complex combinations of the two. Northwest of the Gold Coast in the Senegal valley, for example, politics encompassed a complicated combination of civil war, international war, and invasion by bandits. The states of the eighteenth-century Senegal valley were parts of the former Empire of the Great Fulo, which dominated the valley and many regions outside it through much of the late sixteenth and early seventeenth centuries. But when Great Fulo declined, many formerly independent

regions regained their freedom and competed for regional dominance. Near the Atlantic coast, two such states were Bawol and Kajoor, which sometimes united and sometimes fought, while at the same time the throne of each was occasionally contested by rival candidates. Within the old core of the Empire of the Great Fulo, the state of Futa Tooro was divided into rival contenders and even within each section of the contenders' territories there were civil wars between different factions. In each of these situations, the interstate rivalry intersected with civil wars, so that rival states sometimes supported one side or another in such conflicts. Furthermore, the whole upper western region of Africa was affected by raiding desert nomads from the north, who sometimes were backed by the Sultan of Morocco (who also sent armed forces to the region). Still other raids were launched from Khasso in the east. Raiders did not always function independently; sometimes they were invited to pillage an area by one side in a civil war, or by one state in an interstate rivalry.[16]

Tactics employed by various factions were the Senegalese version of eating the country. As in Gold Coast, it was a strategic advantage to weaken the demographic base of rivals, even if in the long run one hoped these rivals' people would become citizens of a reunited state. This advantage included using the proceeds of the sale of captives to purchase munitions from English and French merchants on the coast or in posts along the Senegal valley. In addition, rulers might actually pay for the services of nomadic raiders from the north or east by allowing them to pillage an area, typically one in the lands of a rival state or contender.

In describing African wars, European visitors sometimes divided them into the "great pillage" and the "little pillage." Great pillages were international wars waged by armies in support of formal goals of a contender or a state, while little pillages were conducted by the same rulers against lands of rivals either within or outside their state. Little pillages were designed to weaken the opposition's population base and to obtain resources through the trade in captives. Little pillage also coincided with invasions of Moors and Arabs from the eastern desert of the Khassonke, raiders whose main interest was obtaining slaves for sale.

Sometimes, instead of provoking or encouraging international rivalry, a civil war's main impact was to destroy internal discipline. This happened with the civil wars that wracked the Kingdom of Congo in central Africa in the

Bronze figurine of slaves chained together in a coffle.
(Sample Pittman Collection, New York City.)

A bronze muzzle for a young female slave.
At forts and along the slave coast, muzzles
were used for various purposes, including
punishing slaves for "insubordination."
(Eugene and Adele Redd Collection.)

A Portuguese musketeer rendered
in bronze and dating from the 1500s.
(British Museum, London.)

late seventeenth and eighteenth centuries. This happened with the civil wars that wracked the Kingdom of Congo in Central Africa in the late seventeenth and eighteenth centuries. The strife was triggered by a succession crisis following the death in 1665 of King António I in the battle of Mbwila against the Portuguese in the colony of Angola.[17] The rival kings established bases in various parts of Congo, and there entrenched they waged wars on one another as each sought to take control of the abandoned capital city of São Salvador. Even after the successful reoccupation of the capital by Pedro IV in 1709, the rivals maintained their bases and periodically destroyed the city. Like the internal wars of the Senegal valley, these also led to the large-scale deportation of people, following the same logic as elsewhere. Selling people weakened rivals and financed munitions and other war costs.

The King of Benin with armed soldiers, early 1700s. (Library of Congress.)

Most enslaved Africans who were not captured in open war were instead waylaid by bandits. Civil war fueled banditry as bands of armed men, often leaderless in a factional struggle, fended for themselves. One such bandit was Pedro Mpanzu a Mvemba, who operated in 1693. Formerly a regional commander for the province, he was dismissed when his overlord was overthrown. Refusing to accept this turn of affairs, with his soldiers Mpanzu a Mvemba took up residence on a local flat-topped mountain and from there raided commerce and villages far and wide. With time he became a local bandit and nuisance, no civil authority having the power to stop him.[18] Nearly a century later, in the 1780s, another bandit known only by his sobriquet of Mbwa Lau (Mad Dog), operated in a similar war in the area just east of São Salvador. He too had begun as a noble commander who, finding his superiors out of power, had taken to crime, preying especially on travelers whom he could sell to slave dealers.[19]

There were places in Africa where extreme political fragmentation was the norm and where banditry could not be checked because no entity ever had enough power to prevent it. The Igbo (Ibo) region of modern Nigeria was in this category. This area was divided into more than fifty small, independent villages, each jealously guarding its independence. Igbos valued their small-scale, open, and opportunity-oriented governmental system and, aside from a nominal and symbolic loyalty to the Emperor of Benin, they were loathe to accept real authority from any warlord. Yet this carefully protected small-scale governance, combined with the fact that their country lay in a heavily forested region that was nevertheless easily penetrable by river, meant that outlaws and bandits, lurking in the woods and highly mobile in watercraft, could strike at will, kidnapping people when they did. To defeat such raiders would have demanded an individual or a coalition of people who would take the matter in hand, an arrangement that does not seem to have developed.

VOICES OF PROTEST

In the final analysis, African political authorities found it logical to support the slave trade, sometimes for reasons rooted in self-interest and greed, on other occasions for strategic reasons. Bandits might have no other motive than personal gain, and there were instances when they could not be checked. Nevertheless, there were times when common people, oppressed by war and enslavement, might protest spontaneously and these protests occasionally shook up the political order.

A sketch showing the residence of the King of Congo, c. 1700. Set on a hilltop, the king's palace dominated a small city that also included Catholic churches and Portuguese forts. Large canoes on the river in the foreground are carrying water to the city from a spring well. (Thomas Astley, ed., *A New General Collection of Voyages and Travels*, vol. 3, London, 1745–47.)

From 1704 to 1706 in Congo, for example, a young woman named Doña Beatriz Kimpa Vita, who believed herself to be possessed by Saint Anthony, led a powerful revival movement intended to stop the wars and restore the kingdom. While she never directly objected to the slave trade, her protest against the unnecessary wars, and the political ambition that underlay them, struck at the root of the slave trade.[20] More explicit in his denunciations was Nasr al-Din, a Senegalese marabout (religious teacher), lawyer, and leader who led the *toubenon* (purification) movement in 1673–77. He began preaching among the desert Arabs and in time counted many of them among his followers. But when he took his message to the Senegal valley he directed his teaching against the political authorities, reminding them that God did not permit them to raid and pillage their own subjects (a reference to the civil wars). Teaching also that Islam specifically prohibited the selling of Muslim slaves to Christian buyers, he temporarily brought the slave trade to a halt. Not that Nasr al-Din opposed the holding or even the selling of slaves—he had slaves himself—but he charged that the changes wrought in the established government by its participation in the slave trade had made tyrants of the rulers who did so.

A century later the same interpretation of Islamic law led Abd al-Qadir, a Muslim leader who seized power in Futa Tooro in 1776, to outlaw the export of Muslims as slaves. His own rise to power had been impelled by exhaustion at the constant raiding by desert Arabs, and he addressed the issue of their wars early in his reign. He also returned to the same themes that Nasr al-Din had broached a century earlier concerning the Atlantic slave trade. In a sharp letter to the British factor on the Gambia River, he rebuked the official for buying Muslim slaves, and ordered that anyone from that region who came to his lands to do so would be killed.[21]

Ultimately, understanding the slave trade and the paradox of enslavement
only comes through a careful examination of African social, political, and
military history. In that study we see that the slave trade was the doing
neither solely of European merchants nor solely of African elites. Although
commercial profit may have played a substantial role, the various decisions of
African rulers to participate in the trade were far more complex. They were
rooted in a complicated series of local situations in which financial, military,
and political considerations conspired to make the capture and export of
people a logical solution. This logic did not operate equally everywhere,
but some version of it operated everywhere the slave trade proceeded at
its highest levels.

Mali handgun. (Danny Drain Collection,
Walterboro, South Carolina.)

This late-eighteenth-century engraving
depicts Danish slave traders negotiating
with the Akwamu king. (P. E. Isert, *Neue
Reise nach Guinea und den Carabischen
Inseln*. By permission of the British Library,
London.)

3

The Middle Passage

Colin A. Palmer

Three-person ankle shackle for a slave ship. The small dimensions of the shackle shown suggest that it was used to restrain women. (Gene Alexander Peters Collection.)

The origin of the term "Middle Passage" cannot be conclusively established. It was probably first employed by English traders during the eighteenth century to describe the second leg of a slave ship's journey, the leg that carried slave cargoes to the Americas. The meaning of "the Middle Passage," however, has been altered over time. It is not certain when this transformation began, but the term now refers exclusively to the slaves' ordeal on their forced journey from the African coast to the Americas. The Middle Passage is now synonymous with the travail of enslaved African peoples, the taking of their freedom, their unspeakable suffering, and their capacity to resist and to survive. It has come to symbolize the profound and anguished sense of loss among the peoples of African descent: the loss of kin, of a homeland, of familiar places, and even of an ancestral ethnic identity. The pain of the Middle Passage has been recalled and commemorated in numerous historical accounts, novels, poems, plays, works of art, and so on.[1] It remains alive in the memories of the peoples of African descent, linking them across the geographic expanse of the diaspora. The horror of the Middle Passage continues to be a terrifying part of the present, resisting any exorcism.

The exact number of people who endured and survived the Middle Passage will never be determined. Modern historians have mined the relevant archives in Europe and the Americas and have produced estimates that seem plausible. Earlier historians had placed the number as high as 100 million, but the emerging consensus appears to reside somewhere between 11 million and 13 million.[2] This figure does not include those who perished on the high seas or shortly after their arrival in the Americas. Estimates of mortality during the Middle Passage vary, but the available evidence suggests that about 40 percent of each cargo died during the sixteenth century, 15 percent during the seventeenth, and between 5 and 10 percent in later years. Taking into account all those who died during their journey from the interior to the African coast, while awaiting transportation to the Americas, or during the Middle Passage, as well as those who survived, the total number of Africans who were enslaved and intended for labor in the Americas may have been as high as 20 million.

The city of Loango was a major departure point for captive Africans about to embark on the Middle Passage in the hold of a slave ship. This lithograph shows the layout of the city in the late 1600s; letters mark the locations of the king's palace and gardens, among other features. In the lower right-hand corner are prisoners awaiting execution. (D. O. Dapper, *Description de L'Afrique … traduite de Flamand*, Amsterdam 1686, in Thomas Astley's *A New General Collection of Voyages and Travels*, vol. 3, London, 1745–47.)

CAPTIVE PASSAGE

If the Middle Passage is defined as the slaves' journey from Africa to the Americas, then it clearly originated in 1518 when Spain's Charles I authorized the direct importation of slaves from Africa. The unfortunate individuals who were destined for transportation to the Americas were confined on the African coast for varying periods of time before their departure. Much depended on when the waiting ships acquired their human cargo and the requisite provisions for them. This, in turn, was a function of supply patterns on the coast and the nature of the competition for the available captives. European traders knew that if African states were at war with one another, the market for slaves would be brisk. Writing from Cape Coast in 1712, for example, one English trader noted with evident relish, "The battle is expected shortly, after which 'tis hoped the trade will flourish."[3]

Captives who remained for long periods on the coast in damp, inhospitable quarters experienced high mortality. Some died from wounds that had been inflicted upon them during their capture. Others fell victim to one of the many diseases that seemed to be ubiquitous on the continent. It may be impossible to determine with any degree of exactitude the extent of this mortality because it may have varied from region to region and over time. One scholar who studied the mortality rates of slaves sent from Loango to Brazil during the eighteenth century observed that the "best estimates suggest that perhaps 40 percent of the slaves bought by Portuguese slave traders in the

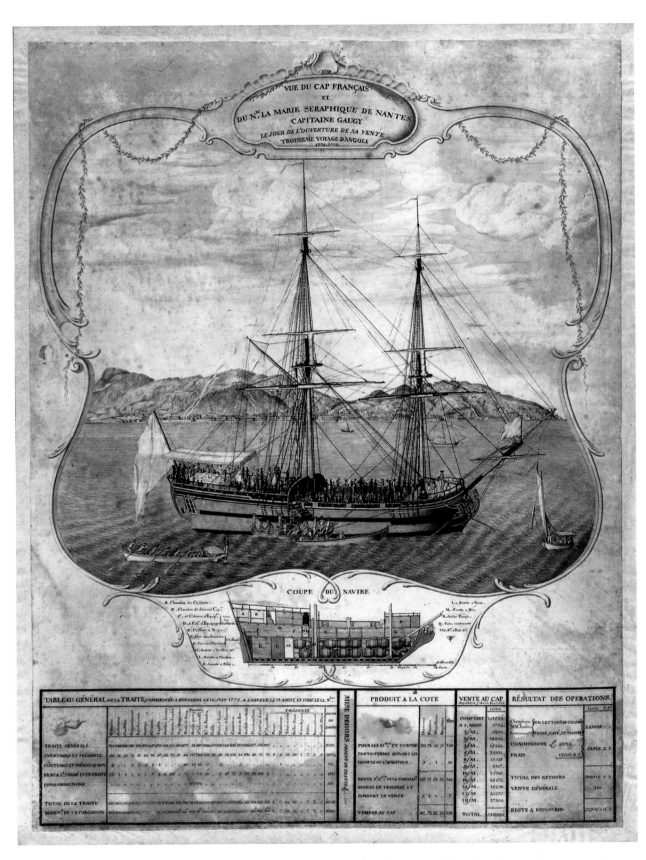

This watercolor painted in 1773 provides a wealth of detail about the French slave ship *La Marie Seraphique*, shown here moored off the island of Hispaniola after completing the Middle Passage from Angola. Close inspection reveals European ladies and gentlemen picnicking on the ship's stern while slave buyers on the forward deck examine a new cargo. (Anonymous; Ville de Nantes, Musée de Chateau des ducs de Bretagne.)

interior died between the time of purchase and the arrival of the survivors six months later at the port towns." An additional 10 percent, this researcher estimated, died in the dungeons in which they were confined on the coast.[4]

These human beings who had lost their liberty had no knowledge of their destination and the fate that awaited them. They had been torn from their homelands and kin and reduced to the status of chattel, bereft of human ties and completely under the control of strangers. The depth of the emotional turmoil caused by their seizure, enslavement, and impending transportation across the sea can only be imagined. Eyewitness reports on the mental state of these people sometimes captured their despair. John Atkins, the Royal Navy surgeon who visited Sierra Leone in 1721, noted that slaves who awaited purchase appeared to be "very dejected."[5] Thomas Trotter, another surgeon, reported that the slaves being brought aboard ship "show signs of extreme distress and despair from a feeling of their situation and regret at being torn from their friends and connections."[6] Mungo Park, who traveled to Africa in the late eighteenth century, was struck by one girl's despair as she was sold. "Never was a face of serenity more suddenly changed into one of the deepest distress," wrote Park. "The terror she manifested in having the load put upon her head and the rope fastened round her neck, and the sorrow with which she bade adieu to her companions, were truly affecting."[7]

Some of the human cargoes had heard fearful rumors that they were being purchased in order to be eaten by the white traders. Captain William Snelgrave, an experienced trader, reported that "these poor People are generally under terrible apprehension upon being bought by white Men, many being afraid that we design to eat them, which I have been told is a story much credited by the inland negroes."[8] Such fears undoubtedly exacerbated the emotional distress of the captives.

Detailed plan of the island of Gorée, situated just south of Cape Verde. Gorée served not only as an embarkation point for slaves but also as a supply depot for slavers about to depart on the transatlantic leg of the triangular trade. It was the first West African slave harbor in which European forms of money—pieces of silver—were used in slave trading. (Thomas Astley, ed., *A New General Collection of Voyages and Travels*, vol. 2, London, 1745–47.)

No modern scholar can fully reconstruct the experiences and emotional travail of those unfortunate people as they were herded onto the slavers shackled, prodded by whips, and terrified as to their future. On the other hand, no modern scholar should treat the experiences of these individuals with such cold detachment that we lose sight of the fact that these "cargoes" were the victims of coercion and mistreatment and members of the human species. They should not be regarded merely as items of trade, similar to gold, textiles, and ivory. Such dispassionate accounts in many contemporary history books do a disservice to the experiences of these people and their descendants in the diaspora.

The ships into which the slaves were herded varied in size and in the space allotted each human captive. Studies show that African slaves occupied a smaller space than other travelers on the ships of the times, even less than that allowed convicts. Historians have found that there was no essential relationship between the tonnage of a ship and the amount of space each slave was

A slave whip with a carved wooden handle. (Danny Drain Collection, Walterboro, South Carolina.)

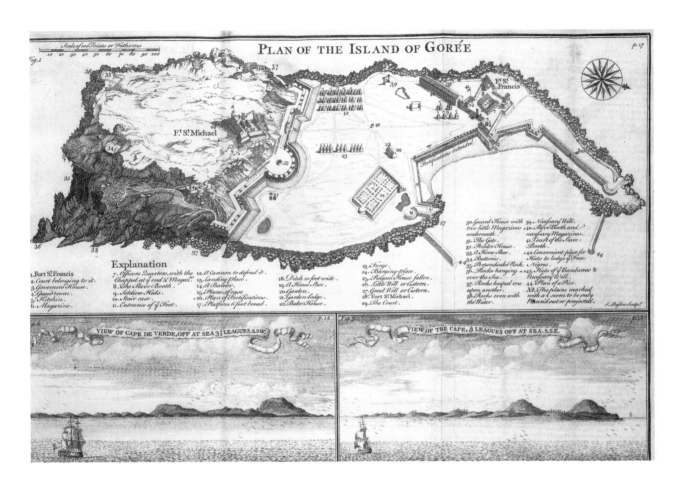

A Royal Business

On September 27, 1672, Britain's King Charles II chartered the Royal African Company, or RAC, to capitalize on a growing commerce with Africa that promised vast economic rewards, especially with regard to the trade in African slaves. The purpose of the enterprise was clear: "to … set to sea such as many ships, pinnaces and barks as shall be thought fitting … for the buying, selling, bartering and exchanging of, for or with any gold, silver, Negroes, slaves, goods, wares and manufactures. …" The RAC's coat of arms included an elephant and images of two "Moors," and its investors included the king, members of England's aristocracy, merchants, and even the philosopher John Locke. Coins struck to recognize the enterprise—using gold purchased in Africa—soon were known as guineas, after the then-popular term for Africa's west coast. The term of the charter was to be a thousand years, its mandate to maximize profits for its investors.

The Royal African Company's charter meant that it possessed an absolute monopoly on British participation in the African trade. It thrived—and kept meticulous records. Between 1672 and 1689, its agents traded the usual assortment of European cloth, beads, iron, rum, and other commodities for nearly 90,000 black Africans, purchased along the coast in such places as Whydah, Angola, and Senegambia. Slaves who survived the Middle Passage were then sold in English colonies like Barbados, Jamaica, and those of mainland North America. By the close of the seventeenth century, roughly 175,000 Africans had made the forced journey to the Caribbean in Royal African Company ships, some 25,000 to Barbadian sugar plantations alone.

After a mere twenty years, however, RAC fortunes began to fade. Like other nationally chartered companies (such as the South Sea Company and the Royal Sénégal Company) the Royal African had plenty of overhead—its home offices, the forts it had to build, staff, and maintain in Africa, and agents who quietly pocketed a portion of the profits. Trade voyages also could easily go awry if cargoes sold for less than anticipated (at either end), if a ship was lost, or if large numbers of slaves perished during the Atlantic crossing. Occasionally, though, slaving trips would succeed wildly, returning handsome dividends on the invested capital.

The potential for substantial profits from the transatlantic slave trade drew a rising chorus of calls for a free trade in slaves—any Englishman or syndicate able to equip a ship and finance a trading voyage wanted a piece of the action. Many in fact did so illegally, coming to be known as "interlopers." By 1698, Parliament gave in to the rising demands and opened the African trade to all comers. Unfortunately for the enslaved Africans, the end of the RAC's monopoly meant that the number of slaves on English ships increased dramatically. By 1700 England led the world in the transport of African captives across the Atlantic Ocean, averaging about 20,000 a year.
—B.C.M.

Coin minted in recognition of the patronage of British King Charles II for the Royal African Company. The small elephant below the king's profile symbolizes the African trade. (British Museum.)

"I have agreed to go to buy the slaves ..."

It was the spring of 1693 when Welsh sea captain John Phillips set out from London in command of the Royal African Company's slave ship *Hannibal*. His first port of call would be the west coast of Africa—or "Guiney," as Britons called it—to trade English guns, gunpowder, cloth, and other goods for gold and slaves. Then the *Hannibal* would make the Middle Passage to the Caribbean islands of St. Thomas and Barbados, where her cargo of Africans would be sold and sugar would be loaded for the return trip to London in 1694. The journal Phillips kept during the two-year sojourn includes the following matter-of-fact account of his purchase of 1,300 slaves from the king of Whidaw (Whydah).

> I have agreed to go to buy the slaves. ... This morning I went ashore at Whidaw, accompany'd by my ... purser and doctor Mr. Clay, the present captain of the East-India Merchant, his ... purser, and about a dozen of our seamen for our guard ... in order to here reside until we could purchase 1300 negroe slaves, which was the number we both wanted to compleat 700 for the Hannibal and 650 for the East-India Merchant, according to our agreement ... with the Royal African Company.
>
> Our factory [trading post] ... stands low near the marshes, which renders it a very unhealthy place to live in ... 'tis compassed round with a mud-wall about six foot high ... within which is a large yard [that includes] a trunk for slaves. ... When we were at the trunk, the king's slaves, if he had any, were first offered to sale ... then the cappshiers [king's representatives] each brought out his slaves according to his degree and quality, the greatest first, etc. ... Our surgeon examin'd them well in all kinds, to see they were sound of wind and limb, making them jump, stretch out their arms swiftly, looking in their mouths to judge of their age ... but our greatest care of all is to buy none that are pox'd, lest they should infect the rest aboard. ... Our surgeon [also] is forced to examine the privities of both men and women [for signs of venereal disease]. When we had selected from the rest such as we liked, we agreed what goods to pay for them ... how much of each sort of merchandise we were to give for a man, woman, child ...
>
> Then we mark'd the slaves we had bought in the breast, or shoulder, with a hot iron having the letter of the ship's name on it, the place before being anointed with a little palm oil, which caused but little pain, the mark being usually well in four or five days, appearing very plain and white after.

At Whydah Captain Phillips purchased a total of 480 men and 220 women for the *Hannibal*'s hold, and after taking leave of the king "with many affectionate expressions on both sides" proceeded to purchase food supplies and depart on the Middle Passage. By his account it was a disastrous crossing:

> What the smallpox spared, the flux [dysentery] swept off, to our great regret, after all our pains and care to give them their messes [meals] in due order and season, keeping their lodgings as clean and sweet as possible, and enduring so much misery and stench so long among a parcel of creatures nastier than swine. ...

Notable in these passages is John Phillips's contempt for his cargo of human beings, and his amazingly sanitized description of the conditions he provided for them during the Middle Passage. In the end, he complained bitterly, "No gold-finders can endure so much noisome slavery as they do who carry Negroes; for ... by their mortality our voyages are ruin'd, and we pine and fret ourselves to death, to think that we should undergo so much misery, and take so much pains to little purpose."

Rendered deaf by disease contracted during the *Hannibal*'s journey, John Phillips never made another slaving voyage.
—B.C.M.

granted.[9] In order to maximize the use of space, the ships would be divided into a number of deck platforms. The slaves would then be herded onto these decks and confined in a pattern roughly similar to books on a shelf. The space separating each deck could be less than five feet, sometimes making it impossible for taller slaves to stand. In 1704, to cite one example, a slave trader stationed at James Island, West Africa, complained that the space allotted to each slave on the *Postillion* was inadequate. "The slaves are so large," he wrote, "[and] it being the general opinion that the slaves could not be healthy in the space of three foot, they broke up one of the platforms which was the reason she couldn't carry more than 100 slaves."[10] Generally speaking, each slave was allowed between five and seven square feet of space regardless of the ship's tonnage or its nation of origin.

Not only were slaves confined to cramped spaces that restricted their mobility, but they were shackled as well, the left foot of one being bound to the right foot of another. This meant, in some situations, that individuals coming from states that harbored ancient rivalries could find themselves shackled together. Women, if they were deemed not to pose a physical threat to the voyage, could be released from their irons as the journey progressed. Children were generally free to move around without restrictions. Slaves confined in irons undoubtedly suffered both physically and psychologically. When a cargo of Africans arrived in Nevis in 1714, for example, the resident trader observed that they "were very feeble and weak at their landing and many having such a contraction of nerves by their being on board and confined in irons that [they] were hardly capable to walk."[11]

Slave traders were fully aware of the fact that slaves needed some form of exercise during the Middle Passage if they were to remain healthy. Accordingly, the slaves were forced to "dance," prodded by the whip. One of the earliest accounts of what was evidently a very bizarre ritual was found in the log of the slaver *Hannibal*, written in 1694. According to this account, the Africans were "linked together [and] made to jump and dance for an hour or two. If they go about it reluctantly or do not move with agility, they are flogged." While some traders reported that such occasions were "full of jollity and good humour" for the slaves, others emphasized its coercive nature, noting that they were "compelled to dance by the cat." Slaves were usually not released from their irons during the "dance," given the possibility of rebellion. The shackles not only restricted their movements but produced discomfort of another sort since "the parts ... on which the shackles are fastened are often excoriated."[12] A poem written in 1790, entitled "The Sorrow of Yoruba," captured the pain and humiliation of the shipboard dance for the enslaved Africans:

> *At the savage Captain's beck,*
> *Now like brutes they make us prance:*
> *Smack the Cat about the Deck,*
> *And in scorn they bid us dance.*[13]

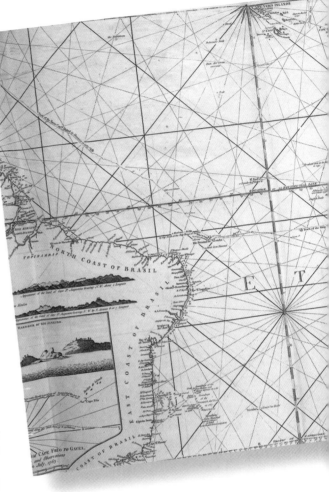

Detail from a book of charts used to guide ships through coastal waters of West Africa and across the Middle Passage. (Robert Laurie, *The African Pilot: Being a Collection of ... Charts ... of Africa*, 1799.)

Opposite:
William Snelgrave's 1754 memoir *A New Account of Guinea and the Slave Trade* details his experiences as a slave captain, which included the suppression of slave revolts at sea. Such memoirs could make money for their authors and serve as information sources for those who wished to enter the trade.

A NEW ACCOUNT OF GUINEA,

And the Slave-Trade,

CONTAINING,

I. The History of the late Conquest of the Kingdom of *Whidaw* by the King of *Dahome.* The Author's Journey to the Conqueror's Camp; where he saw several Captives sacrificed, &c.

II. The Manner how the Negroes become Slaves. The Numbers of them yearly exported from *Guinea* to *America.* The Lawfulness of that Trade. The Mutinies among them on board the Ships where the Author has been, &c.

III. A Relation of the Author's being taken by Pirates, and the many Dangers he underwent.

By Captain WILLIAM SNELGRAVE.

With a new and correct Map of the Coast of *Guinea.*

LONDON:

Printed for J. WREN, at the *Bible* and *Crown*, in *Salisbury-Court*, *Fleet-Street*. 1754.

Slaves on the West Coast of Africa, painted by Auguste Biard around 1833. (Wilberforce House, Hull City Museums and Art Galleries, UK/Bridgeman Art Library.)

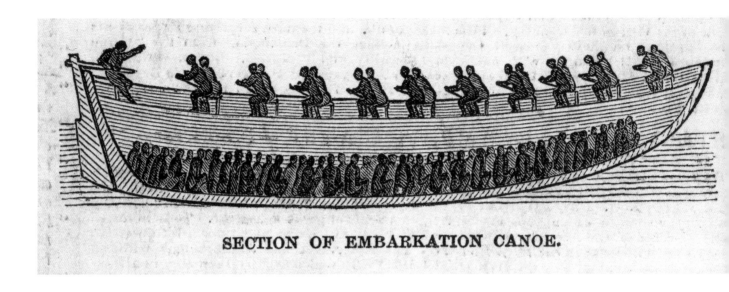

SECTION OF EMBARKATION CANOE.

Cross section of a canoelike craft used to transport slaves from shore to a waiting slave ship. In 1849 the *Illustrated London News*, which ran many articles about the slave trade, published this drawing with the notation that it showed "one of the embarkation boats used by the [Spanish] slave factors" operating on the Gallinas River in Sierra Leone. Such a vessel was 40 feet long by 12 feet across, and could reportedly hold as many as 200 slaves below its deck.

This wood carving shows captive Africans being transported in a canoe. (Gene Alexander Peters Collection.)

Contemporary accounts suggest that slaves were also required to dance in order to entertain the crew, particularly at night. The best dancers received rewards, most frequently alcohol. The records are silent on whether the slaves derived any pleasure from these performances. Still, such dances, performed under very difficult and unusual circumstances, must have drawn upon African traditions and may even have provided the captives with a temporary respite from their travail. But we cannot be certain of this conclusion. All too frequently, modern historians see such activities as muting the pain of enslavement, a questionable and essentially erroneous conclusion when viewed from the perspective of those who had become merely property.

The length of the journey from the different African ports to the Americas varied. Much depended on the point of origin, the destination in the Americas, the type of ship and the speed with which it sailed, weather conditions, and so on. During the sixteenth century, for example, the journey from a West African port to Vera Cruz, Mexico, would have taken between three and four months. By the eighteenth century, with the construction of faster ships, the average sailing time would have been reduced by about one-third to one-half.

The reduction in sailing time as the centuries progressed obviously shortened the shipboard ordeal of the forced immigrants. People familiar with the trade were certain that there was a correlation between sailing time and mortality rates. They were equally convinced that there was a relationship between overcrowding and the death rate. Sir Dalby Thomas, an eighteenth-century trader, pointed out that overcrowding "will occasion a great mortality."[14]

In 1712 the Royal African Company, a British slave-trading company, advised its agents at Cape Coast Castle to dispatch its slavers speedily "though not with their full complement of negroes if upon a survey you find the ship is appointed to take in more negroes than she can conveniently stow. Pray lade no more than are necessary to prevent mortality which has often happen'd by crowding the ship with too many negroes."[15]

Recent scholarship has taken issue with these conventional judgments. Studies of certain branches of the slave trade and of certain time periods appear to indicate that a longer sailing time did not usually result in higher mortality rates. Joseph Miller, who studied the slave trade from Loango to Brazil, found that slaves died at a faster rate in the days immediately following their departure from the African coast. His findings suggested that this high mortality was a consequence of the "pre-embarkation experiences of the slaves in Africa," and not necessarily of their conditions on shipboard and the duration of the voyage. Similarly, the eminent scholar Herbert Klein has questioned whether the "tight packing" of slaves on the ships resulted in a higher incidence of deaths.[16]

Such claims, while they can be supported by hard data for some branches of the trade, should be accepted with a great degree of caution. Much more research needs to be done on these questions since the trade was conducted by several nations and lasted for more than three centuries. Eyewitness accounts

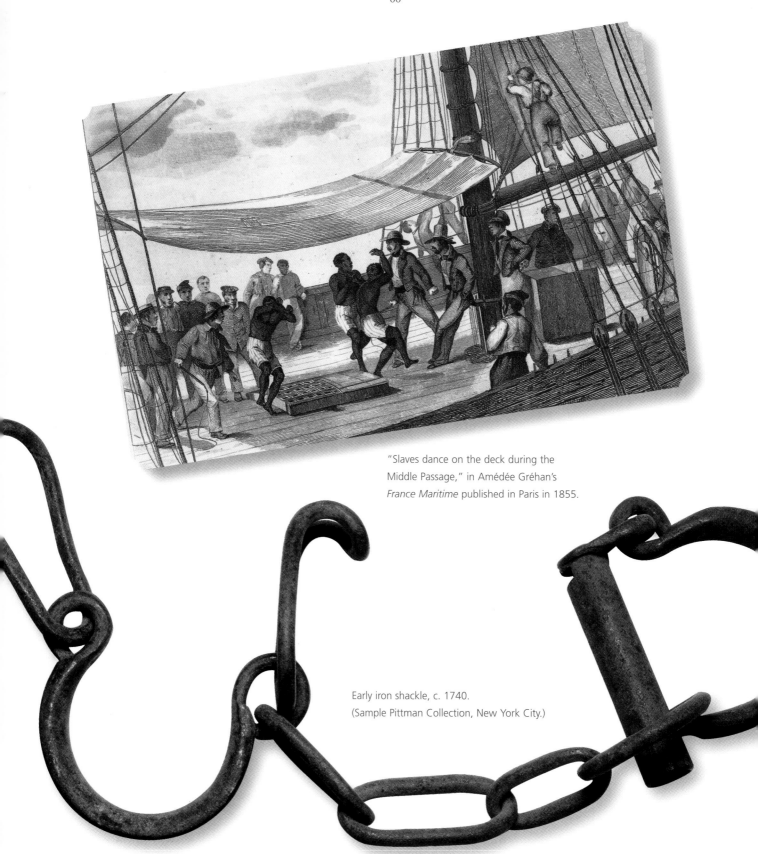

"Slaves dance on the deck during the
Middle Passage," in Amédée Gréhan's
France Maritime published in Paris in 1855.

Early iron shackle, c. 1740.
(Sample Pittman Collection, New York City.)

Opposite:
The slave ship *Brookes* in cross section, showing how slaves were packed in the vessel's
hold. This appears to show "tight packing," the practice of squeezing as many slaves as
possible into the allotted space.

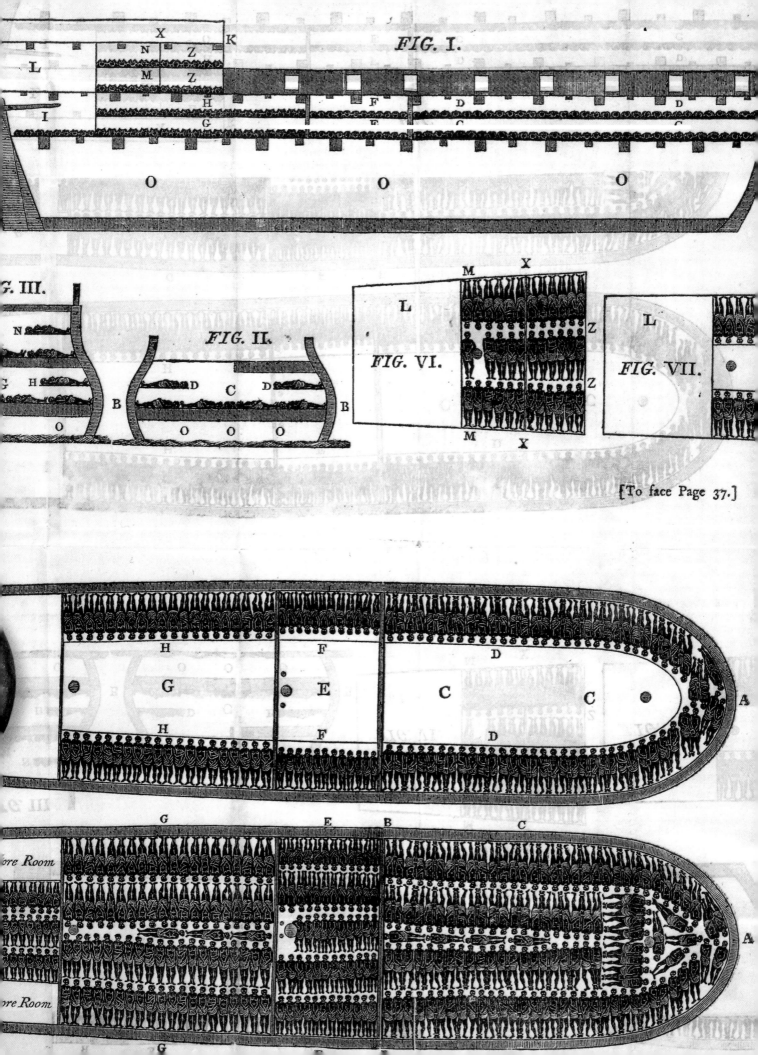

FIG. I.

FIG. III.

FIG. II.

FIG. VI.

FIG. VII.

[To face Page 37.]

of the trade should not be dismissed, nor should generalizations be made on the basis of information derived from limited studies. Nor should we use modern findings to minimize the horror of the Middle Passage.

The slaves' physical comfort and survival or mortality were also related to their diet aboard ship. An experienced captain and his crew understood that an adequate diet and one sensitive to the culinary habits of the human cargo would create a more hospitable environment. Accordingly, they purchased such provisions on the African coast as rice, malaguetta pepper, corn, palm oil, and potatoes. In addition, the ships stocked such supplies as cheese, salt, vinegar, beans, flour, and beef. Some ships also carried such extras as rum, tobacco, and coconuts to serve as "refreshments" for the human cargo.

Before the voyage to Africa began, the ship's owners and the captain had to determine the amount of provisions necessary, based upon the projected size of the slave cargo and the estimated travel time from Africa to the destination in the Americas. It is instructive to examine the kinds of food, the quantity dispatched, and the number of slaves a ship was intended to carry. In 1714, for example, the Royal African Company's ship *Norman* left London with the following supplies for the 300 slaves it hoped to purchase[17]:

150 gallons malt liquor
15 bushels salt
11 1/2 hogsheads vinegar
300 pounds tobacco
10 gross pipes
4 puncheons old beef
310 hundred weight and
10 pounds flour
12 hundred weight of biscuits
40 quarters of beans

The ship undoubtedly took on additional supplies in Africa, thereby meeting the dietary tastes of the captives and simultaneously increasing the amount of provisions. In 1714, for example, the *Dorothy* purchased 128 chests of corn, 100 pounds of malaguetta pepper, 40 gallons of palm oil, and 3 chests of salt on the African coast for its cargo of 200 slaves.[18]

It was obviously in the best interest of the venture's investors to provide an adequate diet for slaves and to ensure that they remained healthy during the transatlantic voyage. Owner captains, in particular, had a deep interest in providing proper food and care since their profits depended on the number of slaves they brought to the Americas alive and in salable condition. In some cases, the captain received a commission from his employers on every slave that he delivered alive. However, despite the claims of self-interest and careful calculations of the amount of provisions that a specific human cargo would require, ships sometimes ran short of food. In such cases, the owners and the captain would have seriously underestimated the necessary food supplies, or the ship's journey across the Atlantic would have taken longer than anticipated. Regardless, the potential outcome was starvation for those on board.

On ships with inadequate supplies the crew had to ration food. In some cases, the result was starvation for the slaves. Slaves on the *Dorothy* experienced starvation during a voyage the vessel made to Barbados in 1709. The ship delivered only 100 slaves after suffering a "great mortality" en route due to

Painted by Francis Meynell, a lieutenant on the antislavery vessel *Albatross*, this watercolor shows emaciated slaves on the slaver *Albanez* surrounded by sacks and barrels of supplies for the journey. ("The Slave Deck of the Albanez, c. 1860." National Maritime Museum, Greenwich, England.)

"povertie for want of provisions, as beefe, oyle, malagetta etc." When the *Pindar* reached St. Christopher in 1715, the agent described its human cargo as being "low in flesh." Agents in the islands frequently reported on the "miserable condition" of the arriving slaves, a euphemism for their being emaciated.[19]

Although not all slave cargoes suffered due to food shortages, sickness and death were the grim companions of every voyage. Modern historians have provided useful statistical evidence on the mortality rates of the slaves and crew for various branches of the trade. Between 1680 and 1688, for example, the Royal African Company shipped 60,783 slaves from Africa but delivered only 46,395. The Middle Passage had claimed the lives of 14,388 Africans, almost a quarter of those originally purchased. Of the 9,949 slaves that the same company transported between 1720 and 1725, 1,311, or 13.2 percent, perished in transit. Dutch traders left Africa with 111,129 slaves between 1700 and 1739, losing 18,787 during the journey to the Americas. Between 1795 and 1811, 170,642 Africans were dispatched to Rio de Janeiro but 15,587 succumbed during the voyage.[20]

Statistics cannot capture the nature of the individual suffering aboard these slavers. The ship's doctor and crew seldom understood the causes of diseases that tormented their human cargo, nor did the slaves receive appropriate medical care, given the time and place. Seasoned captains and crew knew that slaves developed "fevers" during the rainy season, roughly between June and August along the African coast, from which many would later die during the voyage. Accordingly, traders avoided arriving during that season, if they could.

In its continuing search for the causes of sickness and death aboard the ships, the Royal African Company concluded that changes in diet and water were partly responsible. Such was the gist of the company's letter to its agent,

Sir Dalby Thomas, on the African coast in October 1705. "The captains and others" had agreed that while the slaves "are at Cape Coast the water they drink is not good and they are kept short of provisions, and upon alteration in both after [they are] put aboard may occasion the heat of the ship to have a greater influence upon them and cast them into their fatall distempers," the company wrote.[21]

Drinking contaminated water may have been partly responsible for the gastrointestinal disorders that frequently occurred. There is some indication that by 1706 (if not sooner) the Royal African Company had begun to understand a possible relationship between the two. In that year, a company agent at Barbados, Benjamin Bullard, noted that water transported in rum casks was particularly harmful to the slaves who drank it. Bullard reported his observation to the company, which in turn passed it on to Dalby Thomas on the African coast. The company explained that Bullard "writes us they find by experience that rum casks are not fit to be filled with water for the negroes to drink, it gives them the gripes, and occations a mortality amongst them, it may doe well to boile their food, [water?] the fire corrects the ill taste and bad effects of the water." There is no evidence as to whether this advice was acted upon.[22]

Gastrointestinal disorders constituted only some of the afflictions aboard slave ships. Slaves fell victim to smallpox, dysentery, malaria, and a variety of other "fevers." Some suffered from severe dehydration, and to a lesser extent, scurvy. Smallpox was probably the major scourge of the voyages, with dysentery or the "bloody flux" a close second. Traders usually tried to purchase only the most "healthy and merchantable" slaves, but at best it was a matter of guesswork. Some traders took the chance of shipping infected individuals, hoping against their better judgment that the disease would not spread. The Royal African Company's agents at Cape Coast Castle, for example, dispatched the *Elizabeth* in 1713 with 157 slaves, some of whom had smallpox. The agents apparently expected the worst, for they doubted that the ship would make "a good voyage."[23]

The experiences of several voyages illustrate the impact of this dreaded disease. In 1704 Philip Brown, the Royal African Company's agent at Nevis, reported the arrival of a cargo of slaves with "the small pox very hott." In 1706 the *Regard* arrived in Antigua after losing 142 slaves to smallpox, and the *Oxford* arrived in Jamaica in 1713 having lost 95 of its cargo of 521 slaves. The agent informed his superiors in London that "the great mortality was owing to the smallpox which went quite through the ship, not a slave escaping it." The *Indian Queen* lost 140 slaves during its voyage to Buenos Aires in 1716, docking with 45 slaves described as being in the advanced stages of smallpox and another 43 showing the early symptoms.[24]

All slaves, regardless of sex, shared these horrendous experiences. But women had other burdens to bear as well. They were undoubtedly the victims of sexual abuse by the crew, sometimes becoming pregnant as a result. Babies were born during the Middle Passage, although it is difficult to establish when the pregnancies occurred. Others were born shortly after reaching the Americas. Between 1714 and 1718, for example, twenty-five babies were born to enslaved women within a few days of their arrival at Cartagena.[25]

The reports from traders either in Africa or the Americas constitute a dismal catalog of disease, death, and abuse for slaves during the Atlantic crossing. And despite the decline in mortality over time, the Middle Passage

Ottobah Cugoano

There are few accounts of the Middle Passage written by Africans who survived the experience. Those that exist make poignant reading. The following passages are from the autobiography of Ottobah Cugoano of the Gold Coast's Fante people. Born about 1757 in what is modern-day Ghana, Cugoano was kidnapped by African slave merchants when he was about thirteen years old and imprisoned in Cape Coast Castle, where as many as 1,500 slaves awaiting shipment would be housed in a basement dungeon.

> *After I was ordered out, the horrors I soon saw and felt, cannot well be described; I saw many of my miserable countrymen chained two and two, some hand-cuffed, and some with their hands tied behind. … But when a vessel arrived to conduct us away to the ship, it was a most horrible scene; there was nothing to be heard but rattling of chains, smacking of whips, and the groans and cries of our fellow men.*

During the Middle Passage aboard a British vessel bound for the Caribbean sugar island of Grenada, Cugoano took part in an ill-fated attempt at rebellion.

> *And when we found ourselves at last taken away, death was more preferable than life, and a plan was concerted amongst us that we might burn and blow up the ship, and to perish all together in the flames. But we were betrayed by one of our own countrywomen who slept with some of the head men of the ship, for it was common for the dirty filthy sailors to take the African women and lie upon their bodies; but the men were chained and pent up in holes. It was the women and boys which were to burn the ship, with the approbation and groans of the rest; though that was prevented, the discovery was likewise a cruel and bloody scene.*

Cugoano survived whatever punishment the ship's crew exacted from the captives for their efforts to resist enslavement, and after two years in Grenada his master returned to England with the young slave and soon thereafter set Cugoano free. He quickly learned to read and write English and became active in the growing British antislavery movement. In 1787, when Cuguano was about thirty years of age, he published *Thoughts and Sentiments on the Evil and Wicked Traffic of Slavery and Commerce in the Human Species*, one of the first English-language slave narratives. Cugoano apparently died around 1801. —*B.C.M.*

"Transport to the waiting ship." (In M. Chambon, *Le Commerce de L'Amérique par Marseille*, Avignon, 1764.)

continued to be synonymous with human suffering. Yet the Middle Passage also demonstrated that the spirit of the human captives was never vanquished, the capacity to resist never destroyed.

REBELLION

Modern research has shown that rebellions took place on at least 313 slave ships. This figure may be low, because 148 ships reportedly were lost at sea, and some of them may have failed to complete their voyage due to rebellions.[26] But resistance was not confined to slave revolts; the captives manifested their rejection of their condition in other ways as well.

There is evidence to suggest that slaves attempted to run away in Africa, while they awaited shipment to the Americas. Escape was not easy to accomplish, as captives were carefully guarded, but some took advantage of lapses in security. Understandably, even after being loaded on a waiting ship, some Africans also sought to reclaim their freedom by rebelling before the vessel departed for unknown lands. Francis Moore, a seasoned trader, found in Gambia that captives were "apter to rise in a Harbour than when out at Sea, since if they once get Masters of a ship, in the River, their escape to shore is almost certain, by running the ship aground; but at sea it is otherwise, for if they should surprize a ship there, as they cannot navigate her, they must have the assistance of the White Men, or perish."[27] Not many accounts of coastal shipboard rebellions survive, but one recent study discovered seventy such instances.[28]

Slave traders recognized the possibility of such challenges to their power and took appropriate steps to minimize the risk. Heavily armed soldiers constituted a ubiquitous presence on board and the ships' guns were constantly trained on the black captives. Thomas Phillips, who traded for human flesh on the African coast in the

Arriving Africans being sold in a New World market, probably somewhere in the Caribbean.
Apparently taking notice is the slave in the foreground. ("La Vente des Nègres"[the sale of
blacks] in Amédée Gréhan, *France Maritime*, Paris, 1855.)

years 1693–94, recalled that there was "a chest of small arms, ready loaden and prim'd, constantly, lying at hand upon the quarter deck, together with some granada shells and two of our quarter deck guns, pointing on the deck thence, and two more out of the steerage."[29]

Such security measures obviously did not intimidate all slaves, given the incidence of coastal rebellions. The captives took advantage of security lapses or of a crew weakened by disease or death. When the slaves on the *Mary* rebelled in 1708, the resident trader said it was due to the "carelessness" of the crew.[30] This trader, Dalby Thomas, hardly understood the Africans' will to freedom. When Captain William Snelgrave asked a group of slaves why they had rebelled on his ship, they told him rather bluntly that he "was a great rogue to buy them, in order to carry them away from their own country, and that they were resolved to regain their liberty if possible." Seeking to pacify them, Snelgrave denied any responsibility for their capture, coldly informing his human cargo that they had already been reduced to slavery before he purchased them. He also told them that it was futile to escape since they would be recaptured. Hoping to avoid punishment for the uprising, Snelgrave reported that the slaves promised "to be obedient, and never mutiny again." This was undoubtedly an empty promise since the slaves soon began to conspire again, according to Snelgrave.[31]

Despite his own experience with shipboard uprisings, Snelgrave never fully understood the reasons for such resistance, attributing it to the "ill usage" of the crew. He thought that "if a Commander is himself well inclined, and has good officers to execute his orders, the Negroes on board may be easily governed; and many difficulties (which unavoidably arise amongst such numbers) got over with a little trouble."[32] But humane treatment, in the context of the slave trade, did not stymie the will to resist. Snelgrave seemingly was forced to recognize this imperative when he made the questionable observation that a 1722 rebellion was due to the captain's "overcare and too great kindness to the Negroes on board his ship."[33]

Shipboard rebellions frequently resulted in a great loss of lives and injuries for the slaves as well as the crew. The *Tiger* lost forty slaves in rebellion in 1702, and forty slaves were killed in an uprising on the *Duke of Cambridge* in 1714. In 1722 the slaves on the *Ferrers* mutinied, losing almost eighty of their number before the melee was over.[34]

Slaves who did not participate in violence found other means to resist their condition. Some engaged in hunger strikes or committed suicide by leaping into the sea and drowning. One of the most dramatic examples of suicide by drowning occurred in 1737, when more than 100 men on *The Prince of Orange* jumped into the sea while the ship was docked in the harbor at St. Christopher. The crew attempted to rescue them but thirty-three slaves succeeded in taking their own lives. According to a report on the incident, those who perished "would not endeavour to save themselves, but resolv'd to die, and sunk directly down."[35]

In spite of the horror associated with the Middle Passage, survivors forged bonds of friendship born of shared experiences. Shipmates had endured much, and out of their anguish and pain they reached out to their partners in suffering for psychic sustenance. For some, these ties were not easily developed since there were instances when individuals from ethnic groups with traditional rivalries found themselves suddenly thrust in a similar circumstance, even chained together. Yet as the voyage progressed, these ancient animosities would dissolve and a consciousness of a common fate would emerge. Most of those who shared the same shipboard experiences probably never saw one another again after they were separated and sold in the Americas. But those who did never lost their memories of their shared ordeal and nourished emotional bonds that were as sacrosanct as those created by the ties of blood and kin.

The Middle Passage was more than just a shared physical experience for those who survived it. It was and is a metaphor for the suffering of African peoples born of their enslavement, of severed ties, of longing for a lost homeland, of a forced exile. Its meaning cannot be derived solely from an analysis of the tonnage of the slave ships, the cramped quarters of the human cargo, the grim catalog of disease and death, or even the dramatic tales of resistance. It is a living and wrenching aspect of the history of the peoples of the African diaspora, an inescapable part of their present impossible to erase or exorcise. A gruesome reminder of things past, it is simultaneously a signifier of a people's capacity to survive and to refuse to be vanquished.

Seventeenth-century flintlock of Portuguese or Spanish origin. Arms of this sort would have been common on slave ships.
(Eugene and Adele Redd Collection.)

	Ships Names	Mastrs Names	To whom Consign'd	N.º Negroes		Sum
	Leverpool Merch.t	W.m Webster			220	£ 19
ay	Eliz.h (Jn.º Dunn)	John Dunn			176	18
	Blessing	Tho.s Brownbill	M.r W.m Moore		139	13
t.br	Geo. of D.º	Tho.s Tudor			100	19
	Gu.y Pink Mary of D.º	Rob.t Knowles			112	19
y	Guy George	Tho.s Tudor			78	19
	Tryall of D.º D.s	Jos. Appleby			120	29
					945	
pril 16	Abra & Moses Frigg.t	Benj.ª Terry	Isaac and Moses Mendez	470		18
ug. 25	Dolphin	Henry Parson		180		21
pril 19	Ditto	Tho.s Treswarver		172	522	24
July 28	Henrietta Maria	W.m Deacon		188		19
ug. 16	Delight Gally	Francis Martyn		127		21
pril 12	Ann Bonadventure	Ditto Martyn	W.m Shuller Esq.r	378		19
11	Arcania Merch.t	George Lumley		199		19
6.ry 10	Ann Bonadventure	Francis Martyn		474		22
Sept. 2	John Bonadventure	Ant.º Food		435		16
D.º	Elizabeth	Henry Connell		271	1772	16
Jan.ry 1	Fry of New York			135		25
6.ry 1	Fry Ditto		Co. Cordvent	137		24
Oct. 17	Thos. & Shebey			135		25
ury 26	Mary			137		24
July 17	Sarah Gally			151	695	20
Jan.ry 1	Hanover Gally	Jacob Storey	Jos. Swane		173	22
April 20	Betty Frigg.t	John Luke		196		21
ay 28	Sam.l & Henry	John Jacobs	M.r William Godman	184		17
b.º	Betty Frigg	John Luke		160	704	26
May 25	Champion	Rob.t Penington		164		27
e.r 19	Larke Galley		M.r David Creagh	133		26
ug. 13	Ditto			93	226	24
	Mayflower	Edw.d Archer	M.r Zachary Shute	46		18
	Ditto Walter Rust	Walter Rust		148	194	20
Feb.ry	Mary	W.m Connor		235		28
ury	Ditto	Ditto		199		33
Jan.ry	Edwin & Jos:	Edw.d Collins	Co. Carter &	83		29
July	Content	Jos. Thorn		82		28
Nov.r	Edwin & Jos.	Edw.d Collins		82		30
r.n	Mary	John Frankling	Jos. Harbin	230	1424	28
ury	Constance	John Hunt		122		30
July	Edwin & Jos.	Edw.d Collins		59		26
ay	Mary	John Frankling		216		30
						26

4
The *Henrietta Marie*

Madeleine H. Burnside

This oil painting by J. M. Turner bears the evocative title "Slave Ship (Slavers Throwing Overboard the Dead and Dying, Typhoon Coming On), 1840." The vessel depicted was encountering the type of storm that destroyed the *Henrietta Marie*. (Courtesy Museum of Fine Arts, Boston. Reproduced by permission.)

Opposite:
A page from the Barbados Shipping Returns recording the sale of slaves transported on the *Henrietta Marie's* first slaving voyage. The eleventh entry from the top notes that on July 28, 1699 a Barbadian planter named William Schuller purchased the ship's cargo of 188 Africans for approximately £19 each. Entries below it indicate that Mr. Schuller was a regular purchaser of human cargoes. (Public Records Office, London.)

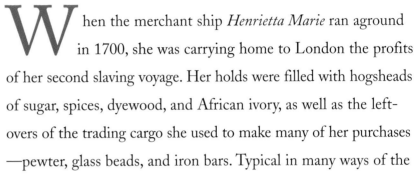

When the merchant ship *Henrietta Marie* ran aground in 1700, she was carrying home to London the profits of her second slaving voyage. Her holds were filled with hogsheads of sugar, spices, dyewood, and African ivory, as well as the leftovers of the trading cargo she used to make many of her purchases —pewter, glass beads, and iron bars. Typical in many ways of the time, she was also unique because slavers of this period had little uniformity.

Caught in a violent storm and driven onto a reef near Key West, Florida, the *Henrietta Marie* took with her evidence of one particular moment in time. While the enslaved Africans she had carried to the Caribbean had been sold in Jamaica, she went down with all the appurtenances of the late-seventeenth-century slave trade. These objects provide the minutiae of everyday life during this pivotal period of slaving and imply the vast increase in the trade that was soon to come. Here are the shackles, some large enough to embrace a grown man's ankle, some so small that only the wrist of a young teen could have been restrained. There is the cookstove on which the Africans' yams were stewed during the Middle Passage; there are the weights, stamped in London, used to measure out the beads that bought human chattel; and there is evidence of the crew: a few cheap coins, some buckles, the scupper that was the officers' toilet.

Ships like the *Henrietta Marie* were common in the Caribbean, where they supplied sugar plantations with labor, although they were not yet familiar to those who lived in the mainland colonies of North America. The artifacts of the *Henrietta Marie* reveal some adaptations made for the slave trade, but the ship was still built as a general merchantman—the refinements with which the swift slaving vessels of the late 1700s were built are not yet present. The evidence of the *Henrietta Marie* shows that the trade was still relatively small and had not yet become the grinding machine that furnished the colonies of the late eighteenth and early nineteenth centuries with their raw human power. Assumptions about people and race had not yet reached a point of consensus. It would be the success or failure of small ventures like the voyages of the *Henrietta Marie* that would drive the decisions of future businessmen to invest in human cargo and human misery.

The English slave trade had begun during the reign of Queen Elizabeth I, with the travels of Sir John Hawkins. Opportunistic rather than planned, such voyages had been very lucrative, and the queen herself was a considerable investor. English involvement in the trade remained haphazard for the next sixty years, with some outspoken repugnance expressed for the idea of Englishmen enslaving anyone; for England this was a period of social ferment and civil war, with concepts of individual rights in the forefront of people's minds. As the upheaval settled and the monarchy was reestablished, more pragmatic views prevailed.

The decline of the Royal African Company in the 1690s marked a turning point in the English slave trade. If the Royal African had retained its monopoly and no one had stepped in to provide efficient delivery of African laborers to English colonies, colonials might have had to look to other arrangements. Alternative forms of labor were already in place, ranging from the indentured servants who were a major resource early in the 1600s, to the genuinely free workers who toiled on smaller farms, such as those in New England. If there had been no independent slave merchants waiting in the wings, as the company's business dwindled sugar production would have gotten underway much more slowly, as would tobacco cultivation, and innovations of England's agricultural and industrial revolutions might have been focused on American crops. Instead, just as the Industrial Revolution was at its height in the late eighteenth century, forced labor prevailed with such ease that mechanical invention for agriculture lagged dramatically behind.

The delay was due to the fact that the nonmechanical solution to the problem of labor demands had been formulated at the turn of the century. The *Henrietta Marie* was already part of it. Her first voyage, in 1697, was as an interloper—outside the purview of the Royal African Company and therefore both highly speculative and semi-illegal, but extremely profitable. She became one of a new class of English slave-trading vessels whose owners had only to pay a 10 percent tax on outgoing and incoming merchandise in order to participate in trade. Known as "ten percenters" or "separate traders," these ships operated with a heavy emphasis on the bottom line; not subject to any preconceived company policies, they could undersell Royal African vessels in Africa and outbid them for slaves. The English slave trade was just beginning to show its potential for profit.

As one thinks of London at the time, the slave trade might seem like an ill-considered sidetrack that eventually became a blind alley, essentially a failure in the history of commerce. In fact, however, it was central to Britain's

The Goree warehouses at St. George's Dock
in Liverpool took their name from the
French island of Gorée off Senegal, a major
embarkation point for slaves and supply
depot for slavers heading westward across
the Atlantic. (By Samuel Austin, 1829.
Courtesy Board of Trustees, National
Museums and Galleries on Merseyside.)

Barrels filled with sugar made by slave labor
on the Caribbean island of Antigua would
be rolled onto a dory, which would carry
them to a slave ship loading cargo for the
return voyage to Europe. (William Clark,
Ten Views of Antigua. Hamilton College.)

international trade strategy and was becoming more important every day. The general public understanding of what the slave trade meant in human terms for Africans varied widely, but few members of the educated classes lacked knowledge of it and most could be said to have profited by it even if only indirectly. Shipwrights were just beginning to be called upon to build faster ships—speed could usually be sacrificed for capacity when merchantmen were built, but a human cargo, confined, suffering, and dying over the course of a voyage, was too fragile for such an approach. Technologies had to be adapted for the slave trade just as they often were in time of war. Forests were felled for the new ships, miners and ironmongers were kept busy, and cordwainers employed workhouse children to recycle old ropes into new. Those who made the cargoes—pewter, glass beads, alcohol, cloth—could all expect profits to rise as new markets prospered overseas.

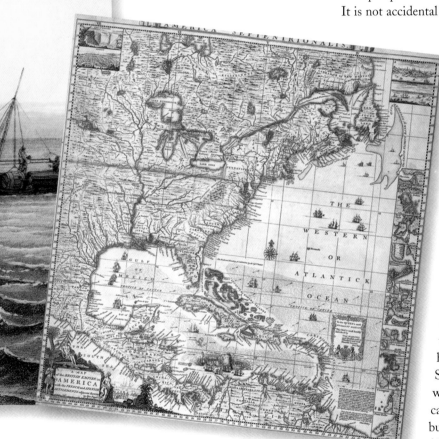

It is not accidental that the Industrial Revolution, the dramatic strengthening of the North American colonies, and the slave trade were all dominated by the English in the latter half of the eighteenth century. All were closely intertwined. As a mercantile endeavor, the slave trade had no obvious precedents, and the essentially new crops it facilitated, such as sugar, tobacco, and later cotton, would reach new markets and ultimately raise the European standard of living.

The combination of the slave trade and the plantation system provided an enormous opportunity for investors. Accordingly, a new breed of profiteers began making their way into the world. One was "Mad Jack" Fuller, who owned a cannon foundry. In 1692–93, demand for these guns was so strong that he expanded his operation, having them made by the Stream Foundry near London, in Sussex, where the *Henrietta Marie*'s cannons were cast. It was the slave trade that sustained businesses like his, and his ability to assess this opportunity was no accident. He was not just an early industrialist but had lived in the colonies and was fully cognizant of slavery as

A map of the British empire in America in 1733. (Henry Popple, engraved by William H. Toms.)

a component of the colonial lifestyle. His diversified portfolio included plantations in Jamaica, and he leased cannons to slave traders to protect their valuable cargoes. It is even possible he lent the *Henrietta Marie* her eight guns as an investment.

If the thirst for exotic African commodities had launched the trade, by the turn of the eighteenth century the demand for slaves drove it. By then, British colonies in the Caribbean were well established and profitable, commanded by sugar planters who dominated Barbados and Jamaica.[1] Mainland colonies in the Americas also showed some profit and more promise if the right combination of crops and labor could be set up. The younger sons of

Suitable Ships

When African slaves first began to be transported to the Americas in the 1440s, a typical European cargo ship was built basically as a shell, its hull a series of planks joined at their edges with internal support pieces being added once the shell was complete. Such a design worked reasonably well for short coastal trips, but it was not adequate for carrying cargoes to and from Europe across the Atlantic. For that, stronger vessels with greater cargo capacity were needed, and the result was a ship-building revolution. First, a reinforced hull skeleton was built, replete with a sturdy keel and supportive post beams fore and aft. The sheathing of wooden planks (typically, oak) was affixed last. The result was a design that offered greatly increased mechanical strength, which in turn permitted hulls to be larger.

Once a hull was complete, a three-masted rigging generally was added. The use of three masts instead of one or two as in earlier times allowed different types and sizes of sails to be rigged to each one—typically, square sails on the fore and main masts with a lateen (triangular) sail at the mizzen mast. Such an arrangement gave captain and crew more options for maneuvering the vessel as winds and currents varied.

Beyond the unavoidable requirement of feeding human beings and disposing of their body wastes, merchants and crews involved in the transatlantic trade in African slaves viewed their human cargoes as little different from other cargoes. Not even the human need to breathe air demanded much in the way of special design, as various other cargoes also needed regular ventilation and vessels designed for carrying them would incorporate ventilated hatch covers as a matter of course. Until the trade was outlawed, slave ships were simply cargo ships adapted as needed to their new use, although as such they benefited from continuing advances in ship-building technology.

In the sixteenth century a standard vessel in the transatlantic trade would have been a three-masted, square-rigged ship. Throughout the 1600s and 1700s, however, important refinements improved seaworthiness and other

With its relatively long, narrow hull, the galleon was stable and could sail closer to the wind than earlier designs. A Spanish innovation, the galleon was quickly copied by England and other maritime nations for both naval vessels and merchantmen. This model has numerous gunports, a feature of naval galleons.
(Kenneth Britten, modelmaker.)

features. Sharpening of the bow and other streamlining measures reduced weight and improved speed. Together with more efficient rigging schemes and taller masts (for larger ships), such engineering changes helped reduce the duration of long voyages, including the Middle Passage—a gain that not only may have helped reduce slave mortality but also allowed vessels to return to Europe with their lucrative American cargoes that much sooner. In the late 1700s, shipowners began to sheath vessel hulls below the waterline with copper, an innovation that dramatically reduced damage from relentless wood-boring mollusks called teredo worms. Eighteenth-century merchant ships also might be equipped with elevated afterdecks on which swivel guns could be mounted. On a slaver, this raised, armed position allowed the crew to more easily monitor the activities of the vessel's human cargo and to defend against rebellion or attacks by pirates.

In the 1850s a British brig called the *Sultana* was engaged in the illegal slave trade from West Africa. With her lines reminiscent of a sleek clipper, the vessel named *Sultana* in this watercolor, which was painted around 1850 by Calvert R. Jones, may be that ship.

Cargo ships, slavers included, became larger as well. Whereas in 1700 a typical British or French slaver might carry up to 70 tons of cargo, by 1800 the average tonnage had risen to around 200–250 tons, with some vessels having a capacity of 400 tons or more.

After 1807, when Britain outlawed the transatlantic trade and began using her formidable navy to enforce the ban, there was a shift in the attributes slave traders began looking for in their vessels. Cargo capacity became less important than speed, the stability to carry cannon, and the maneuverability to elude capture by antislavery patrols. The result was a surge in the building of ultra-sleek, narrow-hulled ships that could race across the Atlantic with a relatively small but highly profitable cargo of slaves and swiftly return to Europe or Africa with goods from the Americas.
—*B.C.M.*

By the time this engraving was made in the 1780s, the skeleton hull had been a standard ship-building design for two centuries. (Honoré Sebastien Vial du Clairbois, *Elémentaire de la Construction des Vaisseaux*, 1787.)

Barbadian and Jamaican settlers, who had the knowledge of how to run a plantation but not the expectation of land, were moving to the Carolinas and Virginia complete with their families, their commercial outlook, and their slaves. Whereas immigrants to the North American colonies, arriving straight from Europe, were accustomed to free labor, these second- and third-generation colonials relied on slaves, particularly where the climate favored a large cash crop over subsistence farming. It was a beginning that would form and rend the thirteen colonies and the country they gave birth to over and over again, down to present times.

The *Henrietta Marie* was not originally intended as a slaver, but as a simple workhorse. About sixty feet long and of 120 tons burthen, she most likely was built in France and spent her early life plying the English Channel with local European wares until becoming embroiled in King William's War, an English-French conflict at the end of the seventeenth century. She was captured by the English, probably in about 1696, and sold off by the Royal Navy in time-honored fashion to support its bottom line. Her new owners renamed her, complicating modern efforts to ascribe specific dates to events in the ship's early life. However, the owners themselves are well documented as a consortium of London businessmen with a knowledge of life in the colonies and some experience in the Africa trade.

Many of the new owners of the *Henrietta Marie* had ties to the colonies. Thomas Starke (1649–1706), who consigned just over £18 worth of bugle beads to the voyage, lived in London and was English born and bred. Nevertheless, he had once been a successful attorney in Virginia, where he still owned five tobacco plantations. In order to better care for his colonial interests, he was part owner of several slaving vessels, including the *Eagle*, the *Concord*, the *Endeavor*, and the *Africa Galley*. Always a litigious man, he was certain that he knew what it took not only to run a plantation but also to command an ocean voyage, and he was known to sue his captains for taking insufficient care of his merchandise.

The major investor was Anthony Tournay, who had made a fortune during the war with France by providing the navy with iron, which was used aboard ship for everything from basic fasteners to barrel hoops. He consigned thirty-three tons of iron to the *Henrietta Marie*'s second voyage, probably in the form of bars. He had been trading in iron to the plantations since 1684 and supplying voyages to West Africa since 1692.[2] The twenty-eight iron bars recovered from the *Henrietta Marie* range from 26.5 to 58 cm, or roughly 10 to 23 inches long. Their average weight is about 1.58 kg, or 3.5 pounds. Several of those found on the *Henrietta Marie* wreck site were interestingly marked, possibly to indicate their source; others are simply blank.

In 1758 a British instrument maker named Thomas Hammond used ivory for the scale of his mahogany quadrant shown here. Any ship of the day that sailed in the transatlantic slave trade would have had a quadrant or similar instrument on board for use in ascertaining the vessel's latitude at sea.

This ivory trade token could have belonged to an English seaman. It is inscribed "John Pepper, brig Highfield, a good man." Trade tokens may have been exchanged as payment pledges or receipts for goods traded. (Courtesy Board of Trustees, National Museums and Galleries on Merseyside.)

Carlisle Bay in Barbados around 1807, with Bridgetown in the background.
The artist was John Waller, a British naval surgeon who lived in Barbados in 1807–08.
(John Waller, *A Voyage in the West Indies*, London, 1820.)

Other investors included the pewterer Thomas Winchombe, who was dabbling for the first time in the slave trade, and Robert Wilson, who consigned not only additional pewter (pewterware being popular in Africa at the time), but also 1,200 copper bars, several cases of alcohol, and four dozen felt hats. Of these investors, Wilson was more interested in ivory than slaves. He did not have a stake in the colonies, but expected to see a handsome profit from ivory turned into cane handles, keys for musical instruments, and other luxury goods prized by fashionable Londoners.

King William's War, fought for eight years against France, had partially interrupted the slave trade of England and France. Conflict in both the English Channel and the Caribbean had made all international commerce more hazardous as warships patrolled routes and blockaded ports, preying on merchants as well as each other for prizes. Meanwhile, the appalling work conditions in even the best colonies such as Barbados depressed the life expectancy of the Africans enslaved there to eight years, so that the plantations' workforce was drastically depleted by the time the *Henrietta Marie* was to sail on her first voyage.

The ship's refitting would have involved repairs of any war-related damages and the addition of sacrificial planking on the outside of the hull to protect it from the notorious teredo worm, a borer that was the bane of wooden ships in tropical waters. The refitting of a similar slaver, the *Daniel and Henry*, cost £550 in 1700.[3] In addition, provisions would have to be made for the half-deck on which the Africans were to lie during the Middle Passage. Wood for these could probably be found in Africa—leaving valuable cargo space open for the first leg of the voyage—but iron fasteners and nails would have to be provided in sufficient quantity to take care of this project as well as the endless round of ship repairs that the long voyage would require. Numerous tools, ranging from sledgehammers to a grinding wheel, were found at the wreck site.

The cargo would have to be calculated. Captains from other ships would have been grilled for information on what goods the Africans were favoring currently. The information was extremely valuable, and sailors such as Jean Barbot and his nephew James sold their memoirs on the basis of it. As the second voyage would prove, outmoded merchandise was a liability unless it could be traded in the colonies also; pewter was a good investment in this way because Africans prized it and colonists welcomed it as a utilitarian but elegant reminder of home. Apart from English pewter, cloth, and hats there would be the Venetian glass beads of various colors and styles used by the Africans to make royal crowns. Beads were cheap in Europe but expensive in Africa, where they typically had to be imported overland through a stream of middlemen.

Finally there were weapons—cutlasses, muskets, and blunderbusses that might be used for defense or barter, depending upon which was most useful at the time.

A SUCCESSFUL FIRST VOYAGE

Only two weeks after the conclusion of King William's War, the *Henrietta Marie* sailed on her first voyage for her new owners, captained by William Deacon. Deacon had already captained two interlopers out of London in 1694–95 and 1695–96; a careful man, even a lucky one, he had survived the danger and constant threat of disease of these earlier voyages and eventually made enough personal profit to become an investor in the *Henrietta Marie*'s second (and last) voyage, as well as the voyages of several other merchant slavers. Among the artifacts found on the wreck was a blunderbuss with Deacon's initials engraved into a butt plate— something to express how close he came to losing his life to the slave trade.

The *Henrietta Marie* probably sailed with a crew of eighteen to twenty-two.[4] On this first voyage were two recruits from Deacon's birthplace of Stepney, outside London: John Scorch, who was probably ranked as boatswain or higher, and Edward Humble, an able seaman. The crew also included a Dane, Peter Christophersen, who died during the Middle Passage, leaving his worldly goods to his countryman and "messmate," Claus (or Claes) Johnsen. The will was witnessed by two other messmates, Christopher Trunifo and James Kedd.[5] Although Christophersen's will was given orally, it was common for literate mariners to prepare a written will for use in case of their demise. The ship's investors prepared in their own way: the crew's specialists, such as the gunner, the carpenter, and the cooper, all traveled with their assistants—a doubling of men that not only spread the workload, but also provided a narrow redundancy that would allow a trained man to step into the position of any mariner who died on the perilous journey.

The crew would also comprise a sailmaker, a cook, and possibly a ship's doctor. The latter would have been versed in only the most basic aspects of seventeenth-century medicine, such as it was. This man would probably have started out as a barber and graduated a small step higher due to his ability to draw blood tidily—bleeding being a common treatment for many ills. A few medically related objects were found in the wreckage of the *Henrietta Marie*, including a pestle for grinding herbs and compounds and some small glass bottles likely to have held salves and powders. Most problems that could be relieved would involve the gastric disorders that increased in number and severity as the poor quality of food aboard ship weakened the systems of sailors and captives alike.

As the ship set sail, Deacon and his senior officers would have used what charts they had, together with Deacon's own considerable experience, to plot his course down Africa's western coast. The bowl and gimbal rings of the ship's compass were found at the wreck site, as were the sounding weights that they would have used to navigate shallow coastal waters and later the Calabar River.

It was December 1697 when the *Henrietta Marie* arrived for the first time at New Calabar, in what is now Nigeria. Internally at peace, New Calabar was situated between warring nations but not threatened by them. This made it an

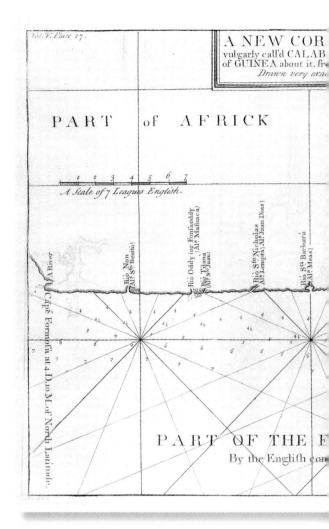

"A New Correct Mapp of Calbar River."
(Awnsham and John Churchill, *Collections of Voyages and Travels*, vol. 5, London, 1732.)

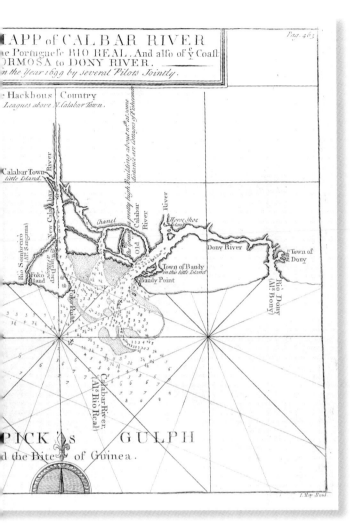

Europeans had myriad uses for African ivory. This Austrian-made
plane, topped with a decorative figure having an ivory head, dates to
around 1680 and would have been used to smooth a ship's planking.

ideal entrepôt for dealing in prisoners of war who could be profitably disposed of as slaves. The *Henrietta Marie*'s small arms might well have been sold in New Calabar, allowing older weapons—whose quality and repair were not well understood by inland nations new to firearms—to be traded for upcountry captives.

As the *Henrietta Marie* was making her way slowly up the Calabar River, the trade in enslaved Africans had been going on for more than 150 years. By this time, trade was starting to focus more narrowly on human cargoes, although the *Henrietta Marie* did carry ivory homeward on both her voyages.[6] The Africa trade had matured, and there were many captains or other sailors who were seasoned Guinea hands. Routes, while not always exactly charted, were well defined and the practical dos and don'ts of the trade had been established.

Africans also had plenty of experience. They knew that every ship that came to their shores was different and that some were dangerous while others were essentially peaceable and certainly profitable. They knew never to go aboard European ships in small numbers, for that could encourage kidnapping. They knew that the Europeans were not all one people, although they

looked alike, and that Europeans could be played against one another. They quickly recognized that as long as European goods were a rare novelty there was an enormous profit to be made in trading for them with surplus African goods, crops, and people. They pressured the Europeans for greater quantities, better quality merchandise, and "new" items. The Europeans had learned the basics from their own vantage point, being well aware that African dignitaries expected to be treated with respect and would simply wait for a different ship if they felt slighted.

The process of purchasing slaves, particularly for a separate trader, was often lengthy and counterproductive. Ships sailing with the Royal African Company would go to the company's various forts and settlements along the coast, where they could expect company "factors"—essentially business agents—to have organized provisions and human cargo. The interlopers, by contrast, had to arrange everything for themselves on the spot.

Once the ship arrived and initial contacts were made, it would often have to wait while the Africans brought in fresh supplies of provisions and even slaves. During this time, the carpenter and his mate would build the half-decks in the cargo hold on which many Africans would be forced to spend the Middle Passage. The captain and the ship's officers would continue to bargain for slaves, sometimes at great length. Meanwhile, the swampy area of New Calabar, which was not particularly healthy for Africans, was often devastating

An English blunderbuss for use aboard ship. Three feet long, this gun has a swivel and bell muzzle, and may have been used as a rail gun. It dates from 1848 and bears the inscription "Barnett," the name of a celebrated family of English gunsmiths that crafted firearms from the early 1620s until 1912.

to Europeans. Tropical diseases caught there were often fatal, a condition anticipated by the captain and the ship's owners; on the *Henrietta Marie*'s first voyage, for example, of the eighteen to twenty-two men who started out with the ship, only nine returned alive to London. Sleep was elusive as the mosquitoes began their nightly attacks, heralding the likely arrival of malaria, yellow fever, and other maladies. Some ships stayed as long as eight months, waiting for a "full" load of enslaved Africans. Often the Africans had no better immunity to disease than the Europeans and died as quickly as the crew, some of which would succumb before even leaving the African shore. Balancing the lives of the crew and human cargo against the bottom line, the captain might have to decide to leave even if the ship was not full.

The voyage from Africa to the Caribbean was the longest leg of the triangular trade. Depending on the weather, it could take up to fourteen weeks—if a ship arrived at all. As a captain made the sometimes desperate decision to leave the African coast, his crew and many of the Africans would already be very ill or dying. In addition to smallpox, ophthalmia was a curse of such voyages, striking both crew and Africans blind for days or weeks, depending

on the severity of the case—long enough, potentially, for the ship to be lost. Other ailments could result in permanent deafness or crippling dysentery, which was quickly followed by dehydration. Fresh water had to be rationed carefully, and the captain usually allowed an insufficient amount for the Africans on the basis that they were not actively involved in ship operations. Dehydration led to depression and often a slow but quiet death—interpreted by writers of the time as the Africans' ability to will themselves to die in order to escape slavery.

Just as there was seldom truly enough water, the food was also highly variable. Foodstuffs would rot, a rough passage might make cooking almost impossible, or an inexperienced captain might try feeding his cargo unfamiliar foods that would give them violent stomach upsets. Sanitation was primitive at best and a rolling sea would make it almost impossible to reach the "necessary buckets" without stepping on someone and causing discomfort or even a fight.

Experienced slavers were careful not to purchase too many people from one village or even one language group. Enemies were a better mix, for they would take many of their frustrations out on one another rather than the crew, and one group could be encouraged to spy on the other for signs of insurrection. In recounting the voyage of the *Hannibal* in 1693, Captain Thomas Phillips described this tactic: "We have some 30 or 40 Gold Coast negroes which we buy ... to make guardians and overseers of the Whidaw negroes ..."[7]

On the *Henrietta Marie*'s first crossing, due to market circumstances that resulted in a low number of captives, the Africans had no privacy but were probably able to stretch out and ease their discomfort. Over the course of the grueling voyage death among the Africans held at less than 10 percent; the crew's mortality rate was a little higher. While no detailed records of this part of the voyage survive, the evidence suggests that the Africans were relatively well treated and escaped the worst elements of disease. Deacon, who had experience, would have known what foodstuffs to buy and, since he had already survived a poorly provisioned voyage with a former employer, he may have made sure that water supplies were also adequate. He may have learned the hard way that less greed and a little more humanity actually paid off financially in the end.

Two of the most telling objects found at the shipwreck site, after the shackles, were the cauldrons. One is small, divided into two compartments, and was probably used to feed the ship's officers or even the depleted crew. The other is massive, ready for preparation of a single stew-type meal that would have been fed to the enslaved Africans.

When Captain William Deacon sailed to the coast of Barbados on July 9, 1698, it was the *Henrietta Marie*'s first voyage as a slaver but Deacon's third. Its prospects were promising. Delivering his cargo to Barbados, one of the first British holdings an arriving slave ship would encounter, Deacon could keep the Middle Passage as short as possible and return home quickly. In addition, the market was strong since the slave trade had been disrupted during the war with France, which was fought throughout the Caribbean.

The number of Africans who survived the voyage was reported by customs officials as 250, but by Nicholas Prideaux, the Royal African Company's agent in Barbados, as 220. On July 28, Deacon consigned 188 Africans to William Shuller for £19 1s. 3d. a head. Shuller was not a plantation owner but a man of some standing who was not only a middleman selling slaves but also justice of the peace for his parish. The fate of the other Africans is unrecorded; perhaps the thirty missing from Prideaux's account were "refuse" slaves, people too ill to be sold at auction and often purchased for a low price by a local doctor for speculative purposes. The captain and senior officers may also have been allowed to carry a few captives on their own account. Such arrangements, which could be curtailed if too many slaves died during the crossing, were common as an incentive to keep all the slaves alive. Instead of using a middle-man, the captain and officers might have sold their slaves directly in an attempt to get a better price.

Many of Deacon's crew were less fortunate: only nine had survived the voyage, a mortality of over 50 percent. Deacon himself would return home once more with his own life and enough profit to invest in the *Henrietta Marie*'s second slaving venture.

In Barbados Deacon probably took charge of the disposition of his human cargo, and while he did so the ship's carpenters would have gone to work knocking out the half-decks on which the slaves had lain during the passage. Room had to be made for the next cargo, sugar, the major crop of Barbados. This year, Deacon would have found that sugar cost more than usual due to a weak harvest, but he was still able to buy 118 hogsheads of brown (muscovado) sugar, 1 hogshead of refined white sugar, and 67 bags of ginger. The value of the sale of the Africans was just over £3,589, some of which would have been used to purchase the new cargo, and Deacon was already carrying "100 elephant's teeth" he had obtained in Africa.[8] When he set sail for London on September 23, Deacon could be sure that the profits would be handsome.

This 1729 engraving of a slave market on the African coast in the early 1700s depicts the kinds of transactions that would have engaged the captains of early English slavers like the *Henrietta Marie*. ("Fort de Maures, sur l'isle Moyella," in Pieter van der Aa, *La Galerie Agréable du Monde*, Leide. Library of Congress.)

LUCK RUNS OUT

The *Henrietta Marie*'s first slaving voyage complete, Deacon was able to step down as captain and look for other opportunities. Possibly he never sailed the triangular route again, but he did remain a player in the trade, investing in various Guinea ventures. A new commander, Captain John Taylor, was appointed to succeed him on the *Henrietta Marie*'s second slaving voyage. Once more the ship had to be refitted and repairs made. The sacrificial planking, now partially destroyed by teredo worms, had to be replaced, and any other worm damage fixed. The barnacles, seaweed, and sea life that had attached to the ship's hull during the previous, year-long voyage would have to be laboriously scraped off. New sails, spars, and timbers would have to be fitted and ropes repaired or replaced. Tools would have been inventoried and checked for durability. A cracked grindstone, for example, could be disastrous because it would mean that no tools could be sharpened and eventually no repairs made—a potential calamity that inspired some ships to carry two of these cumbersome objects.

Gradually, a new cargo was brought aboard. The customs ledgers, long stored in the Public Records Office in London, report that the ship carried "282 lbs Great Bugles [beads], valued at £18:15:6, 33 tons of iron, valued at £449:12:6, 1792 lbs Great Bugles, 60 Short Gurrahs [cloth], 3½ cwt Shot linen, 2½ cwt Broad Germany [cloth], valued at £192, 6 cwt of pewter valued at £34:4:6, 1200 copper bars, 7½ cwt pewter, 4 dozen felts [hats], 70 half cases of spirits valued at £132:5:2 …"[9] Knowing the ship, the investors, and the route, William Deacon consigned beads, gurrahs (coarse Indian muslin), and bundles of linen and rolls of cloth to the *Henrietta Marie*'s next voyage.

Customs delayed the ship's sailing and Captain Taylor took the time to write a will, knowing as he did that Guinea voyages were more dangerous than others. As it turned out, Taylor's prescience in ordering his affairs was well founded.

Taylor, like Deacon, was most likely instructed to make landfall in the Calabar area, where he himself would have done most of the trading. One can imagine him, weakened by fever contracted there, probably impatient and short-tempered, trying to negotiate with the Africans, who had no interest in hurrying the transaction. Fluctuations in the local market had to be accounted for, and values that had worked on Deacon's visit would have shifted with each merchantman that had arrived in the intervening months.

Despite their variations, iron bars were a common currency standard. Judging by the average weight of the *Henrietta Marie*'s bars that were recovered, the thirty-three tons of iron would have been loaded in the form of 1,800 bars at an average value in England of six pence per bar.[10] Trading in bars alone,

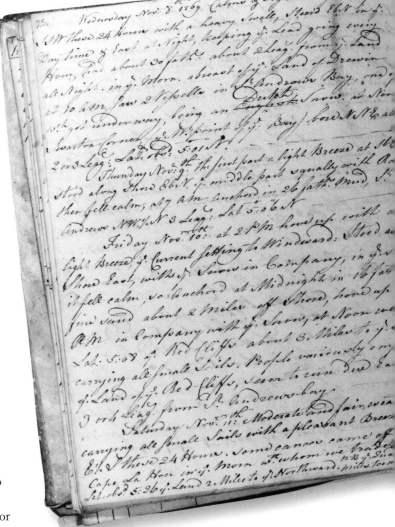

This log book of the Liverpool-based slaver *Unity* describes a slave revolt that occurred during the Middle Passage as the vessel was underway from Cape Coast Castle to Jamaica, the second leg of a voyage that began in 1769. (Courtesy Board of Trustees, National Museums and Galleries on Merseyside.)

A postage stamp recalls slave trading in
the Bahamas, which like Barbados was
colonized by the British.

the *Henrietta Marie*'s captain could have expected to purchase 200 men and an equal number of women and children. In eager anticipation of such a haul, the captain would have directed the sailors to bring up the hundred or so shackles for the men and some smaller ones for unruly women and boys from the hold where they had been stored since the beginning of the voyage.

At this stage of the history of the trade, however, a successful outcome was not taken for granted. Merchants knew that their information about what was in demand in Africa was likely to be outdated. If a ship arrived bearing the same goods as a previous ship in the same season, demand would be soft and goods might be rejected. James Barbot had preceded the *Henrietta Marie* to Africa by only four months, noting in his journal that the Africans he dealt with were not generally interested in pewter[11] or green and yellow beads.[12] When the *Henrietta Marie* was lost, she indeed was bringing home a significant amount of yellow and green beads, for which there must have been no market in the colonies either. As it was, the vessel's £827 in English goods bought ivory, provisions, and only a few more than 200 people. A significant amount of the original cargo was discovered on the ocean floor, indicating that the *Henrietta Marie*'s wares could have purchased more slaves if they had been available.

Captain Taylor was seriously unwell when he gave the order in late January 1700 for the ship to set out on the Middle Passage; no doubt some of the Africans were equally ill. Taylor died during the Atlantic crossing, just one of the bodies slipped into the sea alongside other sailors and the Africans they had come to enslave. Interestingly, Robert Wilson seems to have dropped out of the Guinea trade in 1701; perhaps the death of his friend brought the whole round of tragedy home to him.

Shorthanded and now under Thomas Chamberlain, her new and untried captain, the *Henrietta Marie* arrived in Jamaica on May 18, 1700, with 190 surviving Africans out of the original number purchased. As the captain for the second Atlantic crossing, Chamberlain may have been under different orders or merely looking for a better market. Like Barbados, Jamaica was an English sugar stronghold, but it was deeper within the Caribbean, requiring an additional two weeks of travel. The extra sailing time could mean the loss of Africans who were ill, and a captain had to weigh his owners' suggestions and judge whether prolonging the trip was worth the risk. On the other hand, in the late 1690s, in the outer islands in particular, a ship might face the same challenge in the Caribbean as in Africa—a saturated market. At such times it paid to travel farther for a better price. In addition, Chamberlain had been favored with a mortality of his human cargo of less than 8 percent, compared to an average for the period of 20 percent. This low rate might have been due to the fact that Taylor had laid in rations and had calculated quarters for the number of people he hoped to purchase rather than for the number with which he had had to depart African shores. Better ventilation and more water alone would have made an enormous difference in the slaves' survival. With the number of slaves he had to sell, Chamberlain evidently decided that the extra time required to reach Jamaica would be worthwhile. The decision was justified, for Jamaican planters had recently complained that slaves were selling there as high as £30 a head[13]—almost eight times the purchase price of £4 in Africa.

Like Deacon, Chamberlain probably handled the sale of his cargo and, after he sold the Africans, spent the money he received on his next load of merchandise—sugar. No doubt optimistic, he loaded the ship with eighty-one hogsheads of muscovado sugar, eleven barrels of indigo, fourteen bags of cotton, and twenty-one tons of dyewood.

When he set sail in July 1700, Chamberlain plotted a course that was to take the *Henrietta Marie* home via the Cayman Islands, along the south coast of Cuba, through the Yucatan Channel, and into the Florida Straits. However, July falls in hurricane season, and a major storm overtook the ship as it passed near New Ground Reef, between the Marquesas and the Dry Tortugas, just forty miles from what is now Key West. There were no survivors and the few personal possessions of the crew found on the wreck were meager—buckles used to fasten clothing and some copper coins, remnants of minor players in one of history's major tragedies.

From the sizes of shackles found at the wreck site of the *Henrietta Marie*, it would appear that she had made her transatlantic voyage carrying at least some child slaves. ("Young boys crowded on board ship," *Harper's Weekly*.)

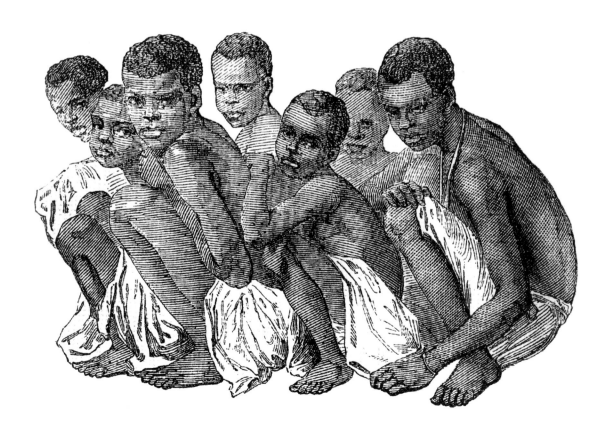

5

The African Diaspora: Resistance and Survival

Linda M. Heywood

The Negroes are so wilful and loth to leave their own country that they have often leap'd overboard and kept under water till they were drowned to avoid being taken up and saved by our boats. ...

I put them all in leg-irons; and if these be [not] enough, I put a collar around their neck, with a chain locked to a ring-on the deck; if one chain won't do, I put two and if two won't do, I put three.

Spiked collar, one of many types of collars and other devices used to restrain and punish slaves. (Gene Alexander Peters Collection.)

Opposite:
Sailor's sea chest with an image of a chained African and his master painted on the underside of the lid. The inscription indicates that the chest belonged to a member of the crew of the brig *Sultan*, which was home-ported in New Orleans and engaged in the then-illegal trade of running slaves in the 1850s.

The male slaves ... possessed themselves a hammer ... with which ... they broke all their fetters in pieces ... they came above the deck and fell on upon our men ... and would certainly have mastered the ship, if a French and English ship had not happened to lye by us ... The Portuguese ... in four years time ... lost four ships in this manner.

The travail of enslaved Africans, which included the horror of the Middle Passage, was both a journey of resistance and defiance and one of creativity and life. It was a time when Africans forcefully taken from their homelands resisted enslavement while rebuilding communities and reformulating their worldviews.

Resistance and defiance were evident from the moment Africans were wrenched from battlefields, farms, and villages, from river houses and coastal crafts, from judicial proceedings and caravan routes; and they persisted as captives were eventually sold to European buyers on the coast. Defiance continued when captives were forced into the bellies of prison dungeons lying astride the west and west-central African coastline. When the enslaved Africans were delivered to ships for the dreaded Middle Passage journey, their attitude did not change, and it endured as they made new communities in European colonies in the Americas. Indeed, the ability of that first generation of Africans to build communities and reshape their worldviews in the Americas exemplified the human spirit of resistance and the will to live. Those two complementary forces became key to captive Africans' survival in the Americas.

Opposite:
Title page of Royal Surgeon John Atkins's memoir *A Voyage to Guinea, Brasil, and the West Indies* published in 1737. In it Atkins recounted details of life aboard the slave ships *Swallow* and *Weymouth* and his experiences in African ports where slaves were acquired.

Painting showing a slave revolt aboard a slave ship, with some Africans diving overboard. From William A. Fox, *A Brief History of the Wesleyan Missions on the West Coast of Africa*, 1851. *(Milton S. Eisenhower Library of The Johns Hopkins University.)*

A VOYAGE TO GUINEA, BRASIL, AND THE WEST-INDIES;

In His Majesty's Ships the *Swallow* and *Weymouth*.

Giving a Genuine Account of the several Islands and Settlements of *Madeira*, the *Canaries*, *Cape de Verd*, *Sierraleon*, *Sesthos*, *Cape Apollonia*, *Cabo Corso*, and others on the *Guinea* Shore; Likewise *Barbadoes*, *Jamaica*, &c. in the *West-Indies*.

Describing the Colour, Diet, Languages Habits, Manners, Customs, and Religions of the respective Natives and Inhabitants.

With Remarks on the GOLD, IVORY, and SLAVE-TRADE; and on the Winds, Tides and Currents of the several Coasts.

By JOHN ATKINS, Gent.

Of *Plaistow*, in *Essex*.

Illi Robur & Æs triplex
Circa Pectus erat, qui fragilem truci
Commisit Pelago Ratem
Primus. ———

HORAT.

THE SECOND EDITION.

LONDON:

Printed for WARD and CHANDLER, at the *Ship*, just without *Temple Bar*; And at their Shops in *Coney-street*, *York*, and the Corner of the *Long-Room-street*, *Scarborough*. 1737. Price 4 s. Bound.

INDEPENDENT SPIRITS

The Africans who were brutally boarded onto slave ships were a study in mixed emotions and attitudes. Of those who exhibited resistance, some did so on a level that surprised their European masters. John Atkins, the Royal Navy surgeon who traveled to Africa in the 1700s, was impressed with the bearing of a tall and stately looking African at the point of departure. He observed that the man appeared to "disdain his fellow Africans for their willingness to be examined ... scorned looking at us, refuses to rise or stretch his limbs as his master commanded."[4] Resistance was certainly in the minds of the slaves who took over the Danish slave ship *Christianburg* on its way to St. Croix in 1787. Paul Isert, a Danish factor accompanying the ship from that nation's outpost at Accra (in present-day Ghana), reported that among the thirty-four Africans who died in the insurrection were men who had jumped overboard while pushing reluctant young boys ahead of them. Isert noted that even when the crew attempted to save them, some "were stubborn even in death, defiantly casting away the rope which had been thrown around their bodies from the ship in order to draw them up, and diving under with force."[5]

African captives showed their independence in other ways as well. In 1751, male slaves aboard the *Duke of Argyll*, which was on its way to Antigua, created a high level of insecurity and fear among the ship's crew when they put a ritual object inside a water cask on deck, giving rise to the rumor that the captives had found a way to poison the water.[6]

Other shipboard accounts reveal responses that reflected a range of survival instincts. In 1668 Father Dionigi Carli da Piacenza traveled from Angola to Brazil on a slaver carrying 630 Africans, and in his writings assigned them to various categories as if they comprised part of a larger community. On the lowest level of the ship were the men, who were relegated to this space because their European captors feared that they would revolt. The priest recorded that even as they lay naked and chained, their sullen, defiant faces instilled fear in the white sailors who had to feed them. He also gave last rites to those who were near death and who would soon be dumped overboard. Yet even the dying were sufficiently alert to engage the priest in heated debate concerning what would happen to them when the ship's food supplies ran out.[7]

On some voyages, deaths among the captive Africans did not exceed a fifth of the ship's cargo, but in other instances the death rate was much higher. Almost one-third of the Igboes leaving Bight of Biafra ports between 1663 and 1713 perished during the Atlantic crossing.[8] Such high mortality indicates that Africans who did survive the journey did so in part because they were physically strong—a conclusion supported by examination of slave traders' records. In addition to addressing concerns about food and water during the passage, investors in slave-trading enterprises gradually came to recognize the need to purchase healthy Africans from the outset. By the late 1700s traders generally tried to buy only slaves who were robust physical specimens.

Alexander Falconbridge, a surgeon who served on slaving vessels in the 1780s, left a vivid description of the care buyers took to ensure that their investments would survive the rigors of the Middle Passage and plantation labor. Writing of the practices at Bonny in the Bight of Biafra region, he observed: "If they are afflicted with any infirmity, or are deformed, or have bad eyes or teeth, if they are lame, or weak in the joints, or distorted in the back, or of slender make, or are narrow in the chest; in short, if they have been afflicted in any manner, so as to render them incapable of much labor, if any of the foregoing are discovered in them, they are rejected."[9]

Rebellion on the Amistad

The rebellion of African slaves transported aboard the Spanish trading vessel *Amistad* has become famous in modern times, in large part perhaps because of the way the affair turned out. It certainly wasn't the first such incident—available evidence speaks of several hundred slave revolts aboard ships, and there must have been many, many more occasions when captive Africans attempted violent resistance while at sea. What helped make the *Amistad* rebellion so different was its success.

The fifty-three Africans aboard the *Amistad* were relative latecomers to the transatlantic slave trade, for they were enslaved in Africa in 1839, more than thirty years after the trade had been outlawed by treaties among former slaving nations such as England and Spain. It was a time when British warships vigorously patrolled the coast of West Africa and when Cuba and Brazil were the major markets drawing slaves directly—and illegally—from Africa. Most of the captives loaded on the *Amistad* had survived the Middle Passage aboard the slaver *Teçora* as part of a group of several hundred slaves to be sold in Havana's slave market. It was there that two Cuban merchants, Pedro Montes and José Ruiz, acquired the *Amistad*'s human cargo: three girls, a boy, and forty-nine men, among them a Mende prince from Sierra Leone named Sengbe Pieh. He would become known to posterity by the name his new owners gave him, Joseph Cinque.

Death of Capt. Ferre

A small coastal schooner less than 70 feet long, the *Amistad* was supposed to carry her captives to the port of Puerto Principe (Port-au-Prince), making a brief stop en route. It was during this first leg of the voyage, when changing weather slowed the ship's progress and rations ran short, that the rebellion unfolded. Terrified by an indication from the ship's mulatto cook that the captives would soon be slain and eaten, Cinque began plotting escape when he discovered a nail on the little vessel's deck. It was all he needed to pick the lock on his own irons, then free the other captives. While a storm buffeted the schooner and distracted the crew, the desperate Africans armed themselves with steel knives meant for cutting sugar cane. Shortly before dawn, they attacked, one of their number being killed by Captain Ramon Ferrer before Ferrer and the cook were struck down and their corpses thrown overboard. Montes and Ruiz, however, were too valuable to kill, for the Africans needed them to guide the *Amistad* back to Sierra Leone.

Weeks passed at sea. Knowing nothing of celestial navigation, Cinque and his compatriots did not realize that the Cubans were secretly guiding the ship north, not east toward Africa. When the *Amistad* finally sailed in view of land, it was off Culloden Point, Long Island, in New York. It was immediately seized by American authorities as a smuggling vessel and Cinque and his band were jailed in New Haven, Connecticut.

There were to be more twists to the plot, however. An appeal by the Spanish government to have the vessel and its cargo returned to them was thwarted when American abolitionists mounted a lawsuit charging that the African "merchandise" could not have been purchased legally in Cuba, as the Spanish claimed. Represented by lawyers that included former president and

e Captain of the Amistad, July, 1839.

Death of the *Amistad's* Captain Ferrer. (John W. Barber, *History of the Amistad Captives*, New Haven, Connecticut, 1840. Connecticut Historical Society, Hartford.)

ardent abolitionist John Quincy Adams, the *Amistad* captives were forced to pursue their case to the United States Supreme Court. There they prevailed. Despite the claims of Spain and sympathizers in the U.S. Congress, Cinque and the other Africans who ultimately had survived the ordeal—thirty-five in all—were released in 1841. The following year abolitionists financed their return to Africa, whence they had been abducted four tumultuous years earlier.
—B.C.M.

Engraving, "Stowing the cargo on a slaver at night." (*Life and Death on the Ocean*.) Henry Howe c. 1855.

Although European slavers occasionally purchased sickly captives, most heeded the market demand for slaves who fulfilled certain requirements. In 1803 one shipowner warned the captain of his vessel to "select only those that are well formed and strong, and do not buy any above 24 years of Age, as it may happen that you will have to go to Jamaica where you know that age would be liable to a duty of #10 pounds per head."[10] Similarly, the powerful cacao planters in early-eighteenth-century Caracas (Venezuela) asked for slaves "of the deepest black (Kongo and Angolans) … without cuts in their faces, nor filed tooth, the men to be well grown to middle stature, not too tall nor too short … the women to be of good stature …"[11]

Mental fortitude also helped enslaved Africans survive the Middle Passage, for they had come from communities that had well-developed world-views, a rational understanding of humankind's place in the universe, and deep insights into human relationships with each other and with the Earth. Of great importance in this regard were notions of the existence of both a spiritual and a physical universe, a belief in a creator God and other deities, and a concept of ancestors as moral beings who protected their descendants. Africans also typically came from hierarchically organized societies in which leaders and institutions held communities together. Despite the wide range of languages, kinship patterns, and religious and political ideas among captive Africans, similarities between these underlying concepts in different African societies allowed those who found themselves captives to open lines of communication, to adopt new patterns of kinship, and to reconfigure their worldviews to explain and cope with their enslavement.

Because male captives had little opportunity to play an active role in shipboard community life, women and children were crucial to networks that helped the captives endure the Middle Passage. On ships where women were allowed on deck, some took to "conversing together, others dancing, singing and sporting after their manner."[12] It was at such times that the humanity of the captives came through and new bonds of kinship took shape. Central Africans in Brazil recognized such connections, using the Kimbundu/Kikongo word *malungu* to describe people who had made the journey from Africa on the same ship, regardless of their African origin. The ties that resulted from the Middle Passage experience called for malungus to observe the same bonds of kinship as if the captives were actually blood relatives.[13] In the English-speaking Americas, the term "shipmates" designated people who came over on the same ship, and in Brazil shipmates had the same kin status as those connected by blood—ties that survived through the generations. For instance, when absentee British planter Monk Lewis visited his Jamaican plantation and inquired of one of his slaves as to whether an older slave with whom he was friendly was an "uncle or your cousin," he noted that the man's reply was "No, he and my father were shipmates."[14] Captives who landed in North America retained such bonds as well.

Depending on when they arrived in the Americas, captives might find themselves being sent to plantations, mines, urban centers, farms, or other locations in the company of their shipmates, some of whom may have been from their own ethnic group or larger region. In some cases captives joined slave communities where members of their ethnic or regional background predominated. For example, in eighteenth-century Chesapeake in Virginia, newly arrived Igboes would have joined their fellow countrymen and women who had been imported there and made up 40 percent of the slave population.

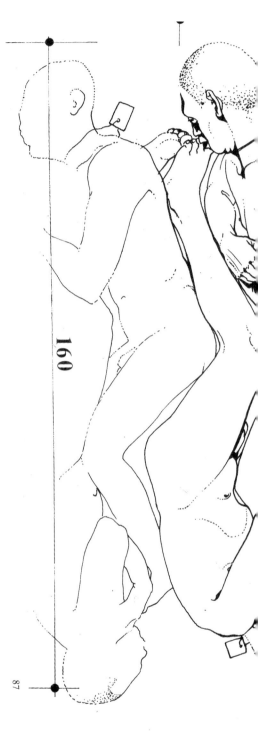

170

Male slaves were forced to assume a
"spoon position" in the hold of the French
slaver *Aurore*. (Line drawing by Jean
Boudriot in *Traite et navires négriers:
Monographie de l'Aurore*. Editions
A.N.C.R.E., Nice, France, 1984.)

Central Africans reaching South Carolina in 1733–44 would also have found themselves in the numerical majority among slaves, for they comprised 60 percent of the slaves imported into the state during those years.[15] But shipmates were often sent to different plantations, and the ethnic community there took precedence. For example, if captives from central Africa went to Jamaica in the 1700s, they would have found themselves outnumbered by slaves from the Gold Coast and the Bight of Benin, who made up more than 50 percent of the eighteenth-century slave population in that colony. Conversely, had they been taken to Rio de Janeiro in Brazil between 1773 and 1777, they would have found themselves in the majority. Indeed, central Africa supplied most of the millions of slaves shipped to Brazil during the course of the Atlantic slave trade.[16]

AFRICAN "NATIONS" IN THE AMERICAS

No matter where they landed, captives had to adjust to their new environment. Initially, they had to assimilate into existing slave communities. All over the Americas, European owners, seasoned enslaved Africans, and their Creole descendants, both slave and free, identified each arriving captive according to his or her "nation." Members of nations already represented in the Americas were supposed to help newcomers adapt to the particular culture in which they would be living and working. For example, enslaved Africans from the Bight of Biafra who went to Jamaica or another English-speaking region joined others who had been identified as belonging to the Igbo, Moko, and Calabar nations, groupings based mostly on language rather than actual political divisions in Africa. Nation identities varied from place to place, however. For instance, had the same group gone to Cuba or Trinidad, they would have been assigned to the Igbo or Carabali nation. Similarly, in the English-speaking Americas captives arriving from the Gold Coast formed the Coromantee (Caramantee), Asante, or Chamba nation, while in Brazil slaves originating from the same area and regions east of it were known as Minas. Likewise, captives from the Slave Coast and the Bight of Benin (a region that today encompasses the Republic of Benin, Togo, and western Nigeria) were identified in the English-speaking Americas as Yarribas, Foulahs, and Hausas. In Cuba, however, the same people were identified as Lucimis, and in Brazil as Whydahs, Ardas, Jejes, Males, Guiné, and Nagos.[17] Throughout the Americas, slaves who had come from central Africa joined groups known as Angolas and Congos; in Brazil the subdivisions were even finer, including regional groups known as Benguelas and Ganguelas, among others.[18]

Although such African "nations" united enslaved Africans from a variety of regions and linguistic backgrounds, they did not necessarily conform to any preexisting nation-state in Africa. A case in point is the Coromantee nation, which included Africans taken from a broad swath of West Africa. Here again, the "nation" identity was based on the fact that the Africans included in it all spoke the same Twi language. The name derived from the small coastal port of Coromantin, located today in Ghana.

As a device for reestablishing the identity that had been stripped from captives, the concept of "nation" provided a basis for social networks. Each nation's reach extended across plantations and individual work sites.

Engraving, "Barbarous Cruelty Inflicted on a Negroe," from *The Curious Adventures of Captain Stedman During an Expedition to Surinam*, 1796. An English gentleman with the military rank of captain, John Gabriel Stedman spent more than five years in the Dutch colony of Surinam in the 1770s, documenting the tropical colony's plant and animal life as well as colonial agricultural enterprises that depended on slave labor.

Voices of the Passage

Oral recollections helped keep the memory of the Middle Passage alive in the folklore enslaved Africans passed on to their American-born offspring. For example, a North American slave known as Uncle Ephraim recalled the vivid memory of survival during the Middle Passage voyage as related to him by his African-born grandfather:

By'n by de wind calm down. Folks got well

an' started eatin'. So dey lets all but de mean

ones come up on deck. Den dey sings. One sings,

an' de res' hum, lak. What dey sing?

Nobody don' know. Dey sing language what

dey learn in Africa when dey was free![1]

Of course, on many slave ships there was little occasion for singing. Father Lorenzo da Lucca, traveling in 1708 on a slaver from Angola to Bahia in Brazil, recounted the depressing situation that the hundreds of enslaved Africans on the ship experienced. He described a scene of utter confusion, with slaves lying side by side in their filth, and wrote that in the chaotic atmosphere aboard ship there was "one shouting on one side, one on the other. Others crying, some lamenting, others laughing."[2]
—*L.M.H.*

1. From Orland Armstrong, *Old Massa's People* (Indianapolis,1931), p.52.

2. From J. Cuvelier, *Relations sur le Congo du Père Laurent de Lucques 1700-1707* (Brussels, Marnixlaan, 1953), p.283.

The existence of nations also helped to subsume regional African dialects under new languages that gradually evolved into the variety of Afro-Creole languages that exist today in the Americas. The nation also allowed enslaved Africans to maintain their beliefs, music, songs, and rituals wherever members gathered. For instance, Jamaican folk songs that recalled enslaved Africans' yearning for home suggest that the communities they left in Africa remained alive in the memories of captives. These were recollections that located captives not in some general Africa, but in specific groupings based on language and ethnic identity. One song's reproachful phrases stressed the importance of these ethno-linguistic groupings and the longing for homeland:

> *If me want for go in a Ebo Me can't go there!*
> *Since dem tief me from a Guinea Me can't go there*
> *If me want for go in a Congo Me can't go there*
> *Since dem tief me from my tata Me can't go there!*

Even in the sad cadence of this song, defiance comes through. The creators of the song put the blame for their removal from their native communities squarely on the shoulders of the European slave traders and plantation owners, an interpretation that Creole folklore emphasized.[19]

The nation identity was so important on many plantations and in mining towns that membership in one or another nation could enhance a slave's status or detract from it. On plantations it was not unusual for a slave to seek honorary membership in a nation that had the dominant reputation. In Jamaica, where membership in the Coromantee nation carried prestige because of the reputed military prowess of the group, Akan day names (names given according to the day a person was born) such as Cuffee, Quacko, Fuba, and Beneba were common, and it was not unusual for Igboes and Congos to carry these day names as well. In fact, interactions between the various nations were commonplace.[20] A survey of Brazilian baptismal and marriage records for some parishes in Rio de Janeiro and the region known as Minas Gerais showed that there, where central African Angolans and Congos predominated and had high standing, slaves showed a high preference for selecting marriage partners from the same ethnic group, as well as a bias toward selecting godparents from similar nations. Elsewhere in the Minas Gerais region many Angolans married Minas and Criolos (Brazilian-born slaves).[21]

On the other hand, members of some nations did not enjoy high standing. For example, in the English-speaking Americas and even in Cuba, members of the Igbo nation suffered from a sullied reputation. European masters considered Igboes to be predisposed to suicide and running away, while fellow slaves of other ethnicities viewed them as "uncivilized" but resourceful. In a similar vein, the former Cuban slave Esteban Montejo wrote that the "Carabalis were like the Mussongo Congolese, uncivilized brutes. They only killed pigs on Sundays and at Easter and, being good businessmen, they killed them to sell, not to eat. From this comes a saying, 'Clever Carabali, kills pig on Sunday'."[22]

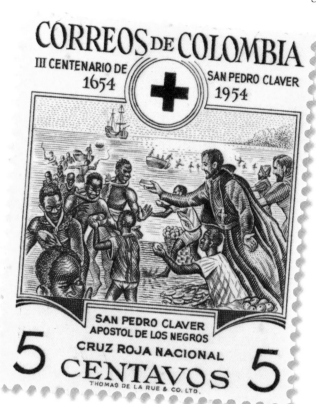

Colombian postage stamp honoring the Jesuit priest Fray Pedro Claver, who worked in the port city of Cartagena from 1616 to 1654. Claver came to be called "apostle of the negroes" for the kindness he showed to arriving African slaves, which included simple medical attention and giving assurances that they would not be eaten.

The influence nations exercised over the cultural norms that emerged on plantations and other localities varied from region to region and from locality to locality. For instance, whereas slaves in eighteenth-century Minas Gerais may have had some leverage over the choice of their partners or godparents, most did not retain their African names but bore Portuguese ones instead. Even in Jamaica, where many enslaved Africans retained Akan day names, a significant percentage responded to fanciful Greek, Roman, and Christian names imposed on them by European overseers and owners.[23]

The solidarity that came with membership in a nation became a rallying point for the political aspirations of slaves who had been born in Africa. Indeed, African-born slaves who were mobilized into nations organized some of the first and most successful resistance movements against American slave regimes. For example, Coromantee slaves fought both the Spanish and English in seventeenth-century Jamaica, and founded maroon settlements there. Their descendants continue to participate in rituals to honor their bravery and independence.[24] Angolan slaves in northeastern Brazil founded and led Palmares, the famous maroon settlement that existed from the early 1600s to 1694.[25] During the eighteenth and nineteenth centuries, the tendency for slaves to organize resistance struggles with members of their own nation was still evident. Coromantee slaves were identified as leaders in several eighteenth- and nineteenth-century Caribbean slave revolts as well as the famous 1712 New York Revolt. The Congo nation spearheaded the 1739 Stono Rebellion in South Carolina, and their countrymen led several guerrilla groups during the Haitian Revolution.[26] In the 1835 Male Revolt, Muslim slaves from the Hausa and Yoruba ethnic groups (called Males and Nagos, respectively) used their Islamic beliefs as the rallying cry for a major revolt in Bahia, Brazil's most Africanized urban metropolis. The uprising was such a serious challenge to Brazilian authorities that several of the conspirators were exiled to Africa, while others were beheaded.[27]

Beyond serving a political role in enslaved Africans' fight for freedom, the existence of nations provided the environment for Africans to shape, maintain, and practice their beliefs and rituals. Griffith Hughes, the mid-eighteenth-century Anglican rector of the parish of St. Lucy in Barbados, observed that all the nations in Barbados were "in much awe of such as pass for *Obeah* Negroes, they being a sort of Physicians and Conjurers, Who can, as they believe, not only fascinate them, but cure them when they are bewitched by others."[28] A report from the same era describing New York's Pinkster festival (an event with roots in the religious celebration of Witsuntide) also pointed to the participation of African nations. It noted how Africans were "divided into Companies, I suppose according to their different nations." Some of the Africans danced "to the Hollow sound of a Drum … others to the grating, rattling noise of pebbles or Shells in a small basket."[29] Similar descriptions refer to African nations participating in public religious celebrations, especially including the nation-based brotherhoods whose members appeared on holy days such as Good Friday and the Feast of Kings in Brazil and Cuba. From various regions of the Americas, there are still other accounts of burial practices, circumcision, secret oath-taking, weddings, naming ceremonies, dancing, singing, and masquerades and other public performances such as John Canoe (juncunoo) and Moko Jumbie. All suggest the central role slave nations played in maintaining and adapting African beliefs and practices in the Americas.[30]

Opposite:

The English poet and artist William Blake illustrated John Stedman's accounts of his sojourn in the Dutch colony of Surinam. Here Blake depicts the impending sale of arriving African slaves, who would subsequently have had to assimilate into the existing slave community there. (John Stedman, *Narrative of a Five-Year Expedition Against the Revolted Negroes of Surinam, 1772–77*, London, 1796.)

A Rebel Negro armed & on his guard.

Constant vigilance was one price of maroon freedom. ("A Rebel Negro armed and on guard." William Blake, in John Stedman, *Narrative of a Five-Year Expedition Against the Revolted Negroes of Surinam, 1772–77*, London, 1796.)

But nations were not the only social networks that African-born slaves developed. Members of the nations had to live, work, and otherwise interact with Creole relatives and with European owners and overseers. Those Africans and their American-born counterparts also often shared in some of the public festivities that took place on the plantations. For example, the English overseer Thomas Thistlewood wrote that on the Jamaican plantation he managed from 1750 to 1786, Christmas for the slaves consisted of nightly festivities with "Creolean, Congo, and Coromantee &c Music & Dancing Enough."[31] Many communities preserved these nation festivities into the twentieth century. Seventy-six-year-old Millicent Griffith, the child of Creole parents, recalled in an interview that when she was growing up in Kanga Wood in Trinidad, older Africans and their descendants formed a distinct community in the village. She noted that they kept a celebration every year that the Creoles called "*Nation Dance*. It was like a feast, where they beat drums and dance ... and if they have people coming from different areas, they would have a special dance."[32]

Members of nations also joined their American-born counterparts in many of the rebellions that challenged the slave systems in the late eighteenth and early nineteenth centuries. Not only did Congo guerrillas fight alongside other nations, Creole slaves, and free blacks and mulattoes during the successful Haitian Revolution, but Monday Cell's Igbo Company was identified as the group that had helped Denmark Vesey plan the 1822 conspiracy in Charleston, South Carolina.[33]

LEGACIES

African-born slaves sometimes accused their American descendants of betrayal to European owners, and those born in the Americas could be suspicious of the strange languages and rituals of their African elders. Yet Creoles, both slave and free, adopted many African values.[34] In their hands, this African heritage underwent further adaptation, melding with European ways to form the dynamic African-American cultures that have come to define Afro-diasporic populations in the Americas. The greatest legacies bequeathed by African-born slaves to their American-born descendants were the religious beliefs and cultural practices they succeeded in preserving.

The religious legacy included rituals connected to burial practices, patterns of worship, and professions of faith. These African roots can be seen in wakes that include songs and rituals meant to ensure that the soul of the deceased passes on properly to the next world—practices that are still common in Trinidad and other West Indian islands. Another example is "second burial," a ceremony common among slaves in the lower south of North America in which they distinguished between "burying" and "preaching the funeral." Following the actual burial of the deceased by as much as a year, second burial has been linked to a similar custom of the Igbo. As James Bolton, a former slave from Olgethorpe County, Georgia, recalled, "When folkes on our plantation died, Marsted always let many of us as wanted to go lay off work 'til the burial. Sometimes it was two or three month after the burying before the funeral sermon was preached."[35]

Patterns of worship that retained African forms were pervasive among Creole slaves and continue to be part of the beliefs and practices of all communities of African heritage in the Americas. The various Afro-Christian

Maroons

Of the many ways enslaved Africans found to resist captivity, running away was one of the most obvious and common. It often was easiest for a slave to elude capture in places where there were comparatively few Europeans and where mountainous terrain or other geographical features provided isolation. Such were the conditions that gave maroon settlements that sprang up in the 1500s in the jungles of South American colonies, and on the larger Caribbean islands such as Jamaica, a chance to take hold and thrive. Such self-sustaining communities of escaped slaves also existed in parts of the American South, although they were small and relatively few in number. There are records of runaway villages in Africa, as well.

Many maroon settlements probably consisted of only a few dozen individuals, or perhaps several hundred. As Captain John Stedman discovered during his sojourn in Surinam in the 1790s, however, they could also be the equivalent of small cities, with populations of 5,000 souls or more. Having found a measure of security in numbers, armed vigilance, and isolation, and despite the tremendous ethnic diversity that might characterize their members, maroon communities successfully developed their own mores and customs, including religious practices that incorporated different African influences. In Surinam and Jamaica, for example, the prevailing religion was essentially Asante but recognized gods of Dahomean and Bantu peoples.

The Spanish used the word *cimarron* to refer to a stray calf or other herd animal that had reverted to the wild; to them the derived term "maroon" was aptly applied to runaway slaves. Determined to retain their freedom, maroons waged what amounted to guerrilla warfare against the militias their former masters sent to subdue them and in turn raided white plantations and settlements. In many places the raids were essential to maroons' survival, because while their inaccessible strongholds offered protection, they were poor locations for farming or other food-producing pursuits. The resulting conflicts between former masters and former slaves typically were extremely violent.

Jamaica became home to three maroon communities when, in 1655, England captured the huge island from Spain. As the British imported African slaves by the tens of thousands for their ever-expanding sugar plantations, the 1,500 slaves left behind by the departing Spanish took to the hills and never looked back. For decades they harassed British planters, escaping after their raids into the surrounding hills and forests. Following one protracted conflict from 1730 to 1740 (the First Maroon War), maroon fighters under the leadership of a clever general known to history only as Cudjoe extracted from the British a formal agreement giving them a section of the island as their own. Like maroons in other places in the Americas, those in Jamaica continued to spar with European colonists, but they survived efforts to eradicate them and their descendants live today. —*B.C.M.*

Maroons in Brazil and Surinam maintained their independence for decades, despite European expeditions mounted in an effort to reconquer them. This engraving depicts such a foray, with still-enslaved Africans being used as bearers. ("March thro' a Swamp." William Blake, in John Stedman, *Narrative of a Five-Year Expedition Against the Revolted Negroes of Surinam, 1772–77*, London, 1796.)

How a female slave styled her hair, and the jewelry she wore, could reflect her particular
native African culture. These sketches by French traveler and writer Jean Baptiste Debret,
entitled "Female Slaves of Different Nations," show slave women in Brazil in 1830. They
appear in volume 2 of Debret's *Voyage Pittoresque et Historique au Brésil*, published in Paris
between 1834 and 1839. (Library of Congress.)

religions—Santeria, Candomblé, Shango, Spiritual Baptist, Vodou, Umbanda, and Afro-Baptist faiths of North America—all were innovations of Africans and their Creole descendants. In reference to the Afro-Baptists of North America, it has been argued that a whole new "Baptist sacred cosmos" developed, based on African principles of direct knowledge of and contact with the other world. In this framework, according to historian Mechal Sobel, dreams, speaking in tongues, and direct knowledge of God and Jesus showed that the believer had "been to Heaven, and *knew* God and *knew* Jesus and *knew* himself saved. African time had become African-American Christian time; past had become future."[36] Bishop Magna Atherly of the Spiritual Baptist faith put it like this in an interview: "At times the service is so high, you speak in tongues, and we dance and enjoy ourselves ... we dance as David before the Ark of the Covenant ... we feel that Christ has taken charge of us and we glorify him ... we have our tambourine and our shak-shak."[37]

In recent times these religions birthed by the African diaspora have attracted growing numbers of adherents, but during the early decades of the twentieth century people of both African and European descent tended to hold them up to derision. In Trinidad, for example, where as in most other regions rituals associated with Afro-diasporic religions were made illegal and the practitioners persecuted, their practices became the subjects of ridicule in calypso songs. Growling Tiger, the popular 1930s Trinidad calypso singer, revealed this attitude at a time when Shango ceremonies were losing their secrecy. He warned:

Everywhere you breathe in the atmosphere
You bound to hear a Shango drum
beating far and near ...
Some fellows dressed in short pants and merino
Those are the drummers in the shango
A fellow with a red cloth tied 'round his head
Like Boris Karloff in The Walking Dead.[38]

Despite being open to scorn, however, the forms of worship and underlying theology of Afro-diasporic religions manifested principles that had much in common with the traditional African belief in the immediacy of the other world—more, in fact, than with the European Christian concept of belief, which large segments of African-descended populations never fully accepted.

The material culture of many communities created by African-born slaves also retained African elements, and recovered artifacts provide telling records of the impact such populations had on their Creole descendants. For example, recent archeological surveys of sites in the Caribbean suggest that artifacts associated with food preparation, musical instruments, religious objects, wood carvings, and even architectural styles of Afro-diasporic communities are heavily influenced by African styles and patterns.[39] Other evidence, such as bottle trees, the presence of grave goods in black traditional cemeteries, and design choices of some African-American sculptors in communities of the American South, leaves no doubt about the lasting influence of African-born captives on their descendants in North America.[40]

Musical forms, dance, and folk knowledge of the enslaved and freeborn African populations also had a significant impact on slave descendants in the Americas. As numerous scholars have pointed out, calypso, modern African-American gospel music, and the varieties of secular music and dance traditions are deeply connected to the experience under slavery.[41]

Ultimately, the legacy enslaved Africans left to their Creole descendants had much to do with the human will to overcome adversity. Whether Africans came on slave ships during the height of the international trade or arrived in its waning years, they had an identity and a worldview that set them apart from their European masters. Today their legacy lives on in the many communities peopled by their descendants that dot every region of the Americas.

Fetishes were objects—often associated with animals—believed to have magical powers from which their owner could benefit; interfering with a person's fetish was a serious offense that could lead to enslavement. As this engraving illustrates, in Africa a fetish could be the focus of village rituals, and belief in the powers of such objects probably made the journey to the New World with many African captives. ("Fetiche dance, Cape Lopez." Thomas Boteler, *Narrative of a Voyage of Discovery to Africa and Arabia* ..., vol. 2, London, 1835.)

West African bead necklace, c. 1750. Beads were highly valued trade items and a necklace such as this one would have been regarded as roughly equal in value to two adult male slaves. (Sample Pittman Collection, New York City.)

A View of CHARLES TOWN the Capital of South Carolina in North America. Vue de CHARLES TOWN Capitale de la Carolina d.
Engraved by C. Canot from an Original Painting of T. Mellish, in the Collection of Mr. John Bowles.

LONDON. Printed for John Bowles at No. 13. in Cornhill, Robt. Sayer at No. 53. in Fleet Street, Thos. Jefferys at the Corner of St. Martins Lane in the Strand, & Carington Bowles at No. 69. in St. Pauls Church Yard.

6

Life in the New World

Philip D. Morgan

Of about 11 million people forcibly removed from Africa for American destinations, roughly half sailed in the eighteenth century and another quarter in the nineteenth; some were still arriving in parts of the Americas in the 1860s.[1] Life for enslaved Africans varied greatly depending on where in the Americas they arrived and lived. Residing on an island was far different from living on the mainland. In mainland North America alone, distinct slave systems emerged in at least eight regions: New England, the mid-Atlantic region of New York and Pennsylvania, the Chesapeake area of Virginia and Maryland, the lowcountry of South Carolina and Georgia, Spanish Florida, French and later Spanish Louisiana, the upper South interior of Kentucky and Tennessee, and last and ultimately the largest, the Deep South interior, that fertile crescent stretching from upcountry Carolina through Georgia and Alabama to the Mississippi Delta.

The contrast was huge between a New England farm and a Virginia tobacco plantation, between the independence of an enslaved black sailor in Philadelphia and bondage on a South Carolina rice plantation, between urban life in New York and New Orleans.

Living in a bustling seaport was a world apart from existence in a remote, interior plantation; an armed maroon or runaway slave inhabiting a swamp or mountainous zone had little in common with a defenseless field hand residing in the plains; a washerwoman in frontier Louisiana would have recognized few similarities between her life and that of the concubine who lived in a great house such as Monticello. Whether slaves resided in tropical lowlands or temperate highlands, on a large plantation or a small farm, surrounded by mostly whites or mostly blacks, whether they toiled in fields or in shops, in manual or skilled labor, in civilian or military occupations, up trees or down mines, on land or at sea—all these factors shaped their experience profoundly.

Enslaved Africans also had markedly different lives according to when they arrived in the Americas. Whereas the earliest African forced migrants were founders who often established customs and patterns of life in their new settings, later African newcomers, particularly in North America, would encounter many native-born African Americans who would educate them to their new situation. They were entering a creole world born or developed in the New World from fragments and influences drawn from the Old.[2]

In spite of these variations, the initial shock of arrival in a new environment following the harrowing physical and mental toll of the Middle Passage was no doubt similar across space and over time. Some newcomers might recall a recent branding on board ship; others might be unable to stand after the long confinement. One noted, "It was more than a week after I left the ship before I could strighten my limbs." Some committed suicide, and for all, the unfamiliar disease environment in the New World dramatically increased the odds of an early death; in some places, as many as a third of arriving slaves died within their first year on American soil. The rest confronted a painful period of adjustment to their situation. Some plainly did not wish to adjust, returning to their site of sale in a forlorn attempt to find a return passage. Disoriented and alienated, many Africans yet demonstrated a measure of camaraderie by running away together, although such fugitives rarely evaded capture for long.[3]

Some slave populations in the Americas grew by natural increase, that is, by births exceeding deaths, whereas others grew only by the influx of forced migrants. The great success story was the North American mainland, where by 1720 the annual rate of natural increase of the slave population was greater than the annual increase due to imports. Overall, by the early 1700s North America's slave population grew faster from natural increase than did its European populations. There were variations in this pattern: Virginia's enslaved population began to grow naturally much earlier than South Carolina's. By contrast, throughout most of the Caribbean and large parts of Latin America, slave populations registered steep natural *decrease* as deaths outnumbered births. Had it not been for the swelling numbers of Africans imported into these areas, their slave populations would have declined.

The reasons why some parts of the Americas were graveyards for slaves and others saw many births are difficult to disentangle. Nevertheless, one major difference seems to be that the fertility of North American slave women was much higher than that of most of their island and South American counterparts. The onerous labor of sugar plantations is a crucial factor explaining why many slave women throughout the Americas never bore a child, or suffered from infertility by their mid-thirties. Wherever slaves were not engaged in sugar production—true of almost all North America, except nineteenth-century Louisiana—their chances of surviving and reproducing were considerably better.[4]

Public Sale of Negroes,

By RICHARD CLAGETT.

On Tuesday, March 5th, 1833 at 1:00 P. M. the following Slaves will be sold at Potters Mart, in Charleston, S. C.

Miscellaneous Lots of Negroes, mostly house servants, some for field work.

Conditions: ½ cash, balance by bond, bearing interest from date of sale. Payable in one to two years to be secured by a mortgage of the Negroes, and appraised personal security. *Auctioneer will pay for the papers.*

A valuable Negro woman, accustomed to all kinds of house work. Is a good plain cook, and excellent dairy maid, washes and irons. She has four children, one a girl about 13 years of age, another 7, a boy about 5, and an infant 11 months old. 2 of the children will be sold with mother, the others separately, if it best suits the purchaser.

A very valuable Blacksmith, wife and daughters; the Smith is in the prime of life, and a perfect master at his trade. His wife about 27 years old, and his daughters 12 and 10 years old have been brought up as house servants, and as such are very valuable. Also for sale 2 likely young negro wenches, one of whom is 16 the other 13, both of whom have been taught and accustomed to the duties of house servants. The 16 year old wench has one eye.

A likely yellow girl about 17 or 18 years old, has been accustomed to all kinds of house and garden work. She is sold for no fault. Sound as a dollar.

House servants: The owner of a family described herein, would sell them for a good price only, they are offered for no fault whatever, but because they can be done without, and money is needed. He has been offered $1250. They consist of a man 30 to 33 years old, who has been raised in a genteel Virginia family as house servant, Carriage driver etc., in all which he excels. His wife a likely wench of 25 to 30 raised in like manner, as chamber maid, seamstress, nurse etc., their two children, girls of 12 and 4 or 5. They are bright mulattoes, of mild tractable dispositions, unassuming manners, and of genteel appearance and well worthy the notice of a gentleman of fortune needing such.

Also 14 Negro Wenches ranging from 16 to 25 years of age, all sound and capable of doing a good days work in the house or field.

Slave auctions typically were advertised in newspapers and on posters. This broadside announced a "Public Sale of Negroes" offered by Richard Clagett of Charleston, South Carolina on March 5, 1833. (Sample Pittman Collection, New York City.)

THE SLAVE'S MATERIAL WORLD

Enslaved Africans and their descendants experienced a spartan material existence, the vast majority of slaves being worse off than the free populations in their societies. To begin with, they generally lived in drafty, dark, dilapidated dwellings, cramped quarters that were sometimes no more than outbuildings. They spent as much of their time outdoors as within and the smell of domestic animals and decaying food pervaded their settlements. The slaves' everyday attire was as mean as their buildings, for New World masters forced slaves to wear cheap, drab, ill-fitting clothes. In addition, slaves were as poorly fed as they were clothed, consuming an extremely monotonous diet that was high in starch and low in protein.

Although most slave housing was small, crudely constructed, and rudimentary in almost every respect, it took many forms. Slaves often built their own houses, incorporating African influences in both materials and shape, perhaps using mud or wattle-and-daub construction, thatch roofs, and earthen floors. Slaves might live in dormitories, particularly on estates that were still in a formative stage and on plantations where a number of recently imported Africans were present. In rural areas they could inhabit work buildings; in towns and cities they often lived above washhouses and kitchens. As slaves formed families, they tended to build separate huts, cabins, or duplexes. Housing therefore evolved from barracks to single or double units, and flimsy structures (with posts placed directly in the ground) slowly gave way to more permanent architectural forms. Over time, slave settlements also tended to become more remote from white oversight and communally oriented. Often slaves had a little garden or yard next to their dwelling, and inside or adjoining their houses they also might have spaces in which to store food, treasured belongings, and stolen goods.

Like the clothing worn by their African ancestors, the essential items of adult dress for many New World slaves were the wraparound skirt for women and the breechcloth or waist tie for men.[5] Despite a trend toward standardized slave clothing, there was no such thing as a slave "uniform." Enslaved people wore too many different fabrics in too many styles for uniformity to prevail, and variety was enhanced by dyes, patches, and trimming. Where slaves made their own clothes, the result was undoubtedly even less uniformity. Slaves also showed a keen interest in sartorial expressiveness, and whites often criticized them for dressing above their station, particularly on Sundays and holidays. Foot and head coverings assumed many types, and artisans and house servants consistently owned more varied clothing than did field hands. Some masters rewarded certain slaves with extra clothing or castoffs and facilitated purchases by others. Conversely, shortages in the availability and distribution of clothing, together with the possible preference accorded some slaves, meant that many were scantily clad and in some instances might even go naked.

There were two main food sources for slaves: either they received rations derived largely from provision crops they grew as part of estate labor, or they grew their own food on their own time. In many parts of the Americas, slaves had access to large garden plots called provision grounds; with such plots they

Iron runaway chain and collar, c. 1820.
(Sample Pittman Collection, New York City.)

A slave branding iron with a large *S*. It was customary for slaves to be branded on the African coast, either with the mark of the ship that would carry them away or with that of the European company to which the ship belonged. When sold again upon reaching a destination in the Americas, many slaves were rebranded with the initials of their new owner, which is the use to which this iron was put.
(Gene Alexander Peters Collection.)

Sugar: King and Killer

Europeans discovered sugar in the Middle Ages when armored Christian crusaders rode to the Middle East to do battle with the believers of Islam. Captivated by the sweet substance, they soon began cultivating sugarcane in Mediterranean plantations. In the 1450s, however, such enterprises shifted to Spanish and Portuguese colonies in the Canary Islands, Madeira, Brazil, and Hispaniola, where the dependably hot and humid growing conditions were more favorable. The westward move was particularly well considered, for by the 1630s Brazilian sugar plantations were exporting more than 20,000 tons of sugar a year. Inexorably, as Dutch and then English interests strove to expand their influence, sugarcane-growing expertise arrived on the shores of Barbados, Jamaica, and other Caribbean colonies including Puerto Rico, Cuba, and Guyana. Scholars estimate that by the mid-1700s the annual exports from those operations totaled nearly 200,000 tons. Staggering as such a quantity must have been in those times, it would more than triple over the next 100 years. In addition to sugar itself, derivatives such as molasses and rum also contributed to the burgeoning commerce.

Growing sugarcane is relatively straightforward: lengths of stalk are simply planted in holes dug for that purpose and, with adequate soil nutrients and water, they grow into mature canes. Yet high profits from sugar production could not be realized without an army of field workers to plant extensive fields and then to do the back-breaking work of cutting the cane with steel knives or machetes. It was in part for this grueling work, performed in stifling heat and humidity on plantations swarming with insects, that millions of African slaves were transported to Brazil and the Caribbean.

Once cane was cut, the next task was processing. Arriving at mills in carts drawn by horses or oxen, the canes were offloaded onto the backs of Africans and fed into the mill, which would grind them to release their juice. Next, that sweet fluid was boiled to evaporate off water and leave behind the pale, caramel-colored crystals. The fires in the boiling house were kept burning virtually around the clock, always attended by slaves sweltering under the oppressive heat. Once the raw sugar was cooled, weighed, and packed in barrels, it was stowed aboard ships bound for Europe—often the same vessels that had recently disembarked a new load of slaves for the plantations.

Sugar plantations needed a steady supply of fresh slave labor because so many of their captive workers died after only a few years in the field and processing operations. Many were simply worked to death during the eight-month harvest season. Others were felled by accidents in the fields or boiling houses. Sugar plantation slaves rarely reproduced at any significant level, a lack of fecundity traceable in part to the physical toll exacted by an appalling workload and in part to the fact that many plantation owners bought mainly male slaves, keeping the relatively few women slaves separate. It was cheaper, in their view, to buy a new slave than to lose the work of a female who became pregnant or was caring for a small child.

Overall, sugar plantations ranged in size from a hundred or so acres to estates of 750 acres or more; they typically required between 100 and 200 slaves. The English sugar plantations of Jamaica, Barbados, and the four Leeward Islands collectively employed approximately 250,000 black slaves by around 1700. Purchased along the coasts of Guinea, Senegambia, and Angola, many had arrived in ships of the Royal African Company. A century later when Britain outlawed imports of African slaves, Jamaica would be the largest sugar exporter in the world, while in Cuba slave-grown sugarcane would blanket some 500,000 acres. And despite official prohibitions, independent traders would continue to carry African captives to those fields until the late 1800s.
—B.C.M.

"Sugar Mill." (Deroy after Lugendas, from *Illustrated London News*, March 1845.)

had to produce their own subsistence even if they also received some rations. The drawbacks of the provision ground system were several. One was the lack of time slaves typically had to tend their gardens due to other labor demands; another was the distance separating slave huts from outlying grounds. The need to produce their own food also put additional pressure on aged, infirm, and young slaves. For all, the extra physical burdens that tending provision grounds entailed could translate into greater ill health, lower life expectancy, and lower fertility. On the other hand, although slaves appear to have been healthier under ration systems, benefits associated with provision grounds included the opportunity for more variety in the slaves' horticultural repertoires, the material rewards that came from selling and bartering produce, and the firm foundation that independent production gave to the slaves' domestic, religious, and community life.[6]

LIVES OF LABOR

The dominant economic experience of most enslaved blacks in the Americas was work on a sugar plantation; about two-thirds of all Africans who reached the New World ended up in sugar colonies. Not until the advent of the modern factory system was it possible to regiment and discipline workers as was done with the slave gangs on sugar estates, where the working conditions were more severe than for any other crop. Harvesting cane in particular was extremely arduous labor. And sugar plantations were as much industrial as agricultural, combining field labor with grinding mills and boiling houses. When the time came for harvesting and grinding cane, slaves worked in shifts day and night. On Caribbean sugar plantations about 90 percent of all slaves worked—probably one of the highest labor participation rates anywhere in the world. Only children under the age of six and a few aged and disabled persons were exempt from toil. Furthermore, few other regions of the world were more exclusively committed to a single economic activity than was the Caribbean. Some islands were little more than one vast sugar plantation.[7]

In North America there was never the same concentration on one crop nor quite the same labor participation rate as on the islands. In the early eighteenth century, slave labor in North America was extremely diverse. In the North most slaves farmed or were domestics; in the Chesapeake region they cultivated tobacco but also tended corn and raised livestock; in the lowcountry and lower Mississippi Valley they grazed livestock, cut wood, and engaged in a variety of other activities. By the 1730s tobacco and rice occupied about four out of ten of the mainland's hands, while the majority were still employed in general farming, in domestic service, in crafts, or in other nonfarm work. Not until the 1760s did about half of the mainland's slaves grow the three main staples—tobacco, rice, and indigo—and even then wheat farming was occupying the time of more and more slaves in the Chesapeake. As the eighteenth century proceeded, and children and the elderly constituted an even greater proportion of the mainland slave population, the labor participation rate fell; by the time of the Revolution, about 80 percent of North America's slaves were active in the labor force.

With the invention of the cotton gin in 1793, cotton emerged as a major crop, although in 1800 only about one in ten U.S. slaves lived on cotton plantations. By 1860, however, in part because about a million slaves were transported from the upper to the lower South, two in three did. Even on cotton plantations, growing and harvesting the crop required only about a

Opposite:

A tobacco plantation in 1788.

(*Federalist Papers.*)

Tobacco Plantation

third of the labor time of slaves; the rest went to tending livestock, growing provisions, home manufacturing, and constructing fences and buildings.

On plantations everywhere, slaves might avoid prolonged field labor if they practiced a trade, supervised other slaves, or worked in domestic capacities, and many did so. In the late seventeenth and early eighteenth centuries, slaves gradually replaced whites as skilled workers, overseers, and house servants. The extent of the replacement depended on the type of crop, the ratio of blacks to whites, and the size of plantations. The shift was most complete in a heavily black sugar colony such as Jamaica, where plantations typically were large, and least complete in a predominantly white tobacco colony like Virginia, where most plantations were small.

Mature slave societies generally allocated their slaves roughly as follows: 70 to 85 percent in field work; 10 to 20 percent in skilled, semiskilled, and supervisory positions; and about 5 to 10 percent in domestic service. These proportions varied considerably from place to place, however. Sugar plantations, for example, often had twice as many skilled personnel but only half as many domestics as did plantations devoted to coffee or cotton. On the mainland, opportunities for skilled work were about one-and-a-half times greater in the lowcountry than in the Chesapeake. Individual slaves were allocated jobs according to gender, age, skin color, physical strength, and birthplace. Men dominated the skilled trades, and women generally came to dominate field gangs; age determined when children entered the workforce, when they progressed from one gang to another, when field hands became drivers or artisans, and when field hands were pensioned off as watchmen. Mulattos were often assigned to domestic work or, in the case of men, to skilled trades, while drivers were taller and often stronger than the men and women they supervised. American-born slaves were more likely to fill craft slots than were Africans, and some African ethnic groups had greater success in avoiding field work than others.[8]

Throughout the Americas those slaves who lived in towns and cities also escaped field labor. The percentage of slaves living in urban places ranged from about 5 percent in most North American regions to 10 percent on most islands to 20 percent in some Latin American societies. Unlike most plantation slaves, slaves in urban areas were often outnumbered by whites and freed former slaves, and they lived on extremely small units under the close watch of a resident master who often was female. Within the urban slave populations women usually outnumbered men, and mulattos were often prevalent, as were (more surprisingly) Africans. Most urban slaves worked as domestics, but hawkers and transport workers (particularly watermen and sailors) were far more numerous in town than countryside, and roughly twice as many skilled tradespeople, fishermen, and general laborers lived in urban as in rural settings.[9]

FAMILY AND SOCIAL LIFE

Despite slaves' status as chattel, it cannot be said that the family was unthinkable to them, or that the nuclear unit was unknown to most. Even so, slavery undoubtedly subjected slaves' familial aspirations to enormous stress, often to the breaking point. Owners generally recognized only the mother-child family tie and bought mostly African men, who then had difficulty finding wives. By sale and transfer, masters separated slaves who did live in families, and they committed sexual assaults on slave women. It is important, however, not to overemphasize the instability, promiscuity, casual mating, disorganization, or

In the Caribbean and elsewhere, slaves typically slept on mats and cooked with simple imple-
ments. They often built their own living quarters, which were spartan at best and might incorporate African styles and techniques, such as thatch roofs. Usually just a single room was
allowed and in many places men were required to live apart from women and children. ("Slave
Quarters Inland," Deroy after Lugendas, *Illustrated London News*, March 1845.)

Field workers on a cotton plantation wore
clothing typical of slaves in such enterprises.
("Negroes Picking Cotton," in *Down to the
Great River*, Captain Willard Glazier, 1888.)

Five generations of slaves on the T. J. Smith
Plantation, Beaufort, South Carolina, 1862.
Photograph from a daguerreotype. (Library
of Congress.)

near-anarchy of slave family life, for the resilience of slave families, the strength of their kinship bonds, and the depth of parent-child affection were impressive. Nevertheless, slaves faced formidable obstacles—most obviously the lack of legal sanction for their marriages—even as they struggled to create and then maintain families.

The possibilities for family life varied enormously over time. Wherever Africans were in the majority, family life was extremely tenuous. In slave populations dominated by African-born slaves, half or more might live not with relatives but with friends or other solitaries, or recognize the "kinship" of shipmates. When Africans did form families, the families tended to be nuclear: such Africans probably saw the two-parent family as the essential building block of extended or polygamous family types rooted in lineage and locality, which were forms common to many of their societies of origin. As the native-born population grew, the larger plantations often became large kinship networks. The typical slave family home comprised a man, a woman, and her children, but kinship ties expanded as cross-plantation mating became common, so that many Creoles tended to live in mother-child units (with a male mate living at a nearby plantation) or in extended units. Family life often centered less on the household or nuclear family than on networks of relationships involving various relatives and spouses.

The family, and particularly the nuclear family, was generally stronger among mainland than among island slaves. The natural growth of the mainland slave population, which occurred earlier in North America than anywhere else, meant that slaves there could find partners more readily and have kin around them. Yet the prospects of sale and transfer increased over time on the mainland, due to a rapidly expanding cotton frontier that led to many family disruptions.[10] It is hard to imagine many slaves in the Americas matching the experience of one Chesapeake woman who, as early as the 1770s, lived on a plantation quarter surrounded by her five children, nineteen grandchildren, nine great-grandchildren, four step-children, and three grandchildren's spouses. She lived enmeshed in one large kinship web.

The family was the key social institution formed by American slaves, but it cannot be divorced from the broader social setting. The slave family was subject to the whim of the master, and life for slaves was similarly regulated by the continuous interaction of free and unfree. Neither slaves nor slave owners can be understood in isolation from each other.

One vital means of institutionalizing interactions between the free and the unfree was the law. Police regulations lay at the heart of the slave system. Thus, common features of the black codes were prohibition and suppression of the unauthorized movement of slaves and of large slave gatherings. Slaves also were not permitted to possess guns or other weapons, to sound horns or beat drums, or to practice secret rituals. Punishment for actual or threatened violence against whites was severe. Special slave-trial courts were established in most regions to provide summary and expeditious "justice." Penal codes varied from place to place, with South Carolina's reputed to be the most severe in North America. In the late eighteenth and early nineteenth centuries, legislation regarding slaves tended to become a little less terroristic. The murder of a slave by a white man, for example, generally became a crime, but such ameliorative legislation was always limited by the sheer fact of planter power.[11]

As the slave trade grew in the eighteenth
century, European merchant ships became
common sights in Caribbean ports. This
view of the harbor of Port au Prince in the
French colony of St. Domingue (now Haiti)
is the work of Nicholas Ozanne, c. 1780.

Slaves who attempted rebellion or committed acts deemed to be crimes might be subjected to horrific punishments or a gruesome execution. Although technically bound by the laws of their home countries with regard to treatment of slaves, in fact the owners and overseers of colonial plantations were typically a law unto themselves, particularly in the early decades of slavery. Renderings of such practices as "The Execution of Breaking on the Rack" eventually became powerful tools in anti-slavery efforts. (William Blake, in John Stedman, *Narrative of a Five-Year Expedition Against the Revolted Negroes of Surinam, 1772–77*, London, 1796.)

In all places custom was as important as law in shaping the black experience. Whereas the way in which slave owners ruled their slaves varied from person to person and from society to society, certain common features held true. One of the most important, a defining characteristic of slavery, was the existence of highly personal mechanisms of coercion; the whip, rather than the law, was the institution's indispensable and ubiquitous instrument. On the plantation or in the household, the master and his delegates used a variety of methods of physical coercion without recourse to, and usually unchecked by, any external authority. Brutality and sadism existed everywhere, but most islands and newly settled areas, where masters felt most isolated and insecure, gained the worst reputations.[12]

Masters hoped that rewards would offset punishments, and in some societies several allowances and privileges became entrenched in both custom and law. These included granting slaves half or full days to tend their provision plots; allowing them to attend extraordinary social functions such as a neighborhood funeral became standard practice. Masters generally allowed slaves time off during Christian holidays. Christmas, in particular, became a time for permissiveness and even social inversion in some slave societies—a black Saturnalia. Special gratuities became routine: an extra allowance of food here, some tobacco there, a ration of rum for completing the harvest, cash payments for Sunday work. Favors and indulgences were disproportionately allocated, however: concubines, domestics, drivers, and tradesmen were the primary beneficiaries. Incentives tended to be most elaborate where plantations were large; the privileges of position within a specialized labor force based on rank and seniority generally did not apply to small-scale farms, which were common in the North and parts of the Chesapeake.[13]

CREATING CULTURE

Although masters and slaves were locked into an intimate interdependence, blacks were not only objects of white action but also subjects who created their own cultures throughout the Americas. At the heart of this cultural development was a common language. The array of languages in Africa was enormous, with about 1,000 different tongues being spoken along the belt of territories that supplied slaves to the Americas. Many Africans spoke more than one language, and not surprisingly several of those languages (or dialects of them) migrated to the New World. In plantation regions where Africans were most numerous, some of them for a time would be able to continue speaking their native language, although more than likely they would also speak a pidgin or trade language. In the towns, among privileged rural slaves, and in societies where Africans were few, many blacks spoke the standard European tongue. In North America alone, some slaves spoke predominantly German, as in parts of Pennsylvania; Dutch, as in New York; French, as in Quebec and Louisiana; Spanish, as in Florida and later Louisiana; and even Gaelic, as in the North Carolina highlands. Without a doubt, blacks were the most linguistically polyglot and proficient ethnic group in the Americas.

In spite of the bewildering variety, the norm was that most African Americans spoke a creolized language that derived much of its vocabulary from a European tongue but incorporated the sounds and syntax of a West African creole or pidgin and, beyond that, of various African languages. In other words, Africans grafted a European vocabulary onto West African grammatical structures that had much in common. Although these Atlantic creole languages shared many structural features attributable to the substrate of African tongues, they were still separate languages. Blacks in the Americas spoke scores of identifiable creoles—many English-based (such as Bahamian, Belizan, Caymanian, Gullah, and Krio), Dutch-based (such as Berbice, Papiamentu), and French-based (such as Haitian, Grenadian, Trinidadian). Some creoles were profoundly influenced by various African languages, but on most of the North American mainland the African influence was much reduced and the forces propelling rapid de-creolization were powerful. By the late eighteenth century, most slaves in the Chesapeake region—the largest congregation of slaves on the mainland—probably spoke a nonstandard English dialect.[14]

In much the same way that a broad spectrum of linguistic forms existed among African Americans, a continuous scale of musical expression, ranging in inspiration from Europe to Africa, also unfolded. The variety began in Africa where, for example, peoples of a large section of Dahomey eschewed harmony in their music, while the Asante in the neighboring Gold Coast employed at least two-part and frequently three- and four-part harmonies for almost all their music. Outside Africa, the variety expanded. At one extreme were those blacks who became integral members of military bands or who played at elite social balls in American cities. At the other extreme were plantation Africans who danced their ethnic dances to their own homeland musical accompaniments—whether banjos, balafos, lutes, gourd rattles, or various kinds of drums. In some places black musical styles were ethnically identifiable, but so-called "Angolan" and "Koromanti" (Coromantee) music usually involved the fusion of different forms. Everywhere, blacks in the Americas invented new music.

Black music developed in ways akin to the formation of creole languages. A basic musical grammar, as it were, with an emphasis on the importance of music and dance in everyday life and the role of rhythm and percussion in musical style, survived the Middle Passage. Even complex musical instruments made the crossing, although more notable is how slaves adapted traditional instruments, invented new ones, and borrowed Euro-American ones. These adaptations, inventions, and borrowings were interpreted and reinterpreted according to deep aesthetic principles drawn from different African musical traditions. Blacks retained the inner meanings of traditional modes of behavior while adopting new outer forms. In musical terms, the key elements of the inner structure were complex rhythms, percussive qualities, syncopation, and antiphonal (responsive) patterns.[15]

Black religious expression also spanned a large continuum. There were major differences in the ways in which African societies explained evil, in the role allocated to a creator divinity, and in the absence or presence of prophetism or spirit possession. Some slaves, particularly from the Upper Guinea coast, were Muslim; some from Congo had been exposed to Catholicism; in most other places a variety of traditional religions existed. Nevertheless, an extraordinary diversity of religious forms coexisted with certain widely shared basic principles. Most Africans, for example, drew no neat distinction between the sacred and the profane, shared assumptions about the nature of causality, and believed in both a high God and many lesser gods as the personification of the forces of nature and destiny. They thought the dead played an active role in the lives of the living, and saw a close relationship between social conflict and illness or misfortune. In the New World a similarly

This engraving of a slave auction in Richmond, Virginia, appears to show a family being sold together. (*Illustrated London News*, 1861.)

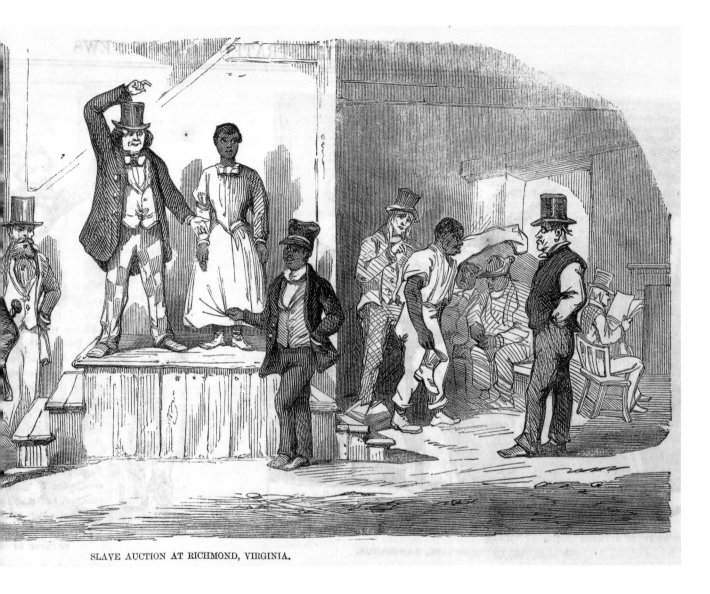

SLAVE AUCTION AT RICHMOND, VIRGINIA.

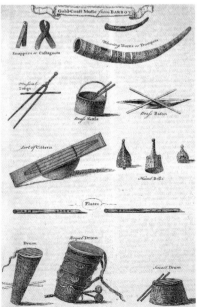

Enslaved Africans in the New World brought with them a variety of musical traditions. These seventeenth-century sketches show drums, snappers (castanets), flutes, horns, bells, and other instruments in common use on the Gold Coast during that time. (Thomas Astley, ed., *A New General Collection of Voyages and Travels*, London, 1745–47.)

enormous variety in black religion existed. Muslim slaves became particularly noted for the power of their magical charms. In the islands, African-style cults such as Jamaican Myal or Cuban Santeria or Haitian Vodou emerged. Some South Carolina slaves may have fled to the Spanish because they were Catholic, and many Louisiana and Florida slaves became devout Catholics. Other slaves in North America especially embraced every form of Protestantism.

A major development in the metaphysics of most slave communities was a shift from the benevolent lesser spirits—the unobservable personal beings so prominent in traditional African cosmologies—to sorcery, the harming of others by secretive means. Because of enforced coexistence with other African groups and because of the serious everyday problems of dealing with harsh taskmasters, slaves turned to those spirits deemed useful in injuring other people. The most common term for sorcery was *obi* or *obia* or *obeah*, which had multiple African origins, including Efik *ubio* (a charm to cause sickness and death) and Twi *o-bayifo* (sorcerer). The term was current among both mainland and island slaves, although on the mainland "conjuring" and "conjuror" were more common. While the boundary between sorcery, folk medicine, and divination was porous, the dominant trend was a powerful concentration on means for injuring people.

Another important development, which became significant toward the end of the eighteenth century and was most fully developed in North America, was the appeal of evangelical Christianity. The message of universal salvation through divine grace, an intensity of feeling and physical expressiveness, and a church structure that was quite egalitarian by the standards of the day, were all reasons why evangelicals were popular among slaves. In the 1760s black Christians were a minority in most American slave populations, but by the late eighteenth century, and gathering pace in the nineteenth, evangelical Christianity made enormous strides among blacks in both islands and mainland, but particularly North America. By the mid-nineteenth century, black Christians were in the majority in most mainland and some island societies.[16]

Creating a distinctive language, music, and religion—in short, a culture— had political implications, but profoundly ambivalent ones. On the one hand, it was an act of resistance, perhaps the greatest act of resistance accomplished by enslaved Africans and their descendants. By carving out some independence for themselves, by creating something coherent and autonomous from African fragments and European influences, by forcing whites to recognize their humanity, slaves triumphed over their circumstances. They opposed the dehumanization inherent in their status and demonstrated their independent will and volition. On the other hand, their cultural creativity eased the torments of slavery, gave them a reason for living, and made them think seriously before sacrificing everything in an attempt to overthrow the system. It thereby encouraged accommodation to the established order.

This ambivalence, which lies at the heart of the political experiences of African Americans, is apparent in slave resistance. List all the plots and rebellions in chronological sequence, and slave resistance appears structurally endemic. Recall the bitter fact that the vicious system of New World slavery lasted for hundreds of years without serious challenge (except in the French colony of St. Domingue, which became Haiti), and its stability seems paramount. No North American region faced a large-scale insurrection that threatened to overthrow slavery. South Carolina's Stono Rebellion in 1739, in which about sixty slaves killed approximately twenty whites and destroyed much property,

Opposite:
Written in Old French, this list gives names, ages, and places of origin of slaves being sold at a Louisiana auction in 1814. (Gene Alexander Peters Collection.)

This bone whistle reportedly belonged to Felipe Chartrand, a coffee and sugar planter in Matanzas, Cuba. At least once, in 1825—after England and Spain had formally but not finally abolished slave trading—Chartrand sailed to Africa in his own bark to secure slaves for his plantations. The whistle may have been used to call slaves to different tasks aboard ship.

179

Territory of Orleans
Parish of Avoyelles

Before me Thomas F. Oliver, Judge of
the Said Parish personally appeared Lemuel
Masters Subscribing witness to the above will
of Morgan Outlaw, who made oath that he
Saw the Said Morgan Outlaw in his life time
Sign the Said Will And Testament, And that
the Said Morgan Outlaw was at the time of
Signing And Acknowledging of the Said Will in
Sound Mind and Memory —

Sworn & Subscribed to
before me this 23 day of } Lemuel Masters —
July 1811.

Thomas F. Oliver J.P.a.

Succession De Marguerite Duplechain

Etat de la Louisianne
Paroisse des Avoyelles

Je Alexandre Planché Juge de la Paroisse
& notaire des Avoyelles ce jourd'hui Septieme du
mois d'octobre de l'annee de Grace mie huit cent
Quatorze me Suis transporté à la demeure de Mr.
augustin Juneau de la Paroisse Su ditte afin d'apposer
Les Sceau Sur les biens delaisse par feu marguerite
Duplechain Epouse de augustin Juneau decedé en
cette Paroisse ab intestat, et faire une inventaire
Provisoire des Su ditte biens, et en presence de
temoins Soussigné Requis à cet Effet Mr. augustin
Juneau présent, ce meme Jour et année de sus

Laborde
Ch. Cappel

A. Planché

Etat de la Louisianne
Paroisse des Avoyelles
Je Alexandre planché Juge et notaire en

Among those featured in this famous painting of a 1786 shipwreck off Dorset, England is a black woman wearing a simple white dress and a tignon—a type of head wrap that was widely worn by female slaves. It would not have been uncommon for a black servant to accompany an affluent European family on a voyage. (George Morland, "The Wreck of the Halsewell," c. 1786.)

was nevertheless small-scale and short-lived. Nat Turner's insurrection in 1831, in which about sixty people died, was a local outbreak confined mainly to Southampton County, Virginia, and lasted two days. By contrast, the Caribbean islands and parts of Latin America were always more brittle. Jamaica experienced many slave rebellions, none more serious than the island-wide insurrection of 1760 that resulted in deaths of 90 whites and 400 blacks, and the exile of another 600 blacks. The slaves of St. Domingue grasped their freedom in the greatest and most successful example of slave resistance in history. And just as slave rebellions varied across space, so they did over time, ranging from events inspired by Africans to events dominated by Creoles, from attempts to secure freedom to attempts to overthrow slavery, from acts of rage to industrial action. Slave resistance was also more than collective violence: it encompassed flight, sabotage, and individual murders. But the cook who put ground glass in the master's food had first to get the job; the slaves who plotted in the marketplaces had first to produce for the market. There is no simple linear gradient from accommodation to resistance.[17]

In sum, life for enslaved Africans and for African Americans was multi-faceted. In certain respects slaves throughout the Americas suffered similar fates. They lived short and impoverished lives, worked most of the time, created fragile families, encountered great brutality, spoke creolized languages, developed distinctive musical styles, believed in magic, and generally accommodated themselves to the system of slavery. But this description is a monochrome caricature, not a richly colored portrait. It fails to do justice to the variations, the subtleties, the many temporal and spatial distinctions in black life. There was no single "black experience." Instead, it varied fundamentally according to time and place and was influenced by a range of factors: the nature of population growth, the type of employment, the size of the slaveholding unit, the level of material well-being, the quality of family life, the patterns of encounters with whites, the extent of black cultural autonomy, and the degree of resistance and accommodation to the system. And yet, drawing upon some shared principles and passing through the fires of enslavement, African Americans everywhere managed to forge separate cultures—an achievement that ultimately formed the core of their experience.

"The Bone Player," painted by William S. Blount in 1856. (Museum of Fine Arts, Boston.)

Opposite:
Quilt made by an African-American slave. The geometrical motif used by the maker may resemble one common in the Asante (Ashanti) region of Africa. (Danny Drain Collection, Walterboro, South Carolina.)

Notice offering a handsome reward of $2,500 for runaway slaves in Mississippi. (Sample Pittman Collection, New York City.)

7

Struggles for Freedom

James Brewer Stewart

In the later eighteenth century, when American abolitionism first took form, the institution of slavery possessed enormous power and legitimacy throughout the Western world. It had been thus for centuries. From the time of ancient Athens, the exploitation of unfree laborers had shaped the economies of western Europe. Slaves by the hundreds of thousands had built the civilizations of classical Egypt, Greece, and Rome. Throughout the Middle Ages, the Renaissance, and well into the eighteenth century, landed aristocrats commanded the labor of millions of peasants and serfs. By the 1600s, the power of slavery to generate wealth from overseas colonies had become apparent to everyone as Spain, Portugal, Holland, France, and England developed immense empires throughout the Western Hemisphere, relying on the forced transshipment of enslaved Africans to create a global economy. Thus when Thomas Jefferson's Declaration of Independence first asserted revolutionary claims of equality in 1776, it did so at a time when sprawling systems of slavery were deeply entrenched and extraordinarily productive. Jefferson himself, of course, owned close to 200 slaves.[1]

This "dress collar" was issued to a slave owned by New Yorker William Clark. This type of collar was worn by slaves at social events that required more formal attire. (Sample Pittman Collection, New York City.)

Nineteenth-century tea caddy made of rolled paper. An inset ivory panel bears bas-relief wax models of chained slaves bracketed by painted designs of two men-of-war. The slaves are kneeling beneath the legend "O Lord, Set Us Free," indicating that this box was created in part to express an antislavery sentiment.

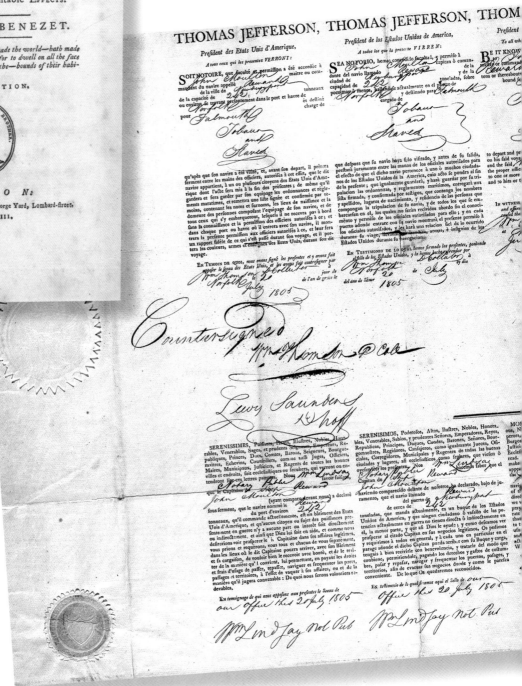

Title page of a 1783 tract on the slave trade by Anthony Benezet, a Quaker pamphleteer who dedicated his life to abolishing slavery.

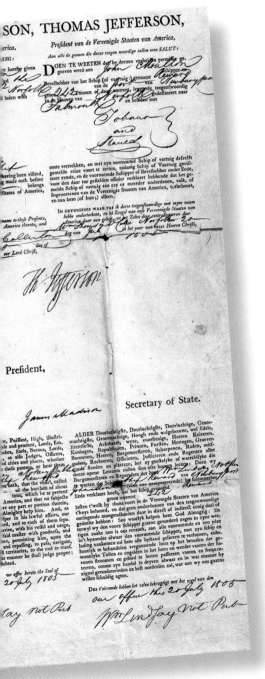

During Jefferson's prerevolutionary years, on Spanish-, English-, and French-held Caribbean islands, as well as in Spanish, Portuguese, and Dutch colonies throughout Latin America, powerful slaveholding elites and huge numbers of enslaved Africans produced sugar, tobacco, rum, coffee, and precious metals. International trading in African slaves had become immensely lucrative. And even as the signers of the Declaration of Independence asserted the right of revolution, every colony, north and south, maintained some system of enslaving African Americans.[2]

Though rural New Englanders generally had few uses for slave labor, elite Yankees confirmed their high status by owning slaves for personal service. In Rhode Island, slave labor was used in agriculture as well, and in New York, New Jersey, Delaware, and Pennsylvania, slavery proved a profitable way to farm on a large scale. In major northern cities, slaves commonly labored in manufacturing concerns and the construction industry. Though the number of African Americans living in the North, free or enslaved, totaled only 4 percent of the population, slavery clearly contributed to the development of the region's economy.

In the southern colonies, meanwhile, slavery exercised a far more pervasive influence, causing that region to develop its own distinctive political culture and economy.[3] Before the American Revolution, in every southern colony an elite group of slaveholders dominated politics, shaped the economy, and defined social norms. From the rice-growing coasts of South Carolina and Georgia to the tobacco plantations of Virginia and Maryland, these distinguished "first families" derived their power from their command over numerous slaves. By 1776 they presided over a region that counted thirty-five African Americans out of every hundred inhabitants. The majority of the South's whites, who were mostly small slaveholders and middling subsistence farmers, often resented these aristocratic "betters" but usually deferred to them, for this was a society based on a clear ordering of unequals: proud over humble, rich over poor, male over female, and above all, white over black.[4]

For this reason, southern whites of all social classes generally concurred with Jefferson that "inalienable rights" and claims of equality did not apply to people of African ancestry. Moreover, from the beginning nearly all English settlers from Georgia to Massachusetts had harbored deep prejudices against dark-skinned Africans that had made their enslavement seem natural and justified. By 1776 such attitudes were becoming deeply ingrained as an almost instinctive white supremacism. The strength of such biases ensured that many white Northerners agreed with their southern counterparts that Jefferson's Declaration should apply exclusively to their own "white race."[5] Thus by 1776, the strength of white racial prejudice posed enormous challenges to those who linked independence with abolitionism. Nevertheless, the colonists' revolt against Great Britain also inaugurated the North American crusade against slavery.

Detail of a clearance document for the ship *Reward* to leave Norfolk, Virginia bound for Falmouth, England laden with tobacco and slaves. It is dated July 20, 1805, and signed by President Thomas Jefferson and Secretary of State James Madison.

OPPRESSION TOO OBVIOUS TO IGNORE

Several factors account for the development of antislavery sentiment in the colonies, and all involved the colonists' revolutionary beliefs. Some prominent figures such as James Otis, Benjamin Franklin, Thomas Paine, Patrick Henry, and Benjamin Rush found strong abolitionist imperatives in the enlightenment rationalism that fueled their hatred of monarchy and aristocracy. Believing that environmental conditions determined the intellectual and moral development of all human beings, not their color or inherited status, such leaders concluded that the contradictions between patriots' demands for liberty and their oppression of black slaves were too obvious to ignore. According to this logic, emancipation would relieve African Americans of their "degraded" circumstances and allow them to "rise," even as white Americans cast off their own corrupting attachments to slaveholding "aristocracy." Other patriotic spokesmen drew their abolitionism from evangelical religion. Calvinist revivalists such as Samuel Hopkins and Jonathan Mayhew joined with Quaker evangelicals such as John Woolman and Anthony Benezet and Methodists such as Francis Asbury to condemn slavery as the foulest transgression of God's will and the main obstacle to independence. Imbibing such sentiments, some prominent planter-politicians in the upper South, such as St. George Tucker and Peyton Randolph, gradually emancipated their own slaves and called on others to follow their examples. In all these respects, the ideology of the Revolution challenged slavery's moral legitimacy as never before.[6]

Just as important, the struggle for independence led African Americans to defy their enslavement, turning the Revolutionary War into what historian Benjamin Quarles has characterized as North America's largest single slave insurrection.[7] In both North and South, many slaves fought as royalists as well as patriots in exchange for promises of freedom. Numerous others took advantage of the disruptions of warfare by escaping to northern cities. All across the North slaves petitioned state legislatures to enact bills of emancipation, bargained with their masters to purchase their freedom, and filed emancipation suits in courts. In all these ways, African Americans not only secured their individual liberty but also embraced political activism, establishing in every northern city communities of color that henceforth supported church and civic organizations and economic opportunity while supplying leadership in struggles against discrimination and slavery.[8]

$50 REWARD.

ABSCONDED from on board a vessel in Nanjemoy creek, a mulatto boy, named William, about nineteen years old, good looking, and has a scar upon his chin, is by trade a blacksmith. The above sum is offered for his delivery to me at Windsor, in King George county, Virginia, or $30 for his apprehension and security in Maryland.   JOHN PARKER.

June 27—dtf

In the North, this black and white activism yielded notable results. By the 1790s, every state legislature north of Virginia and Maryland had enacted bills of gradual emancipation. Though liberation itself was often a painfully slow and partial process because those freed were too often forced into apprenticeships controlled by whites, by the mid-1820s every northern state save New Jersey and Delaware had rid itself of slave holding. In most cases, however, African Americans found their political and civil rights strictly limited in these new circumstances while harsh patterns of discrimination emerged to blight their daily lives. Throughout the antebellum years, as abolitionists

Masters often advertised rewards for runaway slaves, as in this 1850s broadside.

This painting by artist Vernon Wooten depicts British soldiers reading a proclamation by the Earl of Dunmore, Virginia's last royal governor, urging slaves to join him in return for their freedom. Approximately 800 slaves stole sloops, schooners, and scows to join "Lord Dunmore's Ethiopian Regiment." (Colonial Williamsburg Foundation.)

always knew, freedom from slavery for African Americans in the North had little to do with equality.[9]

Meanwhile, the new federal Constitution of 1787 also worked in conservative directions by guaranteeing powerful protections for slavery in the southern states, where voluntary emancipation ultimately made no permanent headway. Constitutional features such as counting slaves as three-fifths of a full person when apportioning representation, guaranteeing the use of federal power to quell slave insurrections, extending the African slave trade for two decades (until 1808), and providing for a federally enforced fugitive slave law all indicated that slavery had been granted formidable legitimacy by the Founding Fathers, who envisioned a strong national government that necessarily suppressed divisive issues like abolitionism.[10]

For all these reasons, as Eli Whitney's cotton gin stimulated an explosive westward expansion of the cotton-growing frontier in the early 1800s, the Revolution's abolitionist legacies all but expired. As several new slave states such as Kentucky, Tennessee, and Alabama entered the Union, the domestic slave trade was thriving. Abolitionist voices had been reduced to a quiet few, largely those of isolated Quakers such as Benjamin Lundy and energetic free black leaders living in northern cities such as Philadelphia's James Forten and Richard Allen, Boston's James Eston, or New York City's John Teasman. Abortive insurrections in Virginia led by free blacks Gabriel Prosser (1800) and Denmark Vesey (1820), as well as the violent black revolution that succeeded in Haiti in the 1790s, had extinguished slaveholders' interest in private manumissions. Such frightening developments had also heightened their fears of local slave revolt and increased interest in the American Colonization Society, which proposed the voluntary repatriation to Liberia of free blacks and emancipated slaves. Benevolent northern whites also joined this organization, regarding it as a moderate way to address their moral concerns about slavery despite their ideological conservatism. Most free blacks in the free states, however, denounced colonization as a gross denial of their right to full citizenship in the United States. Though strong political disagreements pitted southern against northern congressmen over the admission of the slave state Missouri (1819–21), such sectional tensions did nothing to renew the flagging spirit of grass-roots abolitionism. By the later 1820s, slavery had become more entrenched than ever in the nation's economy and political system.[11]

A Slow End to the Brazilian Trade

After the importation of African slaves was officially outlawed in Britain and its North American colonies in 1807, the powerful British navy began patrolling the west coast of Africa and slave ports in the Caribbean and South America. Many governments disputed Britain's right to impose British law on vessels flying other flags, but some South American nations, not wanting to risk disrupting their maritime commerce with England, quickly jumped on the anti-slaving bandwagon: slave imports were banned in Venezuela in 1811 and in Colombia (New Granada) and Argentina in 1812. Mexico (New Spain) and Chile would soon follow suit. None of those nations, however, had a large demand for slave labor. Brazil, by contrast, continued to "require" tens of thousands of newly arrived Africans each year, as well as its existing slave population, to operate sugar and coffee plantations. In a world where antislavery sentiment was growing and, in countries such as France, even becoming fashionable, Brazilian planters were determined to maintain what they viewed as an all-important supply of slaves brought from Africa.

Spurred by ever-increasing pressure from abolitionists at home, in the first two decades of the nineteenth century Britain began pursuing anti-slaving treaties with the other maritime European nations whose flags had flown over slave ships for centuries: Portugal, Spain, Holland, France. These early treaties tended to be honored most in the frequency with which they were evaded; for example, a year after the French government signed an accord with Britain, some sixty French slave ships departed from ports such as Nantes for Africa and thence for the Americas.

For most Brazilians, black slavery seemed altogether part of the normal order of things in the 1820s, when Brazil claimed independence from Portugal. By that time, the forced labor of Africans had been used in Brazil for nearly 400 years. Antislavery organizations had little effect, for many, if not most, political leaders and their supporters were directly or indirectly connected with the slave trade. And for decades, anti–slave trade legislation was routinely ignored. In 1831 the Brazilian government declared slave imports illegal, yet shipping records indicate that between about 1820 and 1860, well in excess of half a million Africans would be transported to Brazil to toil on coffee and sugar plantations, in gold mines, and in the households of the well-to-do. Beginning in the 1840s, some would be transported in steamships—many built in English shipyards—with international crews drawn from Italy, Portugal, and other countries.

Ultimately, factors unrelated to ethics or morality converged to undermine the international trade to Brazil, as well as that nation's reliance on forced labor. For one, nineteenth-century slave traders had steadily increased the prices they charged for African slaves. For another, British merchants were increasing pressure on their Brazilian counterparts to engage, in effect, in "slave-free trade"—maritime commerce that did not include human cargoes nor products made with slave labor. At the same time, throughout the Caribbean and South America slave rebellions were becoming more common.

The last recorded attempt to deliver slaves to Brazil was in January 1856, when Brazilian authorities intercepted the *Mary E. Smith*, an illegal Boston slaver commissioned by Brazilian merchants in the United States. She was loaded with 400 slaves, who ended their voyage as free human beings. Within Brazil, however, pockets of slavery would persist almost until the twentieth century. —*B.C.M.*

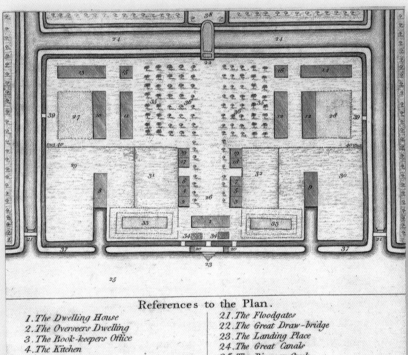

References to the Plan.

1. The Dwelling House
2. The Overseers Dwelling
3. The Book-keepers Office
4. The Kitchen
5. The Storehouse
6. The Poultry-house
7. The Hogs-sty
8. The Boat-house or small Dock
9. The Carpenters & Coopers Lodge
10. The Drying Lodge for the Coffee
11. The Bruising Lodge for do
12. The Negro-houses
13. The Horse Stables
14. The Fold for Sheep & Bullocks
15. The Great Guard house
16. The Hospital
17. The Pigeon-house
18. The Corn-house or Granary
19. The Necessary houses
20. The Sentry Boxes for Watchmen
21. The Floodgates
22. The Great Draw-bridge
23. The Landing Place
24. The Great Canals
25. The River or Creek
26. The Gravel walks
27. The Drying Floor for Coffee
28. The Negro Gardens
29. The Pasture for the Horses
30. The Pasture for the Sheep & Bullocks
31. The Poultry-yard
32. The Hogs-yard
33. The Kitchen Gardens
34. The Flower do
35. The Plantain Trees
36. The Groves of Orange Trees
37. The Dams & Gutters for Draining
38. The Path to enter the Fields
39. The Bridges over the Gutters
40. The Gates, Barriers, &c.

Plan of a regular Coffee Plantation.

Plan of a South American coffee plantation from *The Curious Adventures of Captain Stedman During an Expedition to Surinam*, published in London by Thomas Tegg in 1796. A similar plantation layout might have been used in neighboring Brazil, where by the nineteenth century coffee rivaled sugar as the main export crop.

FREEDOM'S JOURNAL.

"RIGHTEOUSNESS EXALTETH A NATION."

CORNISH & RUSSWURM, *Editors and Proprietors.*

NEW-YORK, FRIDAY, JULY 27, 1827. [VOL. I.--NO. 20.

EUROPEAN COLONIES IN AMERICA.
(Concluded.)

It has sometimes been thought, that the vicinity of one or more independent black states would be dangerous to the internal tranquility of our country; but the experience of more than twenty years in the case of the republic of Hayti, affords a practical refutation of this opinion. There are even some positive advantages attending this circumstance, of no small consequence. A flourishing and prosperous community of this description, would naturally attract from amongst us the free blacks who are found in the slave-holding states to be troublesome members of society, and who would thus obtain abroad an open and inviting field of action. A natural drain of this kind would remove these persons from our territory much more rapidly and effectually than the laborious and expensive efforts of the Colonization Society, which, however well meant, can hardly produce any important results, counteracted as they are by all the motives that ordinarily affec the human mind. The society invites the free blacks to quit a country where they are comfortably situated, and emigrate to another, where they are to encounter great hardships, with no certain prospects for the future. It is obvious that this must be from first to last a forced proceeding; and the least difficulty about it, (though this is not a small one,) is, that the society is under the necessity of defraying all the expenses of this unnatural emigration. In the other case, the emigration, being voluntary and sponta eous, would of course be executed at the expense of the emigrants; and being the effect of powerful motives operating in the ordinary way, might be expected to be rapid and extensive. How far the abovementioned society is likely to accomplish the farther object of removing the slave population itself from our soil, is with me a still more doubtful question, than that of its success with the free blacks. When we consider the natural increase that takes place among the slaves, amounting to not less than thirty or forty thousand a year, and that the society have not yet made arrangements for transporting annually to Africa more than three or four hundred persons, it is easy at least to see, that their arrangements must be very much extended before they will even begin to approach the accomplishment of their purpose. Add to this, that a moderate and regular emigration has in general little or no tendency to diminish the population of a country, and the case will be found to be still more desperate. Finally it may be questioned whether we ought to wish to remove from amongst us, if we could do it peaceably and easy, so large a portion of the working class. The political condition of the blacks is certainly far from being what we could wish it; but such as they are, they are nevertheless industrious and useful labourers, and the southern states would, I apprehend, suffer not a little from the loss of them. The expulsion of the Moors from Spain, and of the Protestants from France, for reasons not unlike those which are now urged for the removal of the blacks, have been commonly considered as among the most impolitic measures that ever were adopted, and a similar result obtained by a special operation *ad hoc* on the minds of the blacks, would be just as impolitic, though somewhat less violent and odious. It is needless, however, to argue against the impolicy of a scheme, of which the accomplishment is obviously and physically impossible. Our duty, as respects the blacks, appears to be in the first place, to make them as happy as we can in their present condition, and then to employ such means as may be most expedient for raising them by a slow and gradual process to a higher one. Of these means, one of the most important is to discourage in every possible way, the idea that any thing can be effected immediately and at once; and the Colonization Society, however respectable from the high character of its members and the purity of their intentions, produces thus far a great positive evil, inasmuch as it keeps up in the public mind an impression, that the situation of the slaves can be violently and suddenly altered for the better, by this expedient of emigration. This opinion engenders a morbid and mistaken sentiment in regard to the whole subject. Mr. King's proposition in the senate is liable to the same objection. In this as in every other project for political improvement, we must assume and build upon the existing state of things. Improve the character of the blacks, and emancipation will come in due time without an effort; whereas, by a premature zeal for formal emancipation, you destroy the possibility of improvement, and thereby defeat your own object. The society may perhaps effect some good by founding a colony on the coast of Africa, although even in this particular its efforts are liable to the same objection which is made habitually with so much justice to those of our missionary institutions, that they employ upon a distant and uncertain object, a part of the time, funds, and good will of the public, for the whole of which there is an ample occupation at home. While therefore, we express our sincere admiration of the honest zeal and generous philanthropy of the members of this body, we may be allowed to wish that these most estimable qualities may receive a different direction, and be devoted to some of the numerous objects of great and undoubted utility which our country offers in such abundance.

HISTORY OF SLAVERY.
(Continued.)

The most important feature of the Mosaic law, in relation to slavery, was its *limited duration.* No sanction is afforded by any precept of that law, to perpetual and hereditary servitude.

To set this subject in its proper light, I shall cite a part of the law, which bears most directly on this subject.

If thy brother that dwelleth by thee be waxen poor, and be sold unto thee, thou shalt not compel him to serve as a bond servant, but as an hired servant, and as a sojourner shall he be with thee, and shall serve thee unto the year of jubilee; and then shall he depart from thee, both he and his children with him, and shall return unto his own family, and unto the possession of his fathers shall he return: They shall not be *sold* as bondmen. Both thy bondmen and thy bondmaids, which thou shalt have, shall be of the heathen that are round about you, of them shall ye *buy* bondmen and bondmaids. Moreover of the children of the strangers that sojourn among you, of them shall ye buy, and of their families that are with you, and they shall be your possession. And ye shall take them as an inheritance for your children after you, to inherit them for a possession, they shall be your bondmen forever: but over your brethren the children of Israel, ye shall not rule over one another with rigour. And if a sojourner or a stranger wax rich by thee, and thy brother that dwelleth by him wax poor, and sell himself unto the stranger or sojourner: After he is sold he may be redeemed again, one of his brethren may redeem him: or, if he be able he may redeem himself. He shall reckon with him that bought him, from the year that he was sold unto him, unto the year of jubilee; and the price of his sale shall be according to the number of years, according to the time of an hired servant shall it be with him. As a yearly hired servant shall he be with him; and the other shall not rule with rigour over him in thy sight. And if he be not redeemed in these years, then shall he go out in the year of jubilee; both he and his children with him. Levit. xxv. 39—54.

These passages, to be properly understood must be taken in connexion with other parts of the law. In the first place we must observe, that these precepts are rather prohibitory than authoritative; that they serve to limit rather than to support the authority of masters over their purchased servants. No obligation to purchase a brother, or permit his sale to a stranger, can be implied. A sale is supposed to have occurred, and to that contingency the rule is adapted.

In the second place, the expression *forever* is frequently used in a limited sense. Thus, Joshua is said to have made Ai an heap forever; and it was said there should not be an old man in Eli's house *forever*; also Jonah declares, "the earth with her bars *was* about me forever." When Moses designed to establish a permanent ordinance, he usually added *throughout your generations.* If in this case a permission only was given, and a limit implied which the text does not clearly define; let us look for an explanation to other positive precepts of the law: Ye shall hallow the fiftieth year, and proclaim liberty throughout all the land, to *all the inhabitants* thereof; it shall be a jubilee unto you; and ye shall return every man to his possession, and ye shall return every man to his family. (Levit. xxv. 10.) But in the case of an Hebrew servant, we have a still narrower limit, for in this case the service is limited to six years; and in the sabbatical year, the Hebrew servant was not only to go out free, but to be liberally supplied from the flock, the floor and the wine press of the master. (Deut. xv. 12, 13; Ex. xxi. 2.) If the servant brought a wife with him, she also was to be free in the sabbatical year. If he had been married, during his servitude, to a servant of his master who was not entitled to her liberty in the sabbatical year, the *marriage* gave her no title to her freedom. Under these circumstances, it is not surprising that under a mild administration, with the privileges frequently enjoyed, the servant should sometimes prefer a continuance with the family in which he had been settled. Hence the provision, that, upon such declaration being solemnly made, his ear should be bored,* in the presence of the judges, and his privilege of freedom in the sabbatical year be withheld. Still the general law, of liberty in the year of jubilee, would reach the bored servant in common with the other branches of his family. (Josephus Ant. Book iv. ch. 8 sect 28.) It therefore appears, that the servants of their brethren, including proselytes as well as Hebrews were to be treated rather as freemen than as slaves, and at furthest to be free in the year of jubilee; that such of them as should be sold to the strangers residing among them, were redeemable at any time between the that the strangers, whom the year of jubilee. But purchase, were liable to be held, without the privilege of redemption, until the jubilee year.

It may be fairly inferred, not only from the unqualified injunction to proclaim a general emancipation in the year of jubilee, but from the text in relation to the heathen bondmen, that perpetual and hereditary bondage was not designed to be tolerated. For no intimation is here given of any right except what should be procured by purchase; those whom they should buy, not those whose parents had been bought, were to be held as a possession. Had an hereditary slavery been intended, the general precept must have been modified, and no doubt, the usual expression, *throughout your generations,* or some other equivalent phrase, have been appended to the grant. The term *forever* may be construed as indicative of the perpetuity of the practice, or that of such they should continue to *buy,* during their own national existence; but not that the servitude should be perpetuated in the person or descendants of the individual purchased.

[*African Obs.*

* The practice of boreing the ears of servants was not peculiar to the Israelites. I was an ancient custom in the east. To this Juvenal refers, when he makes a freedman say,

Though born a slave, ('twere bootless to deny
What these bored ears betray to every eye.)

An expression of Cicero is also noticed, in which he tells a Lybian who pretended he did not hear him, it was because his ears were not sufficiently *bored.* The meaning, if meaning it had, would seem to to indicate that the ears were to be always open or attentive to the directions of the master.

[COMMUNICATED FOR THE FREEDOM'S JOURNAL.]

Our readers who are acquainted with the character of the late lamented, RUSSEL PARROT of Philadelphia, and with his deep concern for his brethren of colour, will readily account for our publishing this effort of his; in defence of their character, and rights.

FROM THE UNION.

A correspondent under the signature of Paul, who seems completely animated with the spirit that filled Saul when he went to persecute the poor Christians, is desirous of knowing 'A Man of Colour's reasons for believing that the interest which the slave states have taken in that fœtus of their own begetting, colonization was engendered in impunity. It shall not be my province to enter into the propriety or merits of a "Man of Colour's" production; this is avowedly the land of liberty, and *here* I know every man can give publicity to his sentiments, holding himself amenable to the laws. I think the article, is superfluous, as it is a mere recapitulation of what we have unitedly said; but honest zeal, no doubt, prompted his individual protest.

The long continuance of our wrongs, the shocking features that have characterised them, have become so familiar to some minds, naturally callous, and dead to sensibility, that they have brought themselves to believe that we have no rights to maintain in society, no interest apart from their cupidity, and that as at first our ancestors were torn from their native land, for the gratification of avarice, that we, their descendants, may, with equal *justice,* be expatriated for expediency; that those virtuous men, whose system Franklin originated and Rush perfected, and which has ranked among its supporters all that is truly good or great in this country, are the dupes of mistaken humanity, and the factious aspirers after mischief. I thank my God that they are not to be driven from the true interest of this country by declamatory libels; but will combat with this monstrous infatuation, until the safety and happiness of these states are placed upon a secure basis.

With an overgrown black population, the frightful amount of which is studiously concealed, groaning under a cruel despotism, gradually advancing towards improvement, in spite of municipal regulation, and feverishly alive to a sense of those rights which God bestowed on them, in common on all mankind, the free black population have become a source of uneasiness to those who are determined to adhere to a ruinous system, to deface over the whole ... the baleful influence of slavery, a system which the united voice of reason and policy have proven to be inconsist... with the spirit of every free government ... prove my assertion, I refer to the l... Virginia, which prevents any inhabita... manumitting a slave; of the Carolina... subjects any assemblage of coloured ... either for religious o mental instruc... be dispersed by flagellation, and the minis... or instructor, punished at the common whipping post; and to top the climax of the inconsistency of these vociferators of liberty, that recent act of Georgia, which, among a dreadful catalogue of wrongs, forbids, under pain of fine, imprisonment, and disgraceful stripes, any white or black teaching a person of colour to read or write. If we search through the wide extended range of creation, we cannot find that its parallel, superstition, and Gothic darkness, would have startled at a measure like this, as too base even for their gloomy policy.

The man who can look at this long chain of barbarous laws, connected with whatever is bad in the ancient colonial policy, must be blind indeed, if he cannot see that the effort which is now making, and which originated with the slave-holding interest, to locate the free blacks in Africa, is to completely and effectually, perpetuate slavery in the southern section of this country.

The people of colour have ever been the victims of misrepresentation—it was maintained, and in many a laborious treatise too, in justification of stealing them from Africa, that they were only a species, but a remove from the brute, with all the bad propensities of man, without one of his good qualities—that it was mercy to rescue them from massacre, to which in their native land they were exposed—their moral and intellectual worth develope themselves in opposition to every effort; they dissipate by force the wilful errors that avarice would propagate, and prove in spite of prejudice, that though the God of Nature diversified the complexion of the human family, created this man white, that brown, and the other black; the heart, the centre of the affections and moral excellence, he formed alike: we have only to look at our ancestors, ignorant and cruel, selling and murdering one another; and the whites, educated and mercenary, stimulating them to these acts of barbarity, and entailing upon a guiltless posterity the ignominy of slavery.

Driven from the ground of inequality of species, they have entrenched themselves behind the subterfuge of expedients; they lament the existence of this monstrous evil, (for an evil is at length admitted to be,) but then it was England that was the cause of

Opposite:

Freedom's Journal, the first black newspaper to be published in the United States, c. 1827. (Collection of the New York Historical Society.)

ADDRESSES AND MEMORIALS

TO

HIS MAJESTY,

FROM THE

HOUSE OF ASSEMBLY AT JAMAICA,

VOTED IN THE

YEARS 1821 TO 1826 INCLUSIVE;

AND WHICH HAVE BEEN PRESENTED TO HIS MAJESTY

BY THE ISLAND AGENT.

PRINTED BY ORDER OF THE HOUSE OF ASSEMBLY
OF JAMAICA.

76678

Published in 1828, this collection of Jamaican appeals to the British king expressed colonial fears that economic turmoil would result from ending the Caribbean slave trade. ("Addresses and Memorials to His Majesty, from the House of Assembly at Jamaica.")

Indeed, throughout the North, the 1820s witnessed an unprecedented spread of antiblack bigotry that strengthened that region's support for southern slavery. Massive immigration from the British isles suddenly put economically vulnerable English, Scottish, and Irish workers into competitive proximity with northern free blacks, stimulating fears about the threat of "white slavery" and creating deep new levels of white working-class prejudice. Among "respectable" middle-class whites, the belief grew that free blacks represented a "naturally degraded race" that needed stringent policing rather than "benevolent" assistance. Free African Americans grew understandably defensive as major antiblack riots erupted for the first time in major cities, and as state and local governments passed harsh new discriminatory legislation even while extending the vote to all adult white males. In newly admitted western "free" states such as Illinois and Ohio, for example, constitutional provisions either prohibited blacks from immigrating or explicitly denied them most civil rights. In 1827, the New York State legislature restricted suffrage to black males having more than $200 in taxable property (a significant sum for ordinary people in the economy of that day), while two years later the white residents of Cincinnati rioted so viciously that many local blacks sought permanent residence elsewhere.[12]

In response to increasing bigotry, besieged black leaders throughout the North gathered their collective strength by founding their own newspaper, *Freedom's Journal*, and their own organization, the Colored Convention Movement (1830), each a vehicle for protesting discrimination, denouncing colonization, and debating the possibility of voluntary emigration to Haiti or lower Canada. In 1829, when Boston's David Walker first published his extraordinary pamphlet *An Appeal to the Colored Citizens of the World, and Most Particularly to Those of the United States* … , his beleaguered black readers understandably embraced his revolutionary call for the use of defensive violence, his scathing criticisms of black Americans' apathy and ignorance, and his wholesale condemnations of the American Colonization Society. As free blacks in the North understood it, the decade of the 1820s was closing on an ominous note of racial crisis.[13]

By 1831, however, this crisis no longer merely threatened. Instead, it exploded as four nearly simultaneous events set off fundamental struggles over slavery and racial equality unprecedented in the nation's history, conflicts that ultimately pointed toward the coming of the Civil War. In addition to the discovery that Walker's *Appeal* was circulating among slaves in the coastal South, 1831 brought with it Nat Turner's bloody insurrection in Southampton County, Virginia, the massive revolt in British Jamaica, dangerous secession threats from South Carolinian "nullifiers" who feared the federal government threatened their right to hold slaves, and, most portentous of all, the publication by Bostonian William Lloyd Garrison of a new abolitionist newspaper, the *Liberator*, which espoused the radical new doctrine of "immediate emancipation." To slaveholders and free northern blacks, to white reformers of all persuasions, and to politicians everywhere it was suddenly clear that slavery constituted a moral question of unprecedented proportions.

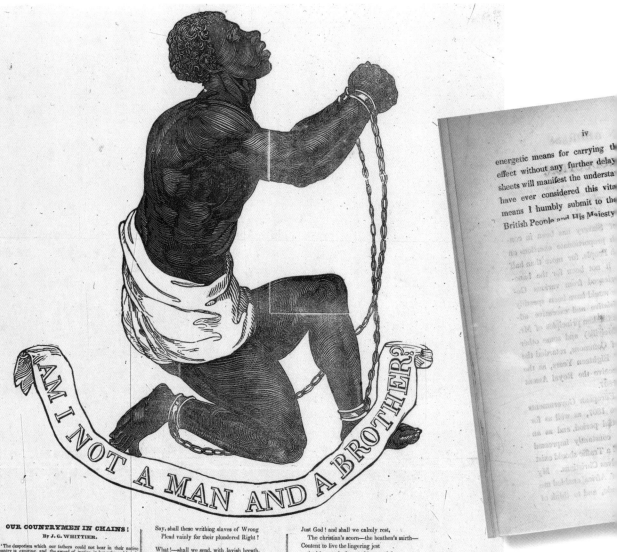

OUR COUNTRYMEN IN CHAINS!
By J. G. WHITTIER.

'The despotism which our fathers could not bear in their native country is expiring, and the sword of justice in her reformed hands has applied its exterminating edge to slavery. Shall the United States—the Free United States, which could not bear the bonds of a king, cradle the bondage which a king is abolishing? Shall a Republic be less free than a Monarchy? Shall we, in the vigor and buoyancy of our manhood, be less energetic in righteousness, than a kingdom in its age?'—Dr. Follen's Address.

Genius of America! Spirit of our free institutions—where art thou? How art thou fallen, oh Lucifer! son of the morning—how art thou fallen from Heaven! Hell from beneath is moved for thee, to meet thee at thy coming!—The kings of the earth cry out to thee, Aha! Aha!—ART THOU BECOME LIKE UNTO US?—Speech of Rev. S. J. May.

OUR FELLOW COUNTRYMEN in chains!
  SLAVES—in a land of light and law!—
SLAVES—crouching on the very plains
  Where rolled the storm of Freedom's war!
A groan from Eutaw's haunted wood—
  A wail where Camden's martyrs fell—
By every shrine of patriot blood,
  From Moultrie's wall and Jasper's well!

By storied hill and hallowed grot,
  By mossy wood and marshy glen,
Whence rang of old the rifle shot,
  And hurrying shout of Marion's men!—
The groan of breaking hearts is there—
  The falling lash—the fetter's clank!
Slaves—SLAVES are breathing in that air
  Which old De Kalb and Sumpter drank!

What, ho!—our countrymen in chains!
  The whip on WOMAN's shrinking flesh!
Our soil yet reddening with the stains,
  Caught from her scourging, warm and fresh!
What! mothers from their children riven!—
  What! God's own image bought and sold!—
AMERICANS to market driven,
  And bartered as the brute for gold!

Speak!—shall their agony of prayer
  Come thrilling to our hearts in vain!
To us—whose fathers scorned to bear
  The paltry menace of a chain;—
To us whose boast is loud and long
  Of holy liberty and light—

Say, shall these writhing slaves of Wrong
  Plead vainly for their plundered Right?

What!—shall we send, with lavish breath,
  Our sympathies across the wave,
Where manhood on the field of death
  Strikes for his freedom, or a grave!—
Shall prayers go up—and hymns be sung
  For Greece, the Moslem fetter spurning—
And millions hail with pen and tongue
  Our light on all her altars burning?

Shall Belgium feel, and gallant France,
  By Vendome's pile and Schoenbrun's wall,
And Poland, gasping on her lance,
  The impulse of our cheering call?
And shall the SLAVE, beneath our eye,
  Clank o'er our fields his hateful chain?
And toss his fettered arm on high,
  And groan for freedom's gift, in vain?

Oh say, shall Prussia's banner be
  A refuge for the stricken slave;—
And shall the Russian serf go free
  By Baikal's lake and Neva's wave;—
And shall the wintry-bosomed Dane
  Relax the iron hand of pride,
And bid his bondmen cast the chain
  From fettered soul and limb, aside?

Shall every flap of England's flag
  Proclaim that all around are free,
From 'farthest Ind' to each blue crag
  That beetles o'er the Western Sea?
And shall we scoff at Europe's kings,
  When Freedom's fire is dim with us,
And round our country's altar clings
  The damning shade of Slavery's curse?

Go—let us ask of Constantine
  To loose his grasp on Poland's throat—
And beg the lord of Mahmoud's line
  To spare the struggling Suliote,
Will not the scorching answer come
  From turbaned Turk, and fiery Russ—
'Go, loose your fettered slaves at home,

Just God! and shall we calmly rest,
  The christian's scorn—the heathen's mirth—
Content to live the lingering jest
  And by-word of a mocking earth!
Shall our own glorious land retain
  That curse which Europe scorns to bear?
Shall our own brethren drag the chain
  Which not even Russia's menials wear!

Up, then, in Freedom's manly part,
  From gray-beard eld to fiery youth,
And on the nation's naked heart
  Scatter the living coals of Truth!
Up—while ye slumber, deeper yet
  The shadow of our fame is growing—
Up—While ye pause, our sun may set
  In blood, around our altars flowing!

Oh rouse ye—ere the storm comes forth—
  The gathered wrath of God and man—
Like that which wasted Egypt's earth,
  When hail and fire above it ran.
Hear ye no warnings in the air!
  Feel ye no earthquake underneath?
Up—up—why will ye slumber where
  The sleeper only wakes in death!

Up now for Freedom!—not in strife
  Like that your sterner fathers saw
The awful waste of human life—
  The glory and the guilt of war;
But break the chain—the yoke remove
  And smite to earth oppression's rod,
With those mild arms of Truth and Love,
  Made mighty through the living God!

Prone let the shrine of Moloch sink,
  And leave no traces where it stood
Nor longer let its idol drink
  His daily cup of human blood:
But rear another altar there,
  To truth and love and mercy given,
And Freedom's gift and Freedom's prayer
  Shall call an answer down from Heaven!

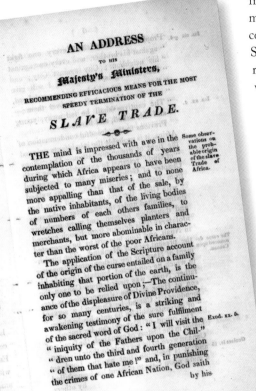

AN ADDRESS

TO HIS

Majesty's Ministers,

RECOMMENDING EFFICACIOUS MEANS FOR THE MOST
SPEEDY TERMINATION OF THE

SLAVE TRADE.

THE mind is impressed with awe in the Some obser-
contemplation of the thousands of years vations on
during which Africa appears to have been the prob-
able origin
subjected to many miseries; and to none of the slave
Trade of
more appalling than that of the sale, by Africa.
the native inhabitants, of the living bodies
of numbers of each others families, to
wretches calling themselves planters and
merchants, but more abominable in character than the worst of the poor Africans.
The application of the Scripture account
of the origin of the curse entailed on a family
inhabiting that portion of the earth, is the
only one to be relied upon;—The continuance of the displeasure of Divine Providence,
for so many centuries, is a striking and
awakening testimony of the sure fulfilment Exod. xx. &
of the sacred word of God: "I will visit the
" iniquity of the Fathers upon the Chil-"
" dren unto the third and fourth generation
" of them that hate me!" and, in punishing
the crimes of one African Nation, God saith
by his

A pamphlet pleading for the "most speedy termination" of trading in human beings. ("An Address to His Majesty's Ministers for Recommending Efficacious Means for the Most Speedy Termination of African Slavery." John Fernandez, 1827.)

Opposite:
In 1837 poet and abolitionist John Greenleaf Whittier published his antislavery poem, "Our Countrymen in Chains." The poem was sold at the Anti-Slavery Office on Nassau Street in New York for two cents a copy, or 100 copies for a dollar. (Library of Congress.)

"IMMEDIATE EMANCIPATION"

Above all, the demand for "immediate emancipation" foreordained this result. The imperative that the "God-defying sin" of owning humans be expunged from the Earth as rapidly as possible originated in Great Britain's abolitionist movement, which was then on the verge of pressuring Parliament to legislate compensated emancipation throughout the Empire's Caribbean sugar colonies. Soon after Garrison adopted immediatism, dozens of influential white reformers throughout New England joined him to form the nucleus of a vibrantly radical white-led crusade that was to continue for at least four decades, even after civil war had finally led to slavery's violent overthrow. In the process, they invited participation by members of the North's African-American communities, who initially joined with great enthusiasm, creating the nation's first biracial social movement. In the atmosphere of mounting racial intolerance so prevalent in the 1820s and 1830s, this eagerness to "mix" black people with white was undoubtedly the most radical feature of immediate abolitionism.[14]

Historians who have examined the motives of white immediatists have usually emphasized the importance of religious revivalism in sealing an initial commitment to "the cause." During the 1820s a popular resurgence of evangelical Protestantism known as the Second Great Awakening swept across the nation, and for certain New Englanders its impact had deep abolitionist implications. Powerful revivalist preachers such as Lyman Beecher and Charles G. Finney propounded doctrines that stressed the individual's free-will choice to renounce sin, to strive for personal holiness, and then, once "saved," to bring God's truth to the "unredeemed" and to combat the social evils that "sin" inevitably perpetuated—drunkenness, impiety, sexual license, and the exploitation of the weak and defenseless. To the ears of certain of Beecher's and Finney's followers, such as Arthur and Lewis Tappan, Theodore Dwight Weld, and Elizur Wright Jr., to evangelical Baptists like Garrison, to neo-Calvinists like Samuel Sewall Jr. and William Jay, or to radical Quakers like Lucretia Mott or John Greenleaf Whittier, each of these doctrines made clear that slavery was the most God-defying of all sins. In what other social system did exploitation of the weak and defenseless occur more brazenly? Where was sexual wantonness more rampant than in the master's debauchery of his female slaves? Where was impiety more openly encouraged than in the masters' refusals to permit their slaves freedom of religious expression? Where was brutality more evident than in the master's heavy use of the whip, or his callous disregard for slaves' ties of family and community? Who beside the slaveholders needed more desperately to respond to the challenge of God's truth that they repent and begin immediately to emancipate those whom they abused so vilely? The answer to all these urgent questions, of course, required preaching the truth of "immediate emancipation" by means of what was termed "moral suasion"—that is, by making peaceful Christian appeals that would awaken the slumbering consciences of southern slaveholders and their unwitting northern abettors.[15]

Advocates of the immediatist cause, though always immensely unpopular, made dramatic initial gains as they multiplied their activities during the early 1830s. Thanks to the efforts of the Tappans, Garrison, the Motts, and other leaders, hundreds of antislavery societies established themselves in towns and

cities in New England, New York State, and Pennsylvania. Farther west, particularly in Ohio, Theodore Weld, Elizur Wright Jr., Beriah Green, and their many co-workers also established a dense network of abolitionist organizations. The denunciatory appeals of Garrison's *Liberator* were quickly amplified by dozens of immediatist pamphlets and newspapers that circulated widely throughout the free states with titles such as *The Slaves' Friend*, *The Emancipator*, and *Human Rights*. Salaried agents crisscrossed the North organizing meetings and denouncing the sins of slave holding in public speeches. The American Anti-Slavery Society, founded in 1833, underwrote these myriad activities and, in addition, developed in 1835 a "great postal campaign" that used the United States mail service to prick the consciences of slaveholders by flooding the South with abolitionist literature. It also set in motion a "great petition campaign" presenting the United States Congress with thousands of petitions, accompanied by tens of thousands of signatures, each praying that Representatives consider enacting specific antislavery legislation. In cities across the North, meanwhile, white abolitionists joined with local African-American activists in daring efforts to "uplift the black race" by founding schools, moral reform societies, manual labor academies, and Sunday school groups. The most enduring of these, Oberlin College, established in Ohio in 1835, represented the nation's first example of multiracial coeducation.[16]

Engraved print of Frederick Douglass at 27, showing broken chains, by J. C. Buttre. (Sample Pittman Collection, New York City.)

As this example and many others made clear, immediatism was, from its inception, a racially "amalgamated" enterprise that included people of both genders. Prominent black leaders such as James Forten, Hosea Easton, and James Barbadoes visibly involved themselves in the American Anti-Slavery Society; Garrison and the Tappans, in turn, entered into the deliberations of the National Colored Convention. The undeniable presence of women of both races in the immediatist ranks, people like the white Lydia Maria Child or the black Sarah Forten, further reinforced impressions among its multiplying opponents that abolitionism sought to undermine every traditional relationship, particularly those that placed masters over slaves, men over women, and whites over blacks. Considering the extraordinary range and radicalism of their endeavors, it is hardly surprising that the abolitionists' peaceful "moral suasion" campaigns provoked unprecedented political repression and organized violence.[17]

Opposite:
Anthony Burns, c. 1855. Burns led a remarkable life as a black man in the United States. He escaped slavery only to be recaptured, then was "ransomed" by abolitionist allies. After regaining his liberty Burns attended Oberlin College in Ohio and eventually became a minister. (Library of Congress.)

The grueling lives of slaves and horrific punishments meted out to them helped fuel not
only peaceful abolitionist fervor but also the violent antislavery activities of the zealot
John Brown. Dogs were commonly used to hunt down escaped slaves, as depicted in this
painting by Richard Ansdell entitled "The hunted slaves." (Courtesy Board of Trustees,
National Museums and Galleries on Merseyside.)

In the South, the "great postal campaign" quickly ended in mayhem as mobs organized by angry slaveholders broke into post offices, burned "incendiary" pamphlets, and hung leading abolitionists in effigy—all with the approval of President Andrew Jackson. In Congress, the petition campaign initially fared no better, resulting in the passage of a controversial "gag rule" that prevented antislavery requests from being debated at all. Meanwhile, between 1834 and 1838, major cities in the free states exploded in racial violence as white mobs attacked African-American communities and abolitionist meetings in cities such as Boston, Philadelphia, Utica, New York City, Hartford, Pittsburgh, and Cincinnati. Encouraging the mobs were commercial and business elites, "gentlemen of property and standing" as abolitionists sneeringly termed them, powerful men who sensed in immediatism comprehensive threats to their traditional moral authority. Leading the attacks on black churches and abolitionist meeting halls were ordinary day laborers, often recent immigrants, who feared deeply that black emancipation would cause their own social and economic "enslavement." Condoning the violence—and blaming the abolitionists for causing it—were representatives of the nation's two great political parties, the Whigs and Democrats, both of whose national organizations required support from southern slaveholders as well as from antiblack voters in the free states. By the late 1830s both political parties, nearly all the nation's leading business and church figures, the vast bulk of the northern working class, and the entire white South had arrayed themselves as one against the abolitionists. As a means for rapidly abolishing slavery, "immediate emancipation" had plainly failed.[18]

A MOVEMENT DIVIDED

To be sure, repression did bring abolitionism some gains, particularly new leaders such as the magnificent orator Wendell Phillips and the millionaire philanthropist Gerrit Smith who were spurred to immediatism by their disgust with proslavery mobs. The suppression of civil liberties such as the rights to petition and peaceful assembly also began leading Northerners in increasing numbers to suspect that slaveholders and their free-state allies conspired against white people's constitutional freedom and political interests, feelings that were to spread rapidly in the 1840s and 1850s during controversies with southern politicians over slavery's role in westward expansion. At the same time, however, the impact of repression also shattered the immediatist movement as warring factions drew conflicting meanings from their trials by violence. For the abolitionists who followed William Lloyd Garrison, repression by church, state, and the political process fostered a deep alienation from all such institutions, a deepening reverence for the sanctity of noncoercive relationships, and a belief in the possibility of human perfectibility. Such axioms, in turn, led most Garrisonians to reject church and state authority, endorse radical pacifism, embrace women's rights, and demand the dissolution of a presumably proslavery Union. These were creeds that most Garrisonians maintained until the eve of the Civil War, and that also directly inspired the founding in 1848 of the first women's rights movement by feminist abolitionists in Seneca Falls, New York.[19]

Garrison's opponents vehemently rejected these new principles, but went separate ways as well. Some attempted to persevere with original "moral suasion" by founding the American and Foreign Anti-Slavery Society, designed to compete with the Garrison-dominated American Anti-Slavery Society. Others

noted rising antisouthern resent-
ments among northern voters over
such issues as the "gag rule," which
prohibited discussions of slavery
issues in the U.S. House of
Representatives, and the possible
annexation of new frontier slave
territories such as Texas. To *these*
anti-Garrisonians, abolitionist duty
dictated plunging into politics by
founding an emancipationist third
party, the Liberty Party, which in
one form or another campaigned in
presidential contests through
Lincoln's election in 1860.[20]

FORCING SLAVERY DOWN THE THROAT OF A FREESOILER

For the next two decades, from
1840 until 1861, these competing
sects of abolitionists pursued their
differing political strategies with
few measurable results. Instead, the
focus of national conflicts over
slavery shifted to Congress, where Whigs and Democrats struggled with
growing sectional discord over slavery's westward expansion. In the complex
process of sectional estrangement that developed in the politics of the 1840s
and 1850s over whether newly acquired western territories should open to
slavery or instead be reserved as "free soil," immediate abolitionists played only
peripheral roles. The annexation of Texas and the Mexican War (1845–48)
first raised this sectional issue, which then exploded in the North in the later
1850s after the Kansas-Nebraska Act and the Dred Scott Decision (in 1857)
seemed to guarantee the unlimited expansion of slavery. As the Whig Party
dissolved and the Democratic Party split along north/south lines, and as a
new Republican Party emerged in the free states pledging to arrest any
further expansion of slavery, abolitionists exercised no discernable power.
Their influence was much greater in more limited northern spheres of politics
as the Civil War drew closer.[21]

On state and local levels, for example, white and black abolitionists sometimes created significant alliances to challenge racial segregation and political
disenfranchisement. Boston in particular witnessed successful biracial efforts
by Garrisonians to desegregate public education, while in New York State,
white and black Liberty Party members campaigned (unsuccessfully) to repeal
unequal suffrage restrictions against black men. During these struggles,
African-American activists developed their own independent crusades against
slavery and discrimination, partly in reaction to expressions of racially tinged
superiority directed toward them by their white abolitionist co-workers.
Impressive new leaders—some escapees from slavery, others free Northerners
such as Frederick Douglass, Henry Highland Garnet, James McCune Smith,
and Sojourner Truth—came to the fore in the 1840s and 1850s to testify
eloquently against slavery and white supremacy. When so doing, they also
infused black abolitionism with rich new ideological visions. These visions
sharpened acutely after Congress passed a stringent new Fugitive Slave Law in
1850, which threatened not only escapees but even free northern blacks with a

This cartoon by John L. Magee of
Philadelphia blames proslavery politicians for
violence against antislavery settlers in Kansas
after Congress passed the Kansas-Nebraska
Act, which specifically allowed slavery in
those territories. (Library of Congress.)

Conclusion in Cuba

In Cuba as in Brazil, international treaties designed to strangle the importation of slaves collided headlong with the interests of planters and slave merchants who had no intention of limiting their imports of captive labor. Between 1820 and 1850 as many as 200,000 new African slaves disembarked onto Cuban soil to work the island's approximately 1,000 sugar plantations. All the while, political machinations in Havana and Madrid would prevent any real progress toward abolition of either the trade or of Cuban slavery itself well into the second half of the century.

Factors that may have helped moderate calls for abolition included Cuban law that made it relatively easy for a slave to purchase freedom, and a common practice among slaveholders of emancipating one or more slaves when the master died. Hence in the 1800s perhaps 10 to 12 percent of the island's blacks were free individuals known as *emancipados*. Many tens of thousands remained in bondage, however, more and more of them employed in steam-powered sugar mills with a mechanized pace that made the work even more debilitating than in earlier times. When Cuban slavery was finally abolished in 1886, the change was wrought in part by the increased threat of rebellion among such brutalized workers and in part by an inescapable combination of international pressure and economic realities. —*B.C.M.*

The port city of Cardenas, Cuba. Like Havana, Cardenas was a major port for exporting Cuban sugar and rum, and it would not have been unusual for one or more of the ships in the harbor to have brought African slaves to sell or exchange for those commodities. In the 1850s when this lithograph was probably created, the buying and selling of African captives was still a thriving enterprise in Cuba. Around this time, Cuban planters also began using steam trains to transport cargoes between port facilities and the countryside, and a train can be seen here, heading inland. (Leonardo Baranano, artist; lithography by Eduardo LaPlante.)

return to bondage. In response, black and white abolitionists united in acts of defiance that sometimes turned to violence, as in Christiana, Pennsylvania, where in 1851 a slaveholder was shot and killed by resisters when attempting to recapture a fugitive. Syracuse, Boston, Oberlin, and Detroit also witnessed such confrontations in the 1850s, with the risk of bloodshed always high.[22]

By embracing confrontation, abolitionists of both races did exercise one surprisingly effective type of political influence in the decade before the Civil War, specifically among the South's slaveholders. Because of resistance to the Fugitive Slave Law, as southern planters judged it, the North in the 1850s seemed to be overrun with law-breaking abolitionists whom authorities could not or would not put down. When protracted guerila warfare between southern and northern settlers broke out in Kansas in the mid-1850s over the possible introduction of slavery there, these suspicions turned into amply substantiated fears. Leading immediatists such as Wendell Phillips, Thomas Wentworth Higginson, and Frederick Douglass gladly became implicated in the frontier bloodshed—especially when sending money and moral support to John Brown and his sons, the abolitionists most responsible for spilling it. After Brown slaughtered several proslavery settlers during the Kansas "wars" of 1855–56, Phillips, Higginson, and Douglass openly endorsed these violent deeds. But such immediatists were hardly alone, because prominent members of the North's emerging Republican Party also proved eager to "save" Kansas from slavery by sending arms to Kansas "free-staters" and endorsing Brown's deeds. Although Republicans denied any intention to dismantle slavery in the South and often affirmed white supremacy, their party platforms consistently registered hostility to slavery's expansion in 1856 elections, and a victorious national plurality for Abraham Lincoln in 1860.[23]

By the time of Lincoln's election, Brown had been hanged for his incendiary attempt to provoke slave insurrection by seizing and distributing weapons from the federal arsenal at Harper's Ferry, Virginia. Slaveholders were now well satisfied that Lincoln and his party were fundamentally no different than Brown, Douglass, and Garrison—"black Republican abolitionists" all. Although three decades of immediatist crusading had produced few measurable results, the abolitionists had exercised an undeniable influence on the decision by frightened slaveholders to leave the federal Union and commence with civil war.[24]

TRIUMPH, TRAGEDY, AND LEGACY

Although a few pacifist abolitionists opposed the onset of war, the vast majority of the original immediatists enthusiastically supported hostilities against the South. Until late 1862, President Lincoln, like most Republicans, understood the war as an effort to restore the Union, not to abolish slavery, a view that abolitionists hotly contested. Their thirty-year crusade against slavery now gave them the status of vindicated prophets in the eyes of many Northerners, a fact they exploited to mold public opinion in favor of emancipation. Douglass, Phillips, and Garrison suddenly became the North's most sought-after public speakers. In their orations they castigated Lincoln's failure to emancipate the slaves and urged the mobilization of African-American fighting units. In private, they cultivated political alliances with abolition-minded Republican congressmen. But when ever-larger numbers of slaves took advantage of the

On June 7, 1850 the U.S. Navy brig *Perry* intercepted the New York–based slave ship
Martha as it neared the West African coast. Already provisioned and with slave decks laid,
the *Martha* was slated to load 1,800 Africans the next day. As the *Perry* approached the
Martha the slaver's captain, using a common ploy, ordered its American flag struck and that
of Brazil hoisted instead; but *Perry* commander Andrew Hull Foote was undeterred. The
confiscated ship and its crew (in irons) were returned to New York. Papers recovered from
the vessel revealed that the majority interest in the venture was held by an American living
in Rio de Janeiro, where the international trade in human cargoes was still a highly
profitable, if risky, undertaking.

chaos of war by abandoning their masters and following the Union armies, they advanced the abolitionists' cause as no congressional representative could.[25]

To force these refugees to return to their masters, traitorous slaveholders who had taken up arms against the Union, was, to Republican Party members, politically unthinkable. The logic of emancipation thus became impossible to deny. But as soon as President Lincoln's Emancipation Proclamation came into force on January 1, 1863, Phillips, Douglass, and the rest next began demanding constitutional amendments that would outlaw slave holding permanently and secure full citizenship to those who were emancipated. Abolitionists also took advantage of massive Union Army conquests in coastal South Carolina by sending into that region ministers, schoolteachers, and businessmen whose task it became to prepare emancipated former slaves for political and social equality. Thanks to the combined efforts of northern abolitionists, black soldiers, and self-liberated slaves, when the war ended in 1865 it had initiated a social revolution in the South. No matter how badly disadvantaged by illiteracy, poverty, and the lack of political rights, every former slave was incontestably free.[26]

It was a revolution that many defeated southern whites immediately attempted to suppress, violently if necessary. Following Lincoln's assassination, former Confederate states recognized the permanence of emancipation by ratifying the Thirteenth Amendment—but then they put so many harsh restrictions on the rights of those who had been liberated that even dispassionate observers could wonder if they were reinstating slavery in another form. Such intransigence, however, played directly into the hands of abolitionists such as Phillips and Douglass and radical Republicans such as Thaddeus Stevens, Charles Sumner, and Benjamin Wade, who truly wished to reconstruct the nation as a biracial democracy by securing the vote for black males and by granting freed slaves farmlands confiscated from leading Confederates. Since many Northerners feared that their hard-won victory would be lost if former Confederates were allowed to return themselves to power, the idea of enfranchising former slaves as voters and protecting them as free laborers seemed not only just, but politically imperative. Thus, most Republicans finally threw their support behind the idea of black enfranchisement.

Though Garrison and some of his supporters argued that the abolitionist mission had been fulfilled with the passage of the Thirteenth Amendment, Phillips, Douglass, Elizabeth Cady Stanton, and many other veterans adamantly disagreed, insisting that the real struggle was only beginning. Until 1870, when Congress and two-thirds of the states had ratified the Fourteenth and Fifteenth Amendments guaranteeing equal legal protection to all citizens and enfranchising all adult black men, these aging radicals never stopped agitating for complete, federally enforced black equality, disagreeing among themselves only on the question of whether to extend voting rights to women of both races. In the process, they led the unsuccessful battle in 1867 to impeach and try Lincoln's successor, President Andrew Johnson, because of his adamant opposition to radical Reconstruction. But when the Fifteenth Amendment did become a reality in 1870, abolitionists concluded that they had at last redeemed the commitments made decades earlier, to sweep away the tyranny of slave holding and to construct instead a society secured by just, uniform principles of racial equality.

In retrospect, the abolitionists' legacy seems far less hopeful. By the 1890s, white counterinsurgents had overturned Reconstruction governments throughout the South. Disenfranchisement, terrorism, sharecropping, and segregation, inflicted in the name of white supremacy, characterized the new order. In most of the North, the dictates of white bigotry also defined the prevailing social order. So it can hardly be claimed that the abolitionists, for all their idealistic persistence, actually inspired the nation to confront its deeper racial tragedy. Yet the abolitionists did discover terrible truths about racial injustice and lay them bare before their fellow citizens. Among themselves they nurtured rich and unprecedented discussions about the meanings of race, gender, and equality. In short, they engaged the world and one another honestly, fearlessly exploring their movement's deeper tensions while indicting the larger society for its deeper injustices. Theirs is, in short, a legacy to which our ongoing struggles for racial justice continue to refer, and which, even today, offers guidance, inspiration, and warnings.

Even as late as the onset of the Civil War, more than half a century after the transatlantic trade was outlawed, slavers were still transporting kidnapped Africans to Brazil and to Caribbean destinations. When the bark *Wildfire* neared Key West on April 30, 1860, her slave deck was packed with more than 400 African captives. ("The slave deck of the bark *Wildfire*," *Harper's Weekly*, June 1860.)

Black Sailors Making Selves

W. Jeffrey Bolster

In our collective consciousness, an image of manacled Africans crammed together aboard slave ships has triumphed as the association of African Americans with the sea. It reinforces whites' belief that blacks were acted on, rather than acting; that blacks aboard ship sailed as commodities rather than as seamen. Yet until the Civil War, black sailors were central to African Americans' collective self, economic survival, and freedom struggle—indeed central to the very creation of black America.

Opposite:
"Ned." A black sailor.
(*Harper's New Monthly Magazine.*)

Many Africans were skilled boatmen, fishermen, and boatbuilders. This picture shows two groups of Africans in war canoes. (In *Boy Travellers on the Congo*, New York, 1888. Harvard College Library.)

On Christmas in 1747 Briton Hammon, a slave to Major John Winslow
of Marshfield, Massachusetts, set out, as he put it, with "an Intention to
go a voyage to sea," and shipped himself "on board of a Sloop, Capt. John
Howland, Master, bound to Jamaica." When the sloop was "cast away on
Cape Florida," only the prodigal Hammon survived, propelled by shipwreck
on a thirteen-year odyssey during which he experienced captivity among
Florida Indians, imprisonment and enslavement in Cuba, Royal Navy service
under fire against the French, hospitalization in Greenwich, England, and
dock work in London. He also came close to making a voyage to Africa as a
cook aboard a slaver. Hammon's *Narrative of the Uncommon Sufferings, and
Surprising Deliverance of Briton Hammon, a Negro Man* became the first voyage
account published by a black American. Like Hammon, enslaved sailors and
nominally free men of African descent rode economic and military currents
to every corner of the eighteenth-century Atlantic world, appreciatively
comparing the regions they bridged. Hammon's work reveals not only the
extent of his travels, but also his multidimensional sense of self. Among a
crew of black and white sailors, he was one of "the people," chiding the
captain. In Spanish Cuba he was both a black Englishman and a slave; in
Indian camps a civilized man; in New England a Negro man; and aboard
the slaver on which he planned to sail, a free seaman on wages or a Briton—
not a captive African. Hammon clearly understood his identity in fluid terms
that were not defined by color alone.[1]

Another black sailor, John Jea, took to the seas after his manumission
from slavery in New York during the 1790s. Born in 1773 at Old Calabar, the
notorious slaving port on the Niger Delta, Jea survived the Middle Passage as
a child. More politicized than Hammon, by about 1800 Jea was on the road
and at sea as an itinerant minister and sailor, a quick-witted and powerful
orator who embodied, according to his biographer, "Methodist evangelism,
revolutionary egalitarianism, and a nascent black nationalism." Jea presented
himself during the era of the Haitian Revolution as "a poor African" or an
"African Preacher." He explicitly cultivated a sense of collective blackness
among black audiences.[2]

Maritime skills and spiritual associations of a different sort shaped the
meanings of self for an elderly African boatman in South Carolina named
Cudjoe. Called "Very artful" by his master at Charleston, Cudjoe had "been
used to the Coasting Business Southwardly" in schooners, canoes, and petti-
augers. Like African vessels he may have known in his youth, canoes and pet-
tiaugers were hollowed from the trunks of prodigious trees; like all African
vessels they carried associations of contact with the spirit world. When five
slaves fled with Cudjoe in 1771, his master had little doubt that the elderly
sailor had "enticed the others away." The master intuited correctly that the
runaways trusted the old patroon's skill. But blind to Africans' spiritual
associations with water and boats, he never entirely fathomed the nature
of that trust.[3]

These sailors' stories suggest some of the processes and components
with which eighteenth-century blacks constructed both a sense of self and a
complex, though not homogenous, African-American identity. Too many
histories assume, as Henry Louis Gates Jr. points out, "that there exists an
unassailable, integral, black self, as compelling and whole in Africa as in the
New World, within slavery as without slavery." In fact, however, whites played
little role in Africa except at coastal castles and slave barracoons. Without
reference to a white "other," the concept of "blackness" was meaningless as a

"Ship's cook prepares a meal."
(In *All Hands: Pictures of Life in the
United States Navy.*)

Opposite:

Frontispiece engraving, *John Jea, African
Preacher of the Gospel,* c. 1800. From
*The Life, history, and unparalleled
sufferings of John Jea, the African Preacher.*
(The Bodleian Library, University of Oxford.)

JOHN JEA.

African Preacher of the
Gospel

Many enslaved African men were able to transfer their skill with watercraft to their New World lives. A notice in the Virginia Gazette in 1772 describes a runaway slave this way: "He calls himself Bonna, and says he came from a place of that name in the Ibo country, in Africa, where he served in the capacity of a Canoe Man." ("Fishing cannoes of Mina, 5 or 600 at a time," engraving by J. Kip. Awnsham and John Churchill, *Collections of Voyages and Travels,* vol. 5, London, 1732.)

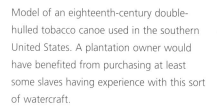

Model of an eighteenth-century double-hulled tobacco canoe used in the southern United States. A plantation owner would have benefited from purchasing at least some slaves having experience with this sort of watercraft.

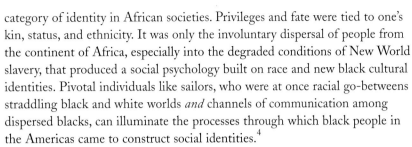

category of identity in African societies. Privileges and fate were tied to one's kin, status, and ethnicity. It was only the involuntary dispersal of people from the continent of Africa, especially into the degraded conditions of New World slavery, that produced a social psychology built on race and new black cultural identities. Pivotal individuals like sailors, who were at once racial go-betweens straddling black and white worlds *and* channels of communication among dispersed blacks, can illuminate the processes through which black people in the Americas came to construct social identities.[4]

Enslaved and free black seamen like Hammon, Jea, and Cudjoe established a prominent presence in every seaport and roadstead lapped by eighteenth-century Atlantic tides. However, the nature of black seafaring changed with time. In 1740 virtually all seafaring blacks were slaves, and the majority of black maritime workers were coastal boatmen in plantation societies. By 1803–04 black men, mostly free, filled about 17 percent of American seamens' jobs. As their numbers grew, black mariners moved from billets as slaves, servants, and musicians to become skilled able seamen, and to define as virtually their own the job of ship's cook. Seamen of color thus fashioned their identities in what was simultaneously a cramped interracial workplace and an expansive international arena.[5]

AFRICAN MARITIME TRADITIONS

African sailors' lives were shaped by various factors, among them seafaring traditions, slave codes, and a multiracial, mobile labor force. Other major influences were their African understandings of and associations with maritime work. That African mental world, constantly evolving as it was, provided sailors like Cudjoe an anchor for the self.

Africans, as historian Igor Kopytoff points out, did not merely believe that ancestors' spirits affected their lives: they *knew* it. For many Africans, watery surfaces appeared as a conduit for communication with ancestors' spirits, and vessels were understood to mediate between this world and the next. For African boatmen enslaved in America, water and vessels were simultaneously historical memories, work environments, and sources of spiritual power.[6]

Long before fifteenth-century Portuguese mariners arrived in western Africa, sub-Saharan peoples had developed extensive commercial networks dependent on canoe mariners. "Not only did the Niger-Senegal-Gambia [river] complex unite a considerable portion of West Africa," writes historian John Thornton, "but the Niger provided a corridor that ultimately added the Hausa kingdoms, the Yoruba states, and the Nupe, Igala, and Benin kingdoms to a hydrographic system that was ultimately connected to the Atlantic." American boat slaves thus looked back to African maritime traditions.[7]

Canoes and other small boats became the heart of the plantation transportation system from the Chesapeake Bay to the Caribbean. For example, the proprietor of Delegal Plantation on Skidaway Island kept a six-oared canoe "painted white outside and red inside, with a black bottom, about 27 feet in length." Vessels like these, similar to African small craft, were vital to slaves' visiting as well as to their work in the Carolina lowcountry, and to a lesser degree in the Chesapeake. Slaves like Billy, "a very black short well made Fellow" who was "very handy at building boats" in Maryland during the

Olaudah Equiano: Slave, Seaman, Writer

According to his remarkable 1789 autobiography, *The Interesting Narrative of the Life of Olaudah Equiano or Gustavus Vassa the African,* Olaudah Equiano's journey into the pages of history began when he was kidnapped as a young boy, probably around 1753, from his Igbo village of Essaka in the region of Benin. Passed from owner to owner in Africa, he eventually was sold to a slaver bound for Barbados. "Reconditioned" there briefly after the harrowing Middle Passage, he was purchased for a plantation in Virginia, where working conditions tended to be more humane than in the sugar colonies. It was the first of several fortunate turns of fate. Renamed Gustavus Vassa by his English master Mr. Campbell, within a year the young Igbo had been resold yet again, this time into the hands of British naval officer Michael Henry Pascal. Traveling to England with Pascal, Equiano now found himself in a situation that would allow him to become educated in the seafaring life and gain other valuable skills. In his autobiography he recalled that in addition to learning the basics of seamanship under Pascal, "I had long wished to read and write and for this purpose I took every opportunity to gain instruction." Both endeavors would serve him well.

For the next few years Equiano served Pascal and, though still a slave, attained the rating of able seaman. In addition to voyaging to Italy, Greece, and points east, he was present at major naval battles during the Seven Years' (French and Indian) War. With the war's conclusion, in 1762 he was sold to a slave trader bound for the West Indies. Apparently quick-witted and resourceful, Equiano carried out his new master's business (which included selling slaves) while managing to buy and sell some trade goods for his own account. While he himself was generally well treated, Equiano could not help but observe the often execrable treatment meted out to slaves in the region. "It was very common in several of the islands … for slaves to be branded with the initial letters of their master's name, and a load of heavy iron hooks hung about their necks. Indeed on the most trifling occasions they were loaded with chains, and often instruments of torture were added," he wrote. "I have seen a negro beaten till some of his bones were broken for even letting a pot boil over."

Frontispiece from *The Interesting Narrative of the Life of Olaudah Equiano … 1745–1774.* (Virginia Historical Society, Richmond, Virginia.)

Free blacks were also subject to abuse and kidnapping, but the risks of freedom were preferable to chattel slavery. With £40 earned from his private business ventures, in 1766 Equiano purchased his freedom, then returned to London after surviving a shipwreck in the Bahamas. He also learned a new trade—that of hairdresser—but soon decided that going to sea was a more lucrative, if more dangerous, profession.

In this next phase of his life Olaudah Equiano would add to his already considerable seafaring resume. In 1773 he signed on with the British expedition of Captain Constantine Phipps to search for a northeast passage through the Arctic Ocean, recalling years later that "I was roused by the sound of fame to seek new adventure, and to find towards the North Pole, what our Creator never intended we should, a passage to India." In the Arctic, Equiano reported, "We saw many very high and curious mountains of ice; and also a great number of very large whales, which used to come close to our ship and blow the water up to a very great height in the air."

After a final trading voyage to Jamaica, in 1777 Equiano returned to London and stayed. Antislavery efforts were strengthening there and he now chose to devote his considerable energies to that cause, becoming a major voice for abolishing both the transatlantic trade and chattel slavery wherever it existed. He was soon to write: "Surely this traffic cannot be good, which spreads like a pestilence, and taints what it touches! Which violates that first natural right of mankind, equality and independency, and gives one man dominion over his fellow which God could never intend!" The publication of his autobiography was a watershed event, the account rivaling in popularity another bestseller of the day, Daniel Defoe's *Robinson Crusoe*. Nine different editions would see print before Equiano's death in 1797. —*B.C.M.*

1760s, undoubtedly felt a sense of proprietorship and possibly a spiritual connection to these vessels.[8]

Eighteenth-century Africans felt the power of water in profound and immediate ways as they envisioned themselves. Intercourse with spirits, both benign and evil, affected all Africans' daily lives.[9] For the Bambara in Senegambia, many of whom were transported to colonial America, an androgynous water spirit called Faro maintained an individual's soul or vital life force after death. Refreshed and purified underwater, the soul would reappear in the next-born member of the family. Igbo peoples from near the Bight of Benin had similar associations with the transmigration of souls in water: a slave in Georgia testified that suicidal Igbos there would "mahch right down in duh ribbuh tuh mach back tuh Africa." For historic Congo peoples a watery barrier called the Kalunga line divided the living from the spirit world. In Congolese minds, Kalunga conveyed powerful associations with the elderly and with those departed who had been exceptionally wise and strong. As anthropologist Wyatt MacGaffey has written concerning twentieth-century Congolese: "The Atlantic Ocean is only one of a number of waters that may serve to represent the ideal barrier, which is called Kalunga. Boats of various kinds are vehicles for transporting souls or for returning to this shore such exceptional individuals as prophets, who are able to come and go."[10]

Beliefs of this sort endured among eighteenth-century Africans transplanted to South Carolina. The quantity of sacred pottery ritually thrown by slaves into South Carolina's rivers, and recently retrieved by archeologists,

An African seaman is barely visible in the upper left-hand corner of this painting of the death of Admiral Horatio Nelson at Trafalgar in 1805. At the time it would not have been unusual for a black to be serving in the British navy. (C. W. Sharpe, engraver; painting by D. Maclise R. A., 1873. Gift of Lily Lambert McCarthy.)

indicates that Kalunga and other spiritual associations with water long remained a psychic compass for Africans set to work in a white-dominated world.[11] They were potent metaphors for life beyond this world that served to draw diverse eighteenth-century Africans and their descendents together as a unified black people in America. African slaves in maritime occupations likewise understood their seafaring experience in an intuitive and symbolic way. And while their allegorical appreciation of the sea did not mitigate the harsh conditions of their work, it did inspire an understanding of the workplace very different from that of white mariners. Nevertheless, blacks still shared certain aspects of white sailors' occupational identity.

TRANSCENDING RACE

In the eighteenth century, black self-consciousness was more complicated than the simple opposition of black and white. Depending upon specific circumstances, blacks defined themselves against other blacks and with other blacks, against whites and with whites. Black seamen built an occupational identity that went beyond race even as it allowed them to express racial self-awareness. Skill, style, mobility, sexual prowess, contact with whites, and reputations as indefatigable runaways shaped individual mariners' sense of self.

Many slaves were skilled in the arts of the sailor. According to their masters, 46 percent of slave mariners in South Carolina between 1732 and 1782 were "sailors" as opposed to boatmen or fishermen—men who either crossed oceans or sailed extensively coastwise. Able to "hand, reef, and steer," these sailors expressed themselves in no small degree through their workplace accomplishments. Experienced sailors like Dick, a slave described in 1788 as "a very good seaman and rigger," instinctively understood ship handling, having internalized the cause-and-effect relationships of wind speed, sail trim, and rudder angle. Their skill and worldliness inspired an occupational identity quite different from that of slaves working in the fields.[12]

Nothing distinguished that identity more than tattoos. Tattooed black sailors generally displayed the same designs as their white shipmates, including initials, anchors, mermaids, dolphins, and crucifixes. Most white seamen, and an even larger proportion of black sailors, were not tattooed. But in an era when tattoos were virtually never seen save on the weather-beaten skin of a seafaring man, they generally spoke to an identity beyond race. Not always, however. One Michael Jones, born in Louisiana in 1774, eschewed conventional designs: he had a figure representing "Justice" pricked into his skin—quite likely a racially specific statement.[13]

As with tattoos, so with clothes: black and white sailors shared a distinctive style that nevertheless allowed room for racial expression. A "bright Mulatto Man slave" named Sam sailed in 1771 aboard the sloop *Tryall* in Virginia. His "Cloathing is such as is worn by Seamen," reported a newspaper's runaway advertisement.[14] Jasper, a Virginian slave "accustomed to work on board vessels" sported "much the air of a sailor." These men presented themselves to the world with occupationally specific clothing, accessories, and style. Even so, contemporary oil portraits, etchings, and documents establish that some blacks set themselves apart from white sailors with bold earrings and other sartorial flourishes. Commander of an all-black crew aboard the whaling schooner *Industry* in 1822, Captain Absalom Boston wore a white shirt and tie indicating command, as well as prominent African-style gold hoops in each ear.[15]

A NEGRO FIGHT IN SOUTH AMERICA.—[SEE PAGE 674.]

Head-butting in a Venezuelan village. (*Harper's Weekly*, August 1874.)

Captain Absalom Boston shown
in an anonymous oil portrait.
(Nantucket Historical
Association, Nantucket,
Massachusetts.)

Along with a shared style, black and white sailors found common ground in the boxing ring and as fencing and wrestling opponents, although it is by no means clear that all of the underlying rules and meanings black sailors attributed to manly sports were identical with those of whites, even in this most common of arenas. For instance, black sailors competed in rough play and fought for real by butting heads. White sailors generally did not.[16]

The African origins of head-butting are clear, and butting survived the Middle Passage to take root in African-American societies from New England to Brazil. And whether fighting pugnaciously or demonstrating martial skill, black seamen propagated the art as they traveled from one region to another.[17] If much of sailors' behavior and style shifted attention away from racial distinctions, butting represented traditions confined almost entirely to people of the African diaspora. It also transcended cultural and linguistic divisions that existed among blacks. For example, tarrying ashore at Guadeloupe in 1787, a group of black and white English-speaking sailors watched a Sunday gathering of slaves entertaining themselves. The males, according to one white sailor, regarded butting as a "favorite amusement … for which purpose their wooly hair is suffered to grow on the top of their heads, whilst that from behind is cut away, and frizzled in amongst that left on top, which forms a kind of cushion, or firm tuft of hair." Circled by onlookers, the "opposing combatants dance[d]" to "African music," before darting "forward, head against head." Intent on reputation, a free seaman of color from Philadelphia named Tom Grace challenged the local champion, a patois-speaking Guadeloupean slave. Grace swore he would "capsize one of these fellows in a crack." He did, his white shipmates watching from the sidelines. But when Grace won, the locals drove him away, and he retreated with the white sailors. Connecting with the Guadeloupean slaves on one level through a characteristically black form of combat, Grace nevertheless remained divided from them by language, region, status, and occupation. As a free seafaring man of color he maneuvered between the two groups, defining himself through transactions of different sorts with foreign blacks and white shipmates.[18]

Sex, like fighting, was central to different individuals' conception of self. Land-based and sea-based black men had opportunities to develop distinctive kinds of sexual identities. Sailors in pursuit of love let the mystique of the water work its magic. Enslaved sailors in Virginia enjoyed the company of women like "a negro wench named Betty … not unacquainted with coasting schooners." There was an "impertinent" black woman fleeing by water from Williamsburg, Virginia to Hampton or Norfolk in 1773: "She is fond of Liquor, and apt to sing indecent and Sailors Songs when so." Ned, a slave whose mistress in Norfolk allowed him to hire himself out during the early 1760s, capitalized on "going by water" to have "a wife at Mr. Parkers on the

Eastern Shore." She would have remained inaccessible to him but for his boat work. All mariners enjoyed mobility that introduced them to many women, permitting multiple sexual contacts. That may have encouraged rakishness; it also may have allowed certain male slaves better chances to practice African-derived polygyny than would ever be the case for land-bound slaves. When Cambridge "ran away from the schooner Sharpe" in 1768, his master believed he had "a wife at almost every landing on the Rappahanock, Mattapony, and Pamunkey rivers."[19]

Blacks might have understood having "a wife in every port" differently than white sailors did; they were certainly more likely to be estranged from their land-based social networks of origin because of sale or flight.

SEAFARERS' MOBILITY AND THE FORMATION OF BLACK IDENTITY

In addition to serving as racial intermediaries straddling black and white worlds, black sailors were traveling men who spent more time moving *between* dispersed black communities than residing in any single one. Situated on vessels connecting all corners of the Atlantic world, black seafarers were newsmongers central to the formation of black America and to the elaboration of a multidimensional black identity. They broadcast accounts from blacks' perspectives regarding the Haitian Revolution, the movements to abolish the slave trade and emancipate slaves, and the debate over colonization that centered on the question of whether people of color would remain in the United States. Outside the pale of these transformative debates and events, the mundane ebb and flow of black sailors' daily lives brought into focus differences among diasporic blacks. A slave named Jim fled down the James River in 1802 to City Point, or Norfolk, and then went "to Philadelphia and New York on board of a vessel," an activity, his master said, "I am inclined to think … he makes a practice of." Seamen like Jim compared the lives of black brothers and sisters in plantations and seaports, and, drawing on storytelling traditions prominent among sub-Saharan Africans and Atlantic seafarers, they talked.[20]

In their travels, black seamen found access to privileges, worldliness, and wealth denied to most slaves. Nothing conveys this more strikingly than the fact that sailors wrote the first six black autobiographies published in English before 1800. Not only did their pens connect oral black culture with what had been an exclusively white world of letters, but theirs was the opening salvo in what would become a barrage of antislavery literature by black authors dedicated to the liberation of all Africans enslaved in the New World.[21]

Early black seafaring autobiographers did not root their personal narratives in American or European locales. In fact, they were detached from place in a way that the authors of many later slave narratives were not, and in ways that few whites wished to be. Olaudah Equiano (in 1789) and James Albert Ukawsaw Gronniosaw (circa 1770) paid substantial attention to their African cultural and geographic origins, thus defining themselves in opposition to the societies in which they currently lived. But with little chance of repatriation to a now strange Africa, these black intellectuals saw themselves as members of an international black community.[22]

Whether professedly British or American or neither, seafarers like Equiano and John Jea recognized that blacks in the Atlantic world could redefine the term "African" in a characteristically creole way. Jea's consistent description of himself as an "African" illuminates the creation of "Africa" itself in the identities of late-eighteenth-century black people, and refers to much more than his birthplace on the continent. Jea could have been born an Igbo, an Efik, or an Ibibio, or into one of the other ethnic groups common in Old Calabar. His family probably had not long considered themselves to be Africans. Nondiscerning Europeans imposed "African" as a label on blacks who actually were native to a host of ethnicities and states. In the ports and plantations of the New World, Igbos, Mandingos, and a multitude of other people refashioned the term into a diasporic black identity. Even so, few eighteenth-century blacks born in Africa recast their identity immediately from their birth ethnicity to "African." Nearly always, they first passed through an intermediate stage of acculturation to Euro-American practices, and reassessment of the role of blackness in the New World. Equiano's autobiography makes this clear. He declines to label himself an "African" in early chapters, referring instead to Benin or Eboe (Igbo). After three years of slavery he had become substantially acculturated to English ways, in a few particulars "almost an Englishman," he wrote, largely because of so much time aboard ship in the company of Englishmen. As his political consciousness developed, however, he referred to himself as "the African," or "the oppressed Ethiopian."[23]

Captain Paul Cuffe. (Drawing by John Pole; engraving by Mason and Mass, c. 1812. Old Dartmouth Historical Society, New Bedford Whaling Museum, New Bedford, Massachusetts.)

The African identity cultivated by worldly diasporic blacks emphasized racial and political realities, and was not particularly in step with that of indigenous peoples of the continent. Nothing reveals this more clearly than the resounding refusal of most free African Americans to embrace their own deportation to Africa as part of the colonization movement. As sailmaker (and abolition activist) James Forten wrote from Philadelphia to Captain Paul Cuffe in 1817, "We had a large meeting of males at the Rev. R. Allen's church the other evening. Three thousand at least attended, and there was not one soul that was in favor of going to Africa."[24]

Grappling with their sense of self and with how that was connected to place, people of color split over the question of blacks' future in America. Captain Paul Cuffe, arguably the most influential black American before Frederick Douglass, ultimately advocated repatriation and colonization of African Americans in Sierra Leone. Only there, he believed after his extensive voyaging to Europe, Africa, and through the Americas, could blacks "rise to be a people." Raised in Massachusetts among his Native American mother's Wampanoag people, and much closer physically to them than to his father's Asante kin, Cuffe eventually favored his identity as an African. "My nature is Musta," he had written around 1773, meaning that he was of African and Native American descent. But by 1809, he stated unequivocally (despite his Wampanoag mother and Native American wife) "I am of the African race." Indians, mustees, and Africans were amalgamated in coastal New England, and boundaries between them difficult to establish. Compared to many plantation slaves in the South or in the West Indies, however, Cuffe was culturally "musta." *Politics*, he recognized, publicly defined him more than did culture. As a prominent man of color he refashioned himself into an African, subsuming his musta identity to a larger cause. Most free blacks in his generation, however, whether they called themselves "black," "African," or "people of color," rejected colonization, defining themselves not only against whites, but against inhabitants of Africa as well.[25]

Of course, eighteenth-century black society defined itself more through common folks' talking than through the extraordinary accomplishments of a handful of prominent leaders like Paul Cuffe. Black storytellers moved easily along the waterfront, where they sought shipping and added their voices to the yarns of men before the mast. Sailors thus became for black people in the Atlantic world what newspapers and the Royal Mail Service were for white elites: a mode of communication integrating local black communities into the larger community of color, even as they revealed regional and local differences.[26]

Many black seamen were both well-traveled and multilingual—talents useful for fostering links between otherwise separate black communities. A "Negro man named Luke" ran off from his master at Cainboy, South Carolina, in 1763. He "has been us'd to the seas, speaks English, French, Spanish, and Dutch, and probably may attempt to get off in some vessel."[27] Multilingual men like these, with extensive knowledge of the Americas, had better-than-average chances to escape from their masters and, perhaps more significant for black peoples' self-awareness, they could spin yarns that dramatized commonalities (and differences) among widely dispersed and linguistically separated people of color.[28]

This is not to suggest that boatloads of multilingual slaves broke down cultural barriers willy-nilly. Many slaves remained provincial. Fundamental to diasporic identity, however, was sailors' recognition that all New World blacks, whether in New England, North Carolina, Nevis, or New Spain (which included the northern half of South America and other territory), inhabited a historically defined common ground. The constant movement of eighteenth-century black mariners became an integral part of the process through which blacks created both a sense of connectedness and of differences within their new black ethnicity.

INSPIRATION AND OTHERNESS IN HAITI

The revolution that began on the scorched northern plain of St. Domingue in the summer of 1791, and that ultimately liberated Haiti from French rule, provided a focal point for black redefinition of self. Revolutionary St. Domingue and republican Haiti became a source of refuge and inspiration for blacks of many nationalities. Epitomizing the demise of slavery, Haiti became a potent symbol for free black spokesmen like Richard Allen, as well as for the group of foreign blacks most intimately familiar with it—free and slave seamen who actually went there. Those men pitted shipmasters and American officials against the Haitian government, finding protection in Haiti simply because they were black.[29] Moreover, transient black seamen from St. Martin, Martinique, London, Baltimore, Boston, and a host of other locales often became "citizens" of Haiti, but "citizens" who returned to the sea and kept moving as roving ambassadors of the pan-African sovereignty that they had found in Haitian ports. Significantly, these men retained their previous national identities while doing so. For many black sailors then, a voyage to Haiti affirmed the value of blackness and helped focus their self-awareness as Atlantic blacks, even as it reaffirmed national and linguistic differences among people of color.

Although desiring foreign men of color to settle there, Haitian officials did not hold them to it. The "Brig Saco, sold here," wrote the American commercial agent at Cape Haitian, "is now Haytien. Her crew (all black) reshipped here as Haytiens, and returned to New York in the same vessel."[24] Having refashioned themselves as "Haytiens," those English-speaking black Americans returned to the United States under the red and black Haitian flag, with stories of resplendent black troops, obliging officials, and a nation where all black people were citizens.

Tales of triumph told by seafaring ex-slaves who had achieved freedom in Haiti reinforced the diasporic consciousness of blacks around the Atlantic world, but they also affirmed a range of black identities. For when black Americans looked at brothers in Haiti, they saw only a partial reflection of their own origins, lives, and experiences.

Perhaps the final word on black sailors' complex selves should belong to Joseph Johnson, an elderly black merchant mariner who frequented London's Tower Hill during the early nineteenth century. Not entitled to a naval pension, and on account of his foreign birth having no claim to parish relief, the old seaman had no choice but to entertain for subsistence. A white Londoner suggested that "novelty … induced Black Joe to build a model of the ship Nelson; to which, when placed on his cap, he can, by a bow of thanks … give the appearance of sea-motion." The aged Johnson tramped the streets with his unique ship model, gracefully dancing his way to a beggar's livelihood. But possibly neither novelty nor necessity alone inspired Johnson's elaborate headgear. We might look instead to his memories of slaves' African-based celebrations. In a classic case of cultural crossover, Johnson appropriated a European artifact, one that had become meaningful to him through his own years of sea service, and reinvested it with African meanings to create a characteristically black cultural hybrid. In many West African cultures, headdresses represented ancestral figures and spiritual power.[30] Most white contemporaries looked at Joe Johnson through the distorting glass of race, and saw an old black sailor cleverly manipulating a full-rigged ship on his head. London blacks, on the other hand, saw an aged mummer bobbing through the streets, connecting them with his coded ship to West Indian and Carolinian slaves, and to people on the Gold Coast and Niger Delta. Forced to represent himself with fawning propriety to white almsgivers, Johnson undoubtedly took psychological refuge in their inability to comprehend him fully, even as he shook his creolized African past in their faces.

"Joseph Johnson with the ship Nelson on his head," by John Thomas Smith, 1815. (In *Vagabondiana, or Anecdotes of Mendicant Wanderers through the Streets of London*, London, 1817. Guildhall Library, London.)

Contributors

Dr. W. Jeffrey Bolster
Assistant Professor of History, University of New Hampshire

Dr. Madeleine H. Burnside
Executive Director, Mel Fisher Maritime Heritage Society

Dr. Linda M. Heywood
Professor of History, Howard University

Dr. Philip D. Morgan
Professor of History, The Johns Hopkins University

Dr. Colin A. Palmer
Distinguished Professor, Graduate Center, City University of New York

Dr. Edward Reynolds
Professor of History, University of California at San Diego

Dr. James B. Stewart
James Wallace Professor of History, Macalester College

Dr. John Thornton
Professor of History, Millersville University

Endnotes

CHAPTER ONE HUMAN COMMERCE

1. This essay places the slave trade and its economic impact in the context of what scholars have called the Atlantic System. Useful studies on the subject include Philip D. Curtin, *The Rise and Fall of the Plantation Complex* (Cambridge, Mass., 1998); Barbara L. Solow, ed., *Slavery and the Rise of the Atlantic System* (Cambridge, Mass., 1991); and John Thornton, *Africa and Africans in the Making of the Atlantic World, 1400-1800* (New York, 1998).

2. Many good works cover the history of the slave trade. See Seymour Drescher, *From Slavery to Freedom: Comparative Studies in the Rise and Fall of Atlantic Slavery* (New York, 1999); David Eltis, *Economic Growth and the Ending of the Transatlantic Slave Trade* (Oxford, 1987) and *The Rise of African Slavery in the Americas* (Cambridge, UK, 2000); J. E. Inikori, ed., *Forced Migration* (London, 1982); Herbert Klein, *African Slavery in Latin America and the Caribbean* (New York, 1986) and *The Atlantic Slave Trade* (New York, 1999); Patrick Manning, *Slavery and African Life: Occidental, Oriental and African Slave Trades* (New York, 1990); Joseph C. Miller, *The Way of Death: Merchant Capitalism and the Angolan Slave Trade, 1730-1830* (Madison, 1989); Vincent Bakpetu Thompson, *The Making of the African Diaspora* (London, 1985); Edward Reynolds, *Stand the Storm: A History of the Atlantic Slave Trade* (London, 1985); and Hugh Thomas, *The Slave Trade: The Story of the Atlantic Slave Trade, 1440-1870* (London, 1997).

3. Studies explaining the demand for the slave trade include that of Luiz Felipe de Alencastro, "The Apprenticeship of Colonization," in Solow, *Slavery and the Rise of the Atlantic System*, pp. 151-76; R. S. Dunn, *Sugar and Slaves* (Chapel Hill, 1972); H. Klein, *African Slavery*; J. Miller, *Way of Death*; Colin A. Palmer, *Human Cargoes: The British Slave Trade to Spanish America* (Urbana, 1981); A. J. R. Russell-Wood, *The Black Man in Slavery and Freedom in Colonial Brazil* (London, 1982); and Peter H. Wood, *Black Majority: Negroes in Colonial South Carolina* (New York, 1974).

4. Various aspects of the Portuguese slave trade are covered in J. Miller, *Way of Death*; Phyllis Martin, *The External Trade of the Loango Coast* (Oxford, 1972); and C. R. Boxer, *The Golden Age of Brazil, 1695-1750* (Berkeley, 1969).

5. The Dutch slave trade is effectively discussed by Johannes Postma in *The Dutch in the Atlantic Slave Trade, 1600-1814* (Cambridge, Mass., 1990); P. C. Emmer, *The Dutch in the Atlantic Economy, 1580-1880: Trade, Slavery and Emancipation* (Brookfield,Ill. 1998); and Willie F. Page, *The Dutch Triangle* (New York, 1997).

6. For a discussion of the British slave trade see Roger Anstey, *The Atlantic Slave Trade and British Abolition, 1760-1810* (London, 1975); Richard Bean, *The British Trans-Atlantic Slave Trade 1650-1775* (New York, 1975); K. G. Davies, *The Royal African Company* (London, 1957); Ralph Davis, *The Rise of the Atlantic Economies* (Ithaca, 1973); Dunn, *Sugar and Slaves*; Robin Law, ed., *The English in West Africa, 1681-1683* (Oxford, 1997); and David Richardson, "The Slave Trade, Sugar and British Economic Growth, 1748-1776," in *Journal of Interdisciplinary History*, vol. 17, no. 4 (1987), pp. 739-69.

7. For the French slave trade, see Stanley J. Stein, *The French Slave Trade in the Eighteenth Century* (Madison, 1979).

8. For information on the Danish trade, see Sven E. Green-Pederson, "The Scope and Structure of the Danish Slave Trade," in *Scandinavian Economic History Review*, vol. 19, no. 2 (1971), pp. 149-97.

9. A good general history of slavery in America is found in Peter Kolchin, *American Slavery*, (New York, 1993). For South Carolina, see Daniel C. Littlefield, *Rice and Slaves: Ethnicity and the Slave Trade in Colonial South Carolina* (Baton Rouge, 1981); and P. Wood, *Black Majority*.

10. For the conduct of the trade, see Manning, *Slavery and African Life*; J. Miller, *Way of Death*; David Northrup, *Trade Without Rulers: Pre-Colonial Economic Development in South-Eastern Nigeria* (Oxford, 1978); James A. Rawley, *The Transatlantic Slave Trade: A History* (New York, 1981); and V. Thompson, *African Diaspora*.

11. See Marion Johnson, "The Ounce in Eighteenth Century West African Trade," in *Journal of African History*, no. 7 (1966), pp. 197-214.

12. Philip D. Curtin, *The Atlantic Slave Trade: A Census* (Madison, 1969); Eltis, *Economic Growth*; Herbert Klein, *The Middle Passage: Comparative Studies in the Atlantic Slave Trade* (Princeton, 1978); Manning, *Slavery and African Life*; and J. Miller, *Way of Death*.

13. Walter Rodney, *How Europe Underdeveloped Africa* (London, 1972), p. 115.

CHAPTER 2 THE SOURCE

1. John Thornton, *Warfare in Atlantic Africa, 1500-1800* (London, 1999), pp. 23-4, 29.

2. David Birmingham, *Trade and Conquest in Angola: The Mbundu and their Neighbours and the Portuguese* (Oxford, 1966), is a good outline; for this interpretation see John Thornton, "Angola," in Joel Serrão and A. H. Oliveira Marques, gen. eds., *Nova História da Expansão Portuguesa*, vol. 10 (11 vols., in progress, Lisbon, 1992-); and Maríla dos Santos Lopes, ed., *O Império Africano* (forthcoming).

3. Thornton, *Warfare*, pp. 56, 84-8.

4. These documents are found in the Public Records Office, Kew, London, T/70 (Records of the Royal African Company); and in *Nederlands Bezittungen ter Kust Guinea*, vols. 84-150, in the Algemeen Rijksarchief (Dutch National Archives).

5. From a communication from Afonso I of Congo to Manuel I of Portugal, October 5, 1514, cited in António Brásio, ed., *Monumenta Missionaria Africana*, vol. 1, series 1 (Lisbon, 1952-88), pp. 294-323.

6. Communication from the King of Dagombe (Adandozan) to the King of Portugal, October 9, 1810, Instituto Histórico e Geográfico Brasileiro, Rio de Janeiro, lata 137 pasta 62, doc. 1.

7. Manning, *Slavery and African Life*, pp. 38-85; and John Thornton, "The Demographic Effect of the Slave Trade on Western Africa, 1500-1850," in Christopher Fyfe and David McMaster, eds., *African Historical Demography*, vol. 2 (Edinburgh, 1981), pp. 691-720. For the special situation in Angola, see Thornton, "The Slave Trade in Eighteenth Century Angola: Effects on Demographic Structures," in *Canadian Journal of African Studies* 14 (1981), pp. 417-27.

8. For this analysis and some proposed examples of how it worked in West Africa, see John Thornton, "Sexual Demography: The Impact of the Slave Trade on Family Structure," in Claire Robertson and Martin Klein, eds., *Women and Slavery in Africa* (Madison, 1983), pp. 39-48.

9. Walter Rodney, "African Slavery and Other Forms of Social Oppression on the Upper Guinea Coast in the Context of the Atlantic Slave Trade," in *Journal of African History* 7 (1966), pp. 431-43.

10. For an assessment of Njinga as a patriot, see John Thornton, "Legitimacy and Political Power: Queen Njinga, 1624-63," in *Journal of African History* 32 (1991), pp. 25-40. A communication from Queen Njinga to Bento Banha Cardoso, March 3, 1625 [ed. 1626], is quoted in correspondence from Fernão de Sousa to Gonçalo de Sousa and his brothers, c. 1630, in Beatrix Heintze, ed., *Fontes para a História de Angola do séulo XVII* (Wiesbaden, 1985-88) vol. 1, pp. 244-5.

11. Werner Peukert, *Der Atlantische Skalvenhandel von Dahomey: Wirtschaftsanthropologie und Sozialgeschichte* (Wiesbaden, 1977), pp. 70-6, 300-4.

12. Thornton, *Warfare*, pp. 76-9.

13. Thornton, *Africa and Africans*, pp. 72-97

14. Traced in Graziano Saccardo, *Congo e Angola con la storia dell'antica missione dei Cappuccini*, vol. 1 (Venice, 1982-83), pp. 332-3.

15. Thornton, *Warfare*, pp. 127-39.

16. This discussion is documented more fully in Thornton, *Warfare*, pp. 19-125.

17. Despite this defeat and the civil war that followed, Congo proved itself still strong enough that attempts by the Portuguese to exploit the situation failed. In 1670, Congo forces crushed an Angolan attempt to install a rival ruler in the country. In the process, the Portuguese suffered losses so great that they refrained from interfering in Congo politics until well into the nineteenth century.

18. For details on effects of the war with Congo, see John Thornton, *The Kongolese Saint Anthony: Doña Beatriz Kimpa Vita and the Antonian Movement, 1684-1706* (Cambridge, Mass., 1998), pp. 94-101.

19. The full account is in material held at the Academia das Cienças de Lisboa, MS Vermelho 296, *Viagem do Congo do Missionario Fr. Raphael de Castello de Vide, hoje Bispo de S. Thomé* (1800, incorporating letters of 1781-88), pp. 294-301.

20. Thornton, *Kongolese St. Anthony*.

21. Boubacar Barry, *Senegambia and the Atlantic Slave Trade* (Cambridge, Mass., 1998), pp. 50-4, 102-6. The original letter is lost, but a 1789 translation (Roi Almany to Mr. Blanchot Mar) is in the French National Archives.

CHAPTER 3 THE MIDDLE PASSAGE

1. Maria Diedrich, Henry Louis Gates, Jr., and Carl Pedersen, eds., *Black Imagination and the Middle Passage* (New York, 1999).

2. See, for example, Curtin, *The Atlantic Slave Trade: A Census;* and David Eltis, David Richardson, and Stephen D. Behrendt, "Patterns in the Transatlantic Slave Trade, 1662-1867," in Diedrich et al., *Black Imagination*, pp. 21-32.

3. The Public Record Office, London (hereafter PRO), Records of the Treasury T 70/5, pp. 18, 86.

4. Joseph C. Miller, "Mortality in the Atlantic Slave Trade: Statistical Evidence on Casualty," in *Journal of Interdisciplinary History*, vol. 2, no. 3 (winter 1981), pp. 385-424.

5. John Atkins, *A Voyage to Guinea, Brazil, and the West Indies* (London, 1735), p. 41.

6. Ibid.

7. Mungo Park, *Travels in the Interior Districts of Africa* (London, 1799), pp. 353-4.

8. William Snelgrave, *A New Account of Some Parts of Guinea and the Slave Trade,* (London, 1734), p. 163.

9. For a general discussion of these issues, see H. Klein, *Atlantic Slave Trade*, pp. 130-60.

10. PRO, T 70/957.

11. PRO, T 70/18, pp. 13, 65.

12. For a fine discussion of these issues and the relevant citations, see Genevieve Fabré, "The Slave Ship Dance," in Diedrich et al., *Black Imagination*, pp. 33-46.

13. Ibid., p. 37.

14. PRO, T 70/14, p. 66; T 70/26, p. 4; T 70/5, p. 6.

15. PRO T 70/52, p. 139. See also Herbert Klein and Stanley Engerman, "Slave Mortality on British Ships, 1791–1979," in Roger Anstey and P. E. H. Hair, eds., *Liverpool, The African Slave Trade and Abolition*, Historic Society of Lancashire and Cheshire, occasional series no. 2 (Bristol, 1976), p. 118.

16. See J. Miller, "Mortality in the Atlantic Slave Trade," pp. 385-424; and H. Klein, *Atlantic Slave Trade*, pp. 130-60.

17. Elizabeth Donnan, ed., *Documents Illustrative of the Slave Trade to America*, vol. 2 (Washington, D.C., 1930-1935), p. 181.

18. PRO, T 70/5.

19. For a discussion of these issues, see Palmer, *Human Cargoes,* pp. 42-56.

20. Ibid., pp. 52-4; and H. Klein, *Atlantic Slave Trade*, pp. 130-60.

21. PRO, T 70/52, pp. 55, 70.

22. Ibid.

23. Palmer, *Human Cargoes*, pp. 42-56; see also PRO, T 70/52, p. 139; T 70/13, p. 50; T 70/8, pp. 16, 33, 34, 55, 85.

24. Ibid.

25. PRO, T 70/957; T 70/19, p. 58. See also Jorge Palacios Preciado, *La trata de los negros por Cartagena de Indias, 1650-1750* (Tunja, 1973).

26. H. Klein, *Atlantic Slave Trade*, p.159.

27. Francis Moore, "Travels in Africa," in Donnan, *Documents*, vol. 2, p. 402.

28. H. Klein, *Atlantic Slave Trade*, p. 159.

29. Thomas Phillips, *A Journal of a Voyage Made in the Hannibal of London*, cited in H. Klein, *Atlantic Slave Trade*, p. 406.

30. PRO, T 70/4, p. 21; T 70/5, p. 45.

31. For a discussion of this uprising and its aftermath, see Snelgrave, *A New Account,* pp.168-85.

32. Ibid., pp.164-73.

33. Ibid., p.184.

34. Donnan, *Documents*, vol. 2; PRO, T 70/13, pp. 21, 31; T 70/890, p. 70; T 70/8, p. 30.

35. Donnan, *Documents,* vol. 2, p. 460.

CHAPTER 4 THE HENRIETTA MARIE

1. Dunn, *Sugar and Slaves,* p. 46.

2. Nigel Tattersfield, "An Account of the Slave Ship *Henrietta Marie* of London," (unpublished manuscript, 1994).

3. Tattersfield, *The Forgotten Trade: Comprising the Log of the* Daniel and Henry *of 1700 and Accounts of the Slave Trade from the Minor Ports of England, 1698-1725* (London, 1991), p. 48.

4. David D. Moore, *Historical and Archaeological Investigations of the Shipwreck* Henrietta Marie (Key West: Mel Fisher Maritime Heritage Society, 1997), III.9.

5. Ibid., III.8.

6. Seven tusks and partial tusks have been recovered from the wreck site. They vary in length from 10.5 cm to 92 cm.

7. Thomas Phillips, *Journal,* cited in George Francis Dow, *Slave Ships and Slaving* (Cambridge, Mass., 1968), p. 76.

8. Tattersfield, "An Account of the Slave Ship *Henrietta Marie.*"

9. Treasury Papers held at PRO Kew, T 70/349, Customs records, July 15–September 1, 1699.

10. Corey Malcolm, "The Price of a Man," *Navigator,* 13.4 (1998).

11. P. E. H. Hair, Adam Jones and Robin Law, *Barbot on Guinea: The Writing of Jean Barbot on West Africa, 1678-1712* (London, 1992), p. 689.

12. Parts of forty-one basins were found at the *Henrietta Marie* site; they were packed in stacks, usually with straw between. They came in two sizes, either 33.3 cm x 8 cm or 38 cm x 9 cm.

13. Hair et al., *Barbot on Guinea.*

14. Malcolm, "The Price of a Man."

15. Tattersfield, "An Account of the Slave Ship *Henrietta Marie.*"

CHAPTER 5 SURVIVAL AND RESISTANCE

1. Phillips, *Journal,* cited in Churchill's *Collection of Voyages and Travels,* vol. 4 (London, 1732), pp. 218-19.

2. C. B. Wadstrom, *An Essay on Colonization,* part 2 (London, 1794), in the David and Charles reprint of 1968, p. 85.

3. William Bosman, *A New and Accurate Description of the Coast of Guinea* (London, 1705), pp. 363-5.

4. Atkins, *Voyage to Guinea.*

5. Selena Axelrod Winsnes, *Letters on West Africa and the Slave Trade: Paul Erdmann Isert's Journey to Guinea and the Caribbean Islands in Columbia (1788)* (London, 1992), p. 179.

6. Sylvia R. Frey and Betty Wood, *Come Shouting to Zion* (Chapel Hill, 1998), p. 37.

7. Michelangelo Guattini and Dionigi Carli, *Viaggio nel Regno del Congo* (São Paolo, 1997), pp. 242-43. Father Carli also recorded that women were placed on the second level of the ship, and from there could hear the voices of their children, who had been left to fend for themselves on the first deck. Several pregnant women were holed up in the poop, giving birth there to infants whom Father Carli baptized.

8. Eltis, *The Rise of African Slavery*, p. 185.

9. Alexander Falconbridge, *An Account of the Slave Trade on the Coast of Africa* (London, 1788), p. 17.

10. Thomas Leyland, "Thomas Leyland and Company to Captain Ceasar Lawson," July 18, 1803, in Donnan, *Documents*, vol. 2, pp. 650-2.

11. H. Thomas, *The Slave Trade*, p. 400.

12. Ibid., p. 421.

13. Robert Slenes, "Malungu, Ngoma vem!" in *África encoberta e descoberta no Brasil*, Museu Nacional da Escravatura (Luanda, 1995).

14. Michael Mullin, *Africa in America: Slave Acculturation and Resistance in the American South and the British Caribbean* (Urbana, 1992), p. 102.

15. See Joseph Holloway, ed., *Africanisms in American Culture* (Bloomington, 1990), p. 6.

16. Katia M. de Queirós Mattoso, *To Be a Slave in Brazil* (New Brunswick, 1979), p. 36.

17. For a discussion on nations see Thornton, *Africa and Africans,* pp. 184-205; see also Mullin, *Africa in America.*

18. The Brazilian case is presented in Livros do Baptismo, 1752-1795 and Iacarejague, Livro 12, various folios, all at Arquivo da Curia Metropolitana do Rio de Janeiro (ACMRJ); see also Mary Karasch, *Slave Life in Rio de Janeiro* (Princeton, 1987).

19. Philip Sherlock and Hazel Bennett, *The Story of the Jamaican People* (Princeton, 1998), p. 99.

20. See, for example, Douglas Hall, *In Miserable Slavery: Thomas Thistlewood in Jamaica, 1750-86* (London, 1992); and Mullin, *Africa in America*, pp. 13-66.

21. ACMRJ, Livros do Baptismo, 1752-1797, Livro 12, various folios; Arquivo Eclesiático da Arquidiocese de Mariana, Cúria Metropolitana, Livro O 26, Livro de Casamentos, Mariana, 1770-1808; see also Colin A. Palmer, "From Africa to the Americas: Ethnicity in the Early Black Communities of the Americas," in *Journal of World History* 6 (1995), pp. 223-36.

22. For more on Igbo runaways in North America, see P. Wood, *Black Majority*, p. 203; and Miguel Barnet, ed., *The Autobiography of a Runaway Slave* (New York, 1968), pp. 14-44.

23. John Thornton, "Central African Names and African-American Naming Patterns," in *William and Mary Quarterly* 50 (1993), pp. 729-40.

24. Mavis Campbell, *The Maroons of Jamaica, 1655-1796: A History of Resistance, Collaboration and Betrayal* (Trenton, 1990).

25. For an early study of Palmares, see R. K. Kent, "Palmares: An African State in Brazil," in *Journal of African History* (1965), pp. 161-75. For more recent studies of Quilombos generally, see João José Reis and Flávio dos Santos Gomes, eds., *Liberdade por un fio: Histório dos Qulombos no Brasil* (São Paulo, 1996); and Stuart B. Schwartz, *Slaves, Peasants, and Rebels: Reconsidering Brazilian Slavery* (Urbana, 1992).

26. See John Thornton, "African Roots of the Stono Rebellion," in *American Historical Review* 96 (1991), pp. 1101-13.

27. Reis and Santos Gomes, *Liberdade* and *Slave Rebellion in Brazil: The Muslim Uprising of 1835 in Bahia* (Baltimore, 1993); and Thornton, " 'I am the subject of the King of Congo': African Political Ideology and the Haitian Revolution," in *Journal of World History* 4, no. 2 (1993), pp. 181-214.

28. Frey and B. Wood, *Come Shouting to Zion*, p. 46.

29. For more on the Pinkster folk traditions, see Shane White, "Pinkster in Albany, 1803: A Contemporary Description," in *New York History* (April, 1989), pp. 191-9, and "Pinkster: Afro-Dutch Syncretization in New York City and the Hudson Valley," in *Journal of American Folklore* 102 (January-March, 1989), pp. 68-75.

30. For a general discussion of African culture in the Americas, see Thornton, *Africa and Africans*, pp. 184-234.

31. Mullin, *Africa in America*, pp. 82-3.

32. Patricia Stephens, *The Spiritual Baptist Faith: African New World Religious History, Identity and Testimony* (London, 1999), p. 210.

33. For a discussion of Creole-type revolts see Michael Craton, "The Passion to Exist: Slave Rebellions in the British West Indies, 1650-1832," in *Journal of Caribbean History* 13 (1980), pp. 1-20.

34. For a discussion of Creole-African relations, see Maureen Warner-Lewis, *Guinea's Other Suns: The African Dynamic in Trinidad Culture* (Dover, 1991), pp. 24-35.

35. David Colburn and Jane L. Landers, *The African American Heritage of Florida* (Gainesville, 1995), p. 62.

36. Mechal Sobel, *Trabelin' On: The Slave Journey to an Afro-Baptist Faith* (Princeton, 1988), p. 245.

37. Stephens, *The Spiritual Baptist Faith*, p. 145.

38. F. I. R. Blake, *The Trinidad and Tobago Steel Pan* (Port-of-Spain, 1995), p. 31.

39. See, for example, Jay B. Haviser, ed., *African Sites: Archaeology in the Caribbean* (Princeton, 1999).

40. Robert Farris Thompson, *Flash of the Spirit: African and Afro-American Art and Philosophy* (New York, 1983), pp. 132-58.

41. Rex Nettleford, *Caribbean Cultural Identity: The Case of Jamaica* (Los Angeles, 1979), p. 7; Gordon Rohlehr, *Calypso and Society in Pre-Independence Trinidad* (Port-of-Spain, 1991), p. 7; Dena J. Epstein, *Sinful Tunes and Spirituals: Black Folk Music to the Civil War* (Chicago, 1977); and Bernice Johnson Reagon, ed., *We'll Understand It Better By and By: Pioneering African American Gospel Composers* (Washington, 1992).

CHAPTER 6 LIFE IN THE AMERICAS

1. David Eltis, "The Volume and Structure of the Transatlantic Slave Trade: A Reassessment," in *William and Mary Quarterly* 58 (2001), pp. 17-46, and *Rise of African Slavery*; and P. Wood, *Black Majority*.

2. Sidney W. Mintz and Richard Price, *The Birth of African-American Culture: An Anthropological Perspective* (Boston, 1992); Ira Berlin, *Many Thousands Gone: The First Two Centuries of Slavery in North America* (Cambridge, Mass., 1998); and Philip D. Morgan, *Slave Counterpoint: Black Culture in the Eighteenth-Century Chesapeake and Lowcountry* (Chapel Hill, 1998).

3. Morgan, *Slave Counterpoint*, pp. 445-7.

4. Robert William Fogel, *Without Consent or Contract: The Rise and Fall of American Slavery* (New York, 1989); B. W. Higman, *Slave Populations of the British Caribbean, 1807-1834* (Baltimore, 1984); Allan Kulikoff, *Tobacco and Slaves: The Development of Southern Cultures in the Chesapeake, 1680-1800* (Chapel Hill, 1986).

5. Morgan, *Slave Counterpoint*, p. 102-45.

6. Ira Berlin and Philip D. Morgan, eds., *Cultivation and Culture: Labor and the Shaping of Slave Life in the Americas* (Charlottesville, 1993).

7. Fogel, *Without Consent or Contract*, pp. 18-28; and Stuart B. Schwartz, *Sugar Plantations in the Formation of Brazilian Society* (Cambridge, Mass., 1985).

8. Fogel, *Without Consent or Contract*, pp. 29-59; and Morgan, *Slave Counterpoint*, pp. 146-254.

9. Claudia Goldin, *Urban Slavery in the American South, 1820-1860* (Chicago, 1976); Richard Wade, *Slavery in the Cities: The South, 1820-1860* (New York, 1964); Higman, *Slave Populations*, pp. 226-59; and Karasch, *Slave Life in Rio de Janeiro*.

10. Herbert G. Gutman, *The Black Family in Slavery and Freedom, 1750-1925* (New York, 1976); B. W. Higman, *Slave Population and Economy in Jamaica, 1807-1834* (Cambridge, Mass., 1976), pp. 156-75, and *Slave Populations*, pp. 364-77; Kulikoff, *Tobacco and Slaves*, pp. 352-80; and Morgan, *Slave Counterpoint*, pp. 498-558.

11. Alan Watson, *Slave Law in the Americas* (Athens, Ga., 1989); Thomas D. Morris; *Southern Slavery and the Law, 1619-1860* (Chapel Hill, 1996); Elsa V. Goveia, *The West Indian Slave Laws of the Eighteenth Century* (Kingston, 1970); and William M. Wiececk, "The Statutory Law of Slavery and Race in the Thirteen Mainland Colonies of British America," in *William and Mary Quarterly* 34 (1977), pp. 258-80.

12. Orlando Patterson, *Slavery and Social Death: A Comparative Study* (Cambridge, Mass., 1982).

13. Robert Dirks, *The Black Saturnalia: Conflict and its Ritual Expression on British West Indian Slave Plantations* (Gainesville, 1987); Higman, *Slave Populations*, pp. 202-4.

14. Mervyn C. Alleyne, *Comparative Afro-American: An Historical Comparative Study of English-Based Afro-American Dialects of the New World* (Ann Arbor, 1980); and John A. Holm, *Pidgins and Creoles* (Cambridge, Mass., 1988).

15. Epstein, *Sinful Tunes*; Kenneth M. Bilby, "The Caribbean as a Musical Region," in Sidney W. Mintz and Sally Price, eds., *Caribbean Contours* (Baltimore, 1985), pp. 181-218; and Richard Cullen Rath, "African Music in Seventeenth-Century Jamaica: Cultural Transit and Transmission," in *William and Mary Quarterly* 50 (1993), pp. 700-26.

16. Albert J. Raboteau, *Slave Religion: The "Invisible Institution" in the Antebellum South* (New York, 1978); Jon Butler, *Awash in a Sea of Faith: Christianizing the American People* (Cambridge, Mass., 1990), pp. 129-63; and Frey and B. Wood, *Come Shouting to Zion*.

17. Eugene D. Genovese, *From Rebellion to Revolution: Afro-American Slave Revolts in the Making of the Modern World* (Baton Rouge, 1979); and Michael Craton, *Testing the Chains: Resistance to Slavery in the British West Indies* (Ithaca, 1982).

CHAPTER 7 STRUGGLES FOR FREEDOM

1. Since modern scholarship on slavery in the United States and its abolition is exceedingly extensive and complex, the notes accompanying this essay make no pretense to completeness. Instead they indicate for general readers what the author deems the most useful, accessible titles related to the subjects discussed in the paragraphs to which they refer. Regarding this particular note, for instance, for up-to-date explanations of the establishment and development of slavery systems in the western hemisphere, see Eltis, *The Rise of African Slavery*; H. Klein, *Slavery in the Americas*; and Berlin, *Many Thousands Gone*. Two syntheses of the abolitionist movement itself are Merton Dillon, *Slavery Attacked: Southern Slaves and their Allies, 1619-1865* (Baton Rouge, 1990); and James Brewer Stewart, *Holy Warriors: The Abolitionists and American Slavery* (New York, 1997).

2. The best recent treatment of the rise and evolution of slavery in British North America's southern colonies is Morgan, *Slave Counterpoint.*

3. For slavery and African-American cultural presence in British New England and the middle colonies, see Edward McManus, *Black Bondage in the North* (New York, 1970); and Edward D. Pierson, *Black Yankees: The Development of an African-American Subculture in Eighteenth-Century New England* (Amherst, 1988).

4. In addition to the titles cited in note #2 above, consult P. Wood, *Black Majority*; and Mechal Sobel, *The World They Made Together: Black and White Values in Eighteenth-Century Virginia* (Princeton, 1987) regarding the rise of planter elites. The fullest discussions of white southern formulations of equality and social ethics are found in Bertram Wyatt Brown, *Southern Honor: Ethics and Behavior in the Old South* (New York, 1982); and Kenneth Greenberg, *Honor and Slavery* (Princeton, 1996).

5. The classic study explaining the historical roots and development of white supremacy in British North America is Winthrop Jordan, *White Over Black: American Attitudes Toward the Negro, 1550-1812* (Chapel Hill, 1968).

6. For analysis of abolitionist feelings and programs accompanying the American Revolution, see David Brion Davis, *The Problem of Slavery in the Age of Revolution* (New York, 1974) and *Slavery and Human Progress* (New York, 1984); as well as Gary B. Nash, *Race and Revolution* (Madison, 1990); Duncan J. McLeod, *Slavery, Race and the American Revolution* (New York, 1974); and James Essig, *The Bonds of Wickedness: American Evangelicals Against Slavery* (Amherst, 1982).

7. Benjamin Quarles, *The Negro and the American Revolution* (New York, 1961).

8. Several excellent recent works explain the development of political consciousness and activism among Revolutionary-era African Americans. See especially Gary B. Nash, *Forging Freedom: The Formation of Philadelphia's Black Community, 1760-1840* (New York, 1988), pp. 1-224; James O. Horton and Lois Horton, *In Hope of Liberty: Culture, Community and Protest among Northern Free Blacks, 1700-1860* (New York, 1997); and Shane White, *Somewhat More Independent: The End of Slavery in New York City, 1770-1810* (Athens, Ga., 1991).

9. In addition to the titles cited in note #8 above, consult Joanne Pope Melish, *Disowning Slavery: Gradual Emancipation and "Race" in New England, 1780-1860* (Ithaca, 1998) for the historical interplay of gradual emancipation and white supremacist feeling in the post-revolutionary North. See also Leon Litwack, *North of Slavery: The Negro in the Free States, 1790-1860* (New York, 1965).

10. The best discussions of relationships between slavery as a political issue and the framing and ratification of the Constitution are found in Donald Robinson, *Slavery in the Structure of American Politics, 1763- 1800* (Boston, 1971); Paul Finkleman, *Slavery and the Founders: Race and Liberty in the Age of Jefferson* (London, 1996); and Nash, *Race and Revolution*, pp. 25-56.

11. For a valuable explanation of free African-American activism in the North and opposition to colonizationism during the early nineteenth century, consult Horton and Horton, *In Hope of Liberty*, chapters 6-8; Paul Goodman, *Of One Blood: The Abolitionists and the Origins of Racial Equality* (Berkeley, 1998), chapters 1-2; and Julie Winch, *Philadelphia's Black Elite: Activism, Accommodation and the Struggle for Autonomy, 1787-1848* (Philadelphia, 1988). The best discussion of the influences undercutting white abolitionist impulses during the early 1800s is found in David Brion Davis, *Revolutions: Reflections on American Equality and Foreign Liberations* (Cambridge, Mass., 1990).

12. The best recent explanations of the intensification of white supremacist feelings and politics in the 1820s and 1830s are Melish, *Disowning Slavery*; and David Roediger, *The Wages of Whiteness: Race and the Making of the American Working Class* (London, 1991).

13. For information on the Colored Convention Movement and the activism sponsoring it, see Winch, *Philadelphia's Black Elite*. For David Walker, see the fine study by Peter Hinks, *To Awaken My Afflicted Brethren: David Walker and the Problem of Antebellum Black Resistence* (College Station, 1997).

14. For discussions of the developments discussed in the above two paragraphs, see Goodman, *Of One Blood*, pp. 36-64; and George Price and James Brewer Stewart, *To Heal the Scourge of Prejudice: The Life and Writings of Hosea Easton* (Amherst, 1999), pp. 1-57.

15. Ronald Walters, *The Antislavery Appeal: Abolitionism after 1830* (Baltimore and London, 1978) is a fine examination of the moral strictures of abolitionist ideology and critiques of slavery. So is Lawrence J. Friedman, *Gregarious Saints: Self and Community in Abolitionism, 1830-1870* (Cambridge, UK, 1982) pp. 11-222.

16. Stewart, *Holy Warriors*, pp. 51-96, offers an extended narrative summary of these various developments.

17. These points are ably emphasized in Goodman, *Of One Blood*, pp. 36-64, 246-60.

18. The coalescence of organized anti-abolitionism and its expression in mob behavior, partisan politics and religious denominations is ably explained in Leonard L. Richards, *Gentlemen of Property and Standing: Antiabolitionist Mobs in Jacksonian America* (New York, 1970); James Brewer Stewart, "The Emergence of Racial Modernity and the Rise of the White North," in *Journal of the Early Republic*, (summer 1998), pp. 181-236; and Larry E. Tise, *Proslavery: A History of the Defense of Slavery in America* (Athens, Ga., 1987).

19. The fullest explanation of the ideological divisions that developed within the abolitionist movement starting in the later 1830s are Aileen Kraditor, *Means and Ends in American Abolitionism: Garrison and His Critics on Strategy and Tactics, 1837-1854* (New York, 1969); and Friedman, *Gregarious Saints*.

20. Richard H. Sewell, *Ballots for Freedom: Antislavery Politics, 1837-1861* (New York, 1976) contains the fullest discussion of abolitionist political parties after 1840.

21. For two excellent histories of these complex political developments, see Eric Foner, *Free Soil, Free Labor, Free Men: The Ideology of the Republican Party before the Civil War* (New York, 1970); and Michael A. Morrison, *Slavery and the American West: The Eclipse of Manifest Destiny and the Coming of the Civil War* (Chapel Hill, 1997).

22. Black political activism in the 1840s and 1850s is well chronicled in Horton and Horton, *In Hope of Liberty*, chapters 6-7; and William H. Pease and Jane H. Pease, *They Who Would Be Free: The Black Search For Freedom, 1831-1861* (New York, 1974), pp. 173-277.

23. These developments are recounted well in James A. Rawley, *Race and Politics: Bleeding Kansas and the Coming of the Civil War* (New York, 1969); and Stephen B. Oates, *To Purge This Land with Blood: A Biography of John Brown* (Amherst, 1984).

24. Three fine studies of slaveholders' understandings and beliefs during the secession crisis of 1860-1861 are Steven Channing, *Crisis in Fear: Secession in South Carolina* (New York, 1970); Michael Johnson, *Toward a Patriarchal Republic: The Secession of Georgia* (Baton Rouge, 1977); and William Barney, *The Secessionist Impulse: Alabama and Mississippi in 1860* (Princeton, 1974).

25. For excellent accounts of these developments, consult two works by James M. McPherson: *The Struggle for Equality: The Abolitionists and the Negro During the Civil War and Reconstruction* (Princeton, 1965) and *The Negro's Civil War: How American Negroes Felt and Acted during the War for the Union* (Urbana, 1982).

26. The most complete modern account of emancipation during the war and its extension into a broader, post-war, political and economic struggle for racial equality is Eric Foner, *Reconstruction: America's Unfinished Revolution, 1863-1877* (New York, 1988), which references most fully the final four paragraphs of this essay.

CHAPTER 8 BLACK SAILORS MAKING SELVES

1. *A Narrative of the Uncommon Sufferings and Surprising Deliverance of Briton Hammon, A Negro Man—Servant to General Winslow, Of Marshfield in New England* [Boston, Green & Russell, 1760] in Dorothy Porter, ed., *Early Negro Writing* (Boston, 1971), pp. 522-28, especially 522, 523, 528. Greg Dening, Ron Hoffman, and Fredrika Teute provided perceptive criticism of an earlier version of this essay. Elaboration can be found in W. Jeffrey Bolster, *Black Jacks: African-American Seamen in the Age of Sail* (Cambridge, Mass., 1997).

2. Graham Russell Hodges, ed., *Black Itinerants of the Gospel: The Narratives of John Jea and George White* (Madison, 1993), pp. 1, 12, 19-29, 126, 128, 145.

3. *South Carolina Gazette*, April 11, 1771, in Lathan Windley, *Runaway Slave Advertisements: A Documentary History from the 1730s to the 1790s*, vol. 3 (Westport, 1983), p. 299.

4. Henry Louis Gates, Jr., *Figures in Black: Words, Signs, and the "Racial" Self* (New York, 1987), pp. 115-6. Most studies of the African diaspora focus on external forces imposed on blacks during their dispersal and reproduction, rather than on the internal workings through which New World blacks came to envision themselves within that process. See, for example, V. Thompson, *African Diaspora*, pp. 1441-1900.

5. Bolster, *Black Jacks*, Table 1, pp. 235-37.

6. This discussion of historic African cosmology draws on Sterling Stuckey, *Slave Culture: Nationalist Theory and the Foundations of Black America* (New York, 1987), pp. 3-97; R. Thompson, *Flash of the Spirit*, and "Kongo Influences on African-American Artistic Culture," in Holloway, *Africanisms in American Culture*, (Bloomington, 1990), pp. 148-84; MacGaffey, "The West in Congolese Experience," in *Africa and the West: Intellectual Responses to European Culture*, Philip D. Curtin, ed., (Madison, 1972), pp. 51-6, and "Kongo and the King of the Americans," in *Journal of Modern African Studies* 6 (1968), pp. 171-81, and "Cultural Roots of Kongo Prophetism," in *History of Religions* 17 (1977), pp. 186-7; Mullin, *Africa in America*; and Igor Kopytoff's contribution, ibid., p. 73.

7. Thornton, *Africa and Africans*, pp. 1-71, especially p. 19.

8. "Pettiauger" or "periauga" referred to a long, narrow canoe hollowed from one tree, or more generally, a boat built of two hollowed tree trunks with a flat bottom inserted between them. Rusty Fleetwood, *Tidecraft: An Introductory Look at the Boats of Lower South Carolina, Georgia, and Northern Florida: 1650-1950* (Savannah, 1982), pp. 30-1, 62. For Billy, see *Maryland Gazette*, April 4, 1765, in Windley, *Runaway Slave Advertisements*, vol. 2, p. 58. For elaboration of Africans' connections to small craft, see Bolster, *Black Jacks*, pp. 47-50, 60-2.

9. Stuckey, *Slave Culture*, pp.12-15; R. Thompson, *Flash of the Spirit*, pp. 72-83, 108-42; and John S. Mbiti, *African Religions and Philosophy* (New York, 1969), pp. 54-5, 78-91.

10. Gwendolyn Midlo Hall, *Africans in Colonial Louisiana: The Development of Afro-Creole Culture in the Eighteenth Century* (Baton Rouge, 1992), pp. 41-55, especially 49-50; William D. Piersen, "White Cannibals, Black Martyrs: Fear, Depression, and Religious Faith as Causes of Suicide Among New Slaves," in *Journal of Negro History* 62 (April, 1977), p. 153; MacGaffey, "The West in Congolese Experience," pp. 51-6, especially p. 55, and "Kongo and the King of the Americans," pp. 171-81, and "Cultural Roots of Kongo Prophetism," pp. 186-7.

11. MacGaffey, "Kongo and the King of the Americans," pp. 173, 177; Leland G. Ferguson, *Uncommon Ground: Archeology and Early African America, 1650-1800* (Washington, D.C., 1992), pp. 109-120; R. Thompson, *Flash of the Spirit*, p. 135, and "Kongo Influences on African-American Artistic Culture," pp. 148-84, especially p. 152; Melville J. Herskovits, *The Myth of the Negro Past* (New York, 1941), p. 232; and Bolster, *Black Jacks*, pp. 62-6.

12. Philip D. Morgan, "Colonial South Carolina Runaways," in *Slavery and Abolition* 6 (December 1985), p. 64 (N=191 enslaved mariners); *Virginia Independent Chronicle*, Jan. 2, 1788, in Windley, *Runaway Slave Advertisements*, vol. 1, pp. 392-3.

13. Ira Dye, "The Tattoos of Early American Seafarers, 1796-1818," in *Proceedings of the American Philosophical Society* 133 (1989), pp. 520-54. Descriptions of the tattoos of fifty-four African-American seamen were kindly made available by Dye.

14. *Maryland Gazette*, March 7, 1771, in Windley, *Runaway Slave Advertisements*, vol. 2, pp. 85-6; *Maryland Gazette*, May 18, 1775, ibid., p. 110.

15. *Virginia Gazette*, November 26, 1767, in Windley, *Runaway Slave Advertisements*, vol. 1, p. 56; *North Carolina Gazette*, March 27, 1778, ibid., p. 449.

16. Elliot J. Gorn, "'Gouge and Bite, Pull Hair and Scratch': The Social Significance of Fighting in the Southern Backcountry," in *American Historical Review* 90 (1985), p. 20.

17. Robert Farris Thompson, foreword to J. Lowell Lewis, *Ring of Liberation: Deceptive Discourse in Brazilian Capoeira* (Chicago, 1992), pp. xii-xiv.

18. William Butterworth, *Three Years Adventure of a Minor in England, Africa, the West Indies, South Carolina and Georgia* (Leeds, 1831), pp. 301-7.

19. *Charlestown Gazette*, January 11, 1780, in Windley, *Runaway Slave Advertisements*, vol. 3, p. 706; *Virginia Gazette*, January 20, 1774, ibid., vol. 1, pp. 142-3; *Virginia Gazette*, January 16, 1761, ibid., vol. 1, p. 33; *Virginia Gazette*, April 21, 1768, ibid., vol. 1, p. 59.

20. *Virginia Argus*, June 23, 1802; ibid., April 9, 1796.

21. The six autobiographies are Briton Hammon, *Narrative of the Uncommon Sufferings* (Boston, 1760); James Albert Ukawsaw Gronniosaw, *A Narrative of the Most Remarkable Particulars in the Life of James Albert Ukawsaw Gronniosaw, an African Prince* (Bath, England, c. 1770; reprinted London, R. Groombridge, 1840); Olaudah Equiano, *Life of Olaudah Equiano* (London, 1789); John Marrant, *Narrative of the Lord's Wonderful Dealings with John Marrant, a Black* (London, 1785); Venture Smith, *A Narrative of the Life and Adventures of Venture, a Native of Africa* (New London, 1798); and Boston King, "Memoirs of the Life of Boston King, a Black Preacher," in *The Methodist Magazine* (March, April, May, June, 1798), pp. 105-10, 157-61, 209-13, 261-5.

22. On African origins, see Henry Louis Gates, Jr., ed., "The Life of Olaudah Equiano" in *Classic Slave Narratives* (New York, 1987), pp. 11-32; and Gronniosaw, *Narrative*, pp. 3-7.

23. Equiano, *Life*, pp. 1, 12, 17, 51, 182.

24. Lamont D. Thomas, *Paul Cuffe: Black Entrepreneur and Pan-Africanist* (Urbana, 1986), pp. 7, 71. See also John David Smith's review of this book in *American Historical Review* 95 (June, 1990), p. 906.

25. Black communication and consciousness around the Atlantic are examined brilliantly in Julius Sherrard Scott, "The Common Wind: Currents of Afro-American Communication in the Era of the Haitian Revolution," (Ph.D. dissertation, Duke University, 1986). See also Paul Gilroy, *The Black Atlantic: Modernity and Double Consciousness* (Cambridge, Mass., 1993). For examples, see *South Carolina Gazette*, November 10-17, 1758, in Windley, *Runaway Slave Advertisements*, vol. 3, p. 167; and Iain McCalman, ed., *The Horrors of Slavery and Other Writings by Robert Wedderburn* (New York, 1991).

26. *South Carolina Gazette*, June 25-July 2, 1763, in Windley, *Runaway Slave Advertisements*, vol. 3, p. 231; *South Carolina Gazette and General Advertiser* August 12-16, 1783; ibid., vol. 3, p. 719.

27. Scott, "Common Wind," pp. 59-113, especially p. 75; N. A. T. Hall, "Maritime Maroons: Grand Marronage from the Danish West Indies," in *William and Mary Quarterly* 42 (1985), pp. 476-98, especially p. 489; Jane L. Landers, "Gracia Real de Santa Teresa de Mose: A Free Black Town in Spanish Colonial Florida," *American Historical Review* 95 (February 1990), pp. 9-30.

28. Nash, *Race and Revolution* (Madison, 1990), pp. 77-8; Floyd J. Miller, *The Search for a Black Nationality: Black Emigration and Colonization, 1787-1863* (Urbana, 1975). For much more complete treatment of black sailors' possibilities for freedom in Haiti, see Bolster, *Black Jacks*, pp. 144-53.

29. *Consular Returns of American Vessels, Jan. 28, 1837*, Consular Despatches, Cape Haitian, microfilm M-9, roll 7, RG 59, N.A.

30. On Johnson, see Paul Edwards and James Walvin, *Black Personalities in the Era of the Slave Trade* (Baton Rouge, 1983), pp. 165-6; Bolster, *Black Jacks*, pp. 66-7. On the role of headdresses in "John Canoe" celebrations, see Matthew Gregory Lewis, *Journal of a West Indian Proprietor* (London, 1823), p. 51; Stuckey, *Slave Culture*, pp. 68-73, 104-6; Judith Bettelheim, "Jamaican Jonkonnu and Related Caribbean Festivals," in Margaret Crahan and Franklin W. Knight, eds., *Africa and the Caribbean: The Legacies of a Link* (Baltimore, 1979), pp. 80-100.

Index

W

X-Y-Z